MISSING PAGE

Copyright © 2023 Eden McGuire
All rights reserved.
ISBN:
ISBN-13:

Cover Designer: Murphy Rae, Murphy Rae Designs, www.murphyrae.com
Cover Artist: Adso Piñurùa

No part of this book may be reproduced or transmitted in any form or by any means, electronic or mechanical, including photocopying, cording, or by any information storage and retrieval system without the written permission of the author, except for the use of brief quotations.
This book is a work of fiction. The characters and events portrayed in this book are fictitious. Any resemblance to real persons, living or dead, or events is coincidental and not intended by the author.

McGuire, Eden 1999-

Follow the author on Facebook and Instagram @edenmcguire and on Twitter @edennmcguire

To four-year-old Eden, who deserved much, much better.

PROLOGUE

THE ROOM SHE WAS PLACED IN WAS COLD, GRAY, AND EERIE. A stale odor wafted from the carpet—the space was as unwelcoming as it was unsettling. It had started sucking the soul from her the second she walked in.

The detective extended his hand, gesturing for her to sit in what appeared to be the world's most uncomfortable chair. Many had sat in it before her, based on the sinking middle and tired leather. *What had they done to get here?* Had they hurt someone, were they the ones hurt?

Once she took her seat—the middle swallowing her as she predicted—she felt small, and utterly helpless. Almost as if by design.

He started a recorder and leaned forward. "This is Detective Shultz. The date is May 26th, 2018. I'm currently here with…"

He looked up, waiting for her answer. She was staring at the recorder, numb.

"It's Lennon, right? Last name Mayfield?" he asked, tapping his pen against the table. She nodded. "How old are you?"

"Twenty-one," she croaked, watching him scribble. She wanted to ask him the same thing. What qualified him to investigate the mysterious death of little girls? He couldn't be more than early thirties, and he didn't look like a superhero; he was just a man.

The cup crinkled in her palm, and he looked up to her.

"Did you want more?"

"No." She wanted him to start already.

He sighed. "Well, firstly, I'm extremely sorry for your loss. Your father told me you two were very close."

Her shock dulled the pain that that his words brought. It was the first time someone had referred to her sister in the past-tense. What was she supposed to say, anyway? *Thank you?*

"Now, if you can, I'd like to hear your version of how things happened yesterday. You were with Page for a good amount of it, right?"

She swallowed tightly, nodding.

"Then let's start from the beginning."

1

WHOOSH.

The quick drop in altitude jolted her awake. She gripped the arms of her seat with enough strength to blanche her knuckles, eliciting a squeal of protest from the plastic underneath. She kept her eyes closed, willing the wall of black to keep her separate from the chaos.

Please, don't let this be the day I die.

The plane leveled out before the seatbelt sign dinged, but the attendant's voice crackled anyway, alerting them of turbulence and their approaching descent.

There were a few things that kept Lennon too anxious to fall asleep on her flights, though none of them involved the flight itself. While she did think that people accepted being suspended at thirty-six thousand—*thousand!*—feet too easily, she was mostly concerned about sleeping sober. It never ended well for her, or the people in her vicinity. Without some sort of sedation, nightmares as vivid as hers usually produced flailing limbs, fighting off the monsters buried in her subconscious.

By a stroke of Vegas luck a few vacations ago, she'd forgotten to take her weed pen out of her purse and learned how easily they were mistaken for vapes. Now she could sneak away to the bathrooms before boarding to coat her lungs in a thick layer of THC, and pray it put her in a sleep deep enough to keep her neighbors safe.

"We're fine," an older man next to her said assuringly, noticing her sweaty brow. He reached over, patting her shoulder. "Probably just hit an air pocket. Back in my golden days, I used to..."

Her eyes stayed on his lingering hand while he spoke. It only took a few moments for the message to get across, and soon both his smile and hand faded away. She made sure to give a pointed look at the gold band glinting on his thick, square finger before pulling a pair of sunglasses from her sling bag and sliding them up the bridge of her nose. Lennon slumped down into the chair, using her tits as a table to cross her arms over. The man *hmph'd*, confirming her intuition, and begrudgingly returned to his phone.

Unable nor willing to go back to sleep, Lennon drew another breath, counting down from ten. She'd had the same dream for almost two decades, but it always produced the same effects. When had she even fallen asleep?

She remembered scanning her ticket, nodding hello to the flight attendants before crossing over the plane's threshold—tugging her hat low off their stares. She certainly remembered how comfy the eight hundred dollar seat felt under her ass. But after take-off, ten minutes into Wizard of Oz...*poof*.

Shadows still floated behind her lids, banging its fists against the frosty spheres of her eyes. The dream always started the same; a dark room with hushed whispers, cut off by the sharp sound of scraping metal. Lennon could feel the leftover dread thrashing like a scared kid in her stomach; it'd been a long time since weed had been able to make her completely dreamless. Compared to her old habits, marijuana looked like Ibuprofen, but at least it kept her limbs at bay.

It's just nerves, she assured herself. Coming home had a way of doing that.

Lennon flipped the window cover up, letting the sun wash away the last few lurking shadows. Her eyes were too dry to maintain anything more than a squint against the blinding light, but John Wayne Airport's green fields eventually came into view. Next were the palm trees, providing little shade from the California sun. The heat was bearable, for now. May was much more gentle than her summer counterparts.

With three bumps of the landing gear against pavement, her chest cautiously deflated. *Rough start, but not terrible.* The belt dug into her abdomen as the brakes moved into action, straining her full bladder under its pressure. Her thumbs danced across the screen while her phone woke up, eager to swipe away the airplane symbol. It wasn't long before notifications interrupted her music in quick succession—three, to be exact.

> DAD
> Can't wait to see u kiddo. Don't forget our fishing trip Tuesday
>
> HART ROGERS
> You got this baby. I'll call you around noon?:)
>
> MOM
> Not gonna be able to pick u up, still @ hair appt.

Lennon huffed at the last one, staring down at the phone. It wasn't out of character for her mother to bail on her last minute, but frustrating nonetheless. *You should've known better,* she thought to herself scoldingly. Responsible was not a word in Cash Mayfield's vocabulary; whatever made her life the most enjoyable took priority, no matter her obligations.

She sent Hart a plane landing emoji and her dad a thumbs up, but something kept her hovering over her mother's name. It had been five months since she'd last seen her family, and couldn't even make it home before Cash let her down.

> Thx for the warm welcome.

She tucked her phone into her pocket after pressing send, watching with amusement as passengers stood impatiently from their seats, a few banging their heads in the process.

"You can go ahead." The man nodded, sitting back in his seat. "I'm in no hurry."

Lennon resisted rolling her eyes, but just barely. He wasn't smart, after all—he was just a man, hoping to get a face full of what he'd nearly broken his neck over earlier. *All in the noble name of chivalry.*

"Me neither," she responded, tightening her arms.

She waited until he'd shuffled out to reach for her carry-on, and then rushed down the walkway. The amount of urine bearing down on her bladder had soiled her desire to enjoy the weather; she couldn't be bothered with the cooling breeze welcoming her sweaty forehead or the sunrays warming her sleeves frozen by a direct stream of airplane AC. Beelining to the closest bathroom and shoving her biker shorts down to her ankles, Lennon sighed in relief once her bare skin touched porcelain. Her bladder emptied while she fished for a slender black stick from her crossbody bag, fingers clumsy with desire.

Though a cloud of smoke rose above the stall, nobody seemed to notice, or at least care enough to complain. Her phone chimed again, but this tone was unique to the ones preceding it. While those bells normally incited excitement, in this moment she felt only dread. Lennon lifted her screen into view, chewing her lip. Surely Cash could keep *one* thing...

PAGE MAYFIELD
> mom spilled the beans. omg!! so excited to see you

Great. Not only had Cash left Lennon to fend for transportation, but now the surprise she'd worked so hard to keep secret the past two weeks was ruined. She stood and shimmied her shorts over her hips, faced with a poster taped to the door. A picture of a scared young girl, with a child abuse hotline number displayed above her head. Her large, glassy eyes peered helplessly, mouth open in a silent cry.

Lennon scoffed. It was hard to take those seriously, and it'd never sat right with her; manufacturing suffering when it already ran rampant. She couldn't imagine being the mother, taking a check for making her child cry.

The stall door swung shut behind her, followed by the faucet squeaking to life. Lennon scrubbed her hands red before embarking toward baggage claim, groaning when her phone buzzed again.

> MOM
>
> The world doesn't revolve around u, Lennon. You'll live

The carousel shuddered to a start, grinding at the same frequency as Lennon's teeth. She locked her phone, refusing to let her mother get under her skin through a text message. Cashmere was a master at minimizing feelings and guilt-trips; Lennon knew better than to pick a fight with her. She wasn't nicknamed *Cashmanian Devil* for nothing.

A pair of matching red suitcases dropped down to the metal panels. She muscled them to the floor, grunting with the effort. During her two years at college, she'd lost most of the muscle high school volleyball had built. It wasn't anything to worry over; the amount of biking she was about to do was sure to put her back into shape in no time. Lennon didn't like to drive high, and walking gave her too much time to think. But for now, she'd have to struggle and attempt to drag the overweight suitcases toward the taxi bay while ordering an Uber.

She squinted at the photo of her driver and sighed, anxiety shooting through her foot in a quick, steady rhythm. A Tesla slowed in front of her four minutes later, the passenger window rolling down to reveal a perspiring man. She leaned down, foot still tapping.

"For who?"

"Le-non?" he answered, accent thick. She nodded, walking around the back to stow her bags, double checking the license plate in the meantime. He opened his door to help, but the last suitcase thudded against the trunk's floor before he could reach her.

"I got it," she breathed, nodding. He wiped his brow, slightly confused, before opening her door in a final act of service. She ducked inside, sucking in her dimpled cheek and sliding to the other side.

"To Laguna Beach, huh?" His eyes found hers for a moment in the rearview mirror. She nodded, making a show of placing the black headphones over her ears and pulling her hood up for emphasis. There wasn't anything playing over them, save for the noise-canceling waves. Lennon wasn't much of a talker, especially to strangers—if he couldn't take the hint, she'd force feed it to him.

Ding!

HART
Miss ur face pretty girl.

Lennon stared at the screen, the turmoil leftover from her mother now liquifying inside of her.

Texts like these used to feel so carefree, but now that blue bubble settled like expired food in her stomach. Hart had started off as a casual crush, but was now solidifying into something more serious; Lennon wondered if she might genuinely, truly *like* him, and the idea alone made her want to red-button his memory and disappear. She'd already sunken too deep, far past comfort; she knew and liked his friends, and his family even more.

She quit drugs—the hard ones, anyway—months ago, but Hart was something else, all his own. Every time they were together she'd promise herself it was the last time, but the idea of quitting him was becoming harder and harder to imagine. Being apart this summer would help. In fact, she was counting on it. It was a tale as old as time; they'd get some space between them, he'd get bored or find someone else, and then her head and heart could go back its normal, ice-cold temperature. These sweet moments were starting to feel like quicksand, dragging her back into its depths. Lennon had a special ability to turn the greenest flags into red; when every door felt like a trap, there was no remorse over shutting it in someone's face.

She'd been grounded over this, once. Four different boys had asked her to the winter formal once, and she'd said yes to every one of them. It was amusing to her, as she'd never intended to go to the dance in the first place. It was even funnier when they all showed up to the Mayfield's house, asking for her with matching confused expressions. She hid upstairs with her little sister, wearing her favorite sweats and T-shirt, shoveling icecream into her mouth between giggles. Her dad couldn't keep a straight face as he bore the news, but her mom didn't find it nearly as humorous, and barred Lennon from social events for the rest of the school year. She'd just turned fifteen.

Even though they weren't technically official—by her choice, not his—Hart had been her longest relationship. Lennon and her feelings changed with the seasons, but something about Hart felt evergreen. He was unprecedented, and she had no idea what to do with him. Or how to respond to his adorable, stupid text messages.

Ducking out of the driver's view, she lifted the camera up to snap a quick picture of herself. There wasn't much to see, which was the point. She loved challenging his attraction. Most of her choppy jet-black hair was concealed by her hoodie, and his favorite feature of hers, a pair of chronically sleepy, icy eyes, were just barely peeking over her sunglasses. Although they—and the rest of her, for that matter—were exquisitely beautiful, there was an unsettling awareness hidden behind them, sharp and calculating. They looked out of place on her otherwise youthful face.

Ten seconds later, three heart-eye emojis lit up her screen. She locked her phone and focused on the view outside her window, cursing the warmth that coursed through her.

Lunch traffic added an extra fifteen minutes to the drive from John Wayne to the Mayfield residence. It allowed her time to admire the greenery of the rolling hills, the growing number of palm trees and exotic flowers. Rather than the fishy smell most beach towns adopted, Laguna's air was a mix of fresh honeydew and florals, greeting its residents at every corner.

Though Laguna's Main Street was short, it was teeming with life. It consisted mostly of tourists shops and art galleries, with a few overpriced restaurants for whoever was hungry and desperate enough.

The Tesla turned the corner, and the dozens of lemon-haired heads bobbing around the main square disappeared as quickly as they appeared. Down the street, he slowed in front of a three-story Mediterranean-style home, and she leaned to check the dash. May 25th, 2018, 11:27 AM. She'd made it back with three minutes to spare.

"We're here?" he asked, unsure.

"Yes," she answered, with the weight of both relief and dread. She allowed the man to get her bags for her this time, nodding in thanks.

"Do you need help taking them—?"

"No," She shook her head, busy with her phone. "I'm good."

A small scowl puckered his lips. Lennon turned for the entrance, pushing back her hood and slipping her sunglasses into her bag.

"...*bunch of spoiled brats*..." he muttered under his breath.

His phone chimed, cutting off his complaint. A three-digit number glinted in his bulging eyes, the shiny dollar sign drawing an involuntary squeak from his throat.

"Ma'am," he started, sure she'd made a mistake.

"Consider it a donation from the Flaky Mom Organization." A dimple in her left cheek punctuated a hypnotic smile, and suddenly her concealment made sense. She was naturally distracting, and dangerously enchanting. "Thanks again."

He blinked, fighting the warmth spreading over his cheeks. Finally, he ducked inside his car, descending the driveway with a few careful glances in the rearview mirror.

Missing Page

She waited for the Tesla to reach the end of the drive before approaching the door, punching in the memorized code and waiting for the melody at the end. She faltered with a frown when it blinked red instead, blaring an unpleasant tone.

She entered the numbers again, slower this time. 1-1-1-3-9-7, her birth date. Another flash of red, followed with the one-note song of unacceptance.

Her brows knitted as frustration oxidized beneath her chest. She concentrated, trying to put herself in Cash's line of thinking post-Christmas...

Eyes opening with an idea, she punched in a new set of numbers.

0...7...

Perhaps it was low of her to try this.

1...1...

Would her mom really do it?

0...3

The note she'd been expecting finally sounded with a victorious flash of green. Lennon stood still for a moment, processing. The code was someone's birthday, all right—her sister's.

Petty? Yes. Surprising? Not in the slightest.

Lennon swung her luggage against the door like a battering ram, hit with the delicious scent of teakwood and tobacco as the living room opened before her. The smell was nostalgic, instinctively spiking her adrenaline. *You're home,* it half-cooed, half-warned.

It was eerie when this house was so quiet. It looked like it belonged to a nice family; one who took evening walks and had dinner together every night. But Lennon remembered what she'd left, and why she hadn't been back since Christmas—nobody could put on a pretty face like a Mayfield.

"Hello?" she called out. Pairs of feet bounded up the stairs from the bottom floor, nails scraping against the wood. The family's German Shepherd attacked her with wet kisses and excited whines, bursting with puppy-like energy despite his graying chin. Lennon bent down, shaking her fingers through his coat.

"Kaiser, my boy!" she gushed.

He broke away to start up the second set of stairs, whining impatiently at the top. She'd paused to look at the set of photos lining the wall, a new visual pathway to the mother-in-law suite. Each was magnified in mind-boggling detail; the first was a dew drop, each facet reflecting the emerald leaf it rested on, glinting like a gemstone in the light. The second revealed metallic blue streaks in a young girl's eye, breaking the sapphire hues like cracks in a lake of ice. The last was an angelic view of a coastline, using a slow shutter speed to melt the ocean into the sand. Each was signed in thin white Sharpie at the bottom— S.M.

Stacy Mayfield was a well-known and highly successful photographer, even by Laguna's standards; he also happened to be Lennon's father. It started as a hobby, as most of these things did, but Stacy had a particular talent for finding beauty in the small things. Who could predict that after only four years, people would dish five, sometimes six figures to bring these single-frame moments into their home?

Ascending the rest of the stairs, Lennon dropped her bags in the mini kitchen, promptly shutting herself in the bathroom. She started a small symphony of her own—the swish of clothes falling to the tile, shower knobs squeaking after months of nonuse. The glass fogged before she could fully take in her appearance, but even through the haze, she could see the weariness in it.

A gratifying hum rolled through her as scalding water snaked through her hair and high-pressure streams pelted her skin from either side. Lennon preferred hot showers, as hot as the knobs would allow; she liked seeing her flesh turn red, flushing away everyone's touch from the day, and knowing she was completely clean. She'd even hung a small mirror from the head so that she could make sure she was free of hidden dirt or leftover shampoo. It was a small way to simulate control over a body that had never really felt like hers.

Today was her first official day of summer. It was going to be a good one—she'd make sure of it. The plan was simple: nap on the

Missing Page

deck, smoke the joints tucked into her sock, and, most importantly, see her sister.

She ventured onto the bathmat shortly after the water cut off, padding across the terracotta tiles to the sink. Salty air had already curled her dark layers into wild waves. Back in Oregon, vibrant hues of blue, green, or red were popular hair colors. But in this town's abundance of blondes, Lennon and Page stuck out like sore thumbs.

An incoming call vibrated loudly against the marble, startling her with a jump. She pressed her hand to her heart after checking the photo shaking within the glass margins, displaying a handsome young man in an Elvis costume.

The first thing that came to mind when Lennon thought of Hart Rogers was *fun*. Almost every person that knew him claimed him as their best friend; no one could resist his magnetic charisma. He smiled and greeted every person he saw, somehow always knowing them some way or another. Everyone except for Lennon.

For an entire year he'd only nodded at her, occasionally curling his lips in the smallest of smiles. Because of his distance, she was genuinely surprised when he asked her to dinner after a lecture. She remembered how uncharacteristically shaky his voice sounded, how his six feet and three inches had suddenly lost its power. Where had that confident, charismatic man gone?

She learned in a cherry-leather booth that it was not arrogance that had kept him distant, but nerves. He'd been building the courage to talk to her for a year through those small nods and rare *hellos*. Their conversation flowed easily over sushi and sake, if not a little more quiet than Hart was used to. He'd clear his throat any time she looked at him a little too long, stiffen whenever their fingers accidentally brushed. People were usually much more eager to talk about themselves. However, though she was quiet, by no means was she shy. Lennon did most of her talking through her eyes, and it was electrifyingly intense.

It was she who made the first move after two and a half gruelingly platonic weeks, kissing him after he walked her to her door for the fifth night in a row. If she were being honest, she'd done it as a humorous experiment rather than a profession of feelings. What she *hadn't* expected was the pleasant way their lips fit together, or the soft yet firm touch of his hands. The intimacy threw her off; she felt naked. To balance that, she pulled him into her dorm where she would be covered in darkness, and proceeded to unzip his jeans and give him—his words, not hers—the best blowjob of his entire life.

The key to a life-altering blowjob might be more simple than one would think. Most girls were concerned about seeming delicate, polite, *pretty*. Lennon, however, knew how animalistic men could be. They didn't want a pair of well-mannered lips around their cock, with a finale that could be wiped away with a quick swipe of the hand. Girls filtered men through their own beautiful lens, crafted from romance books they'd read, or movies they'd seen. Lennon knew better than to think that was reciprocated; men wanted nasty, downright disgusting acts of nature. They loved when you gagged—an easy boost to their ego. Liquids coming out of every orifice, mascara-ruining tears, snot mixed with the pool of saliva stretching from your mouth to their dick like hot cheese on pizza.

It was only later that she realized Hart didn't care about any of those things; he was different. Lennon thought the most she'd ever feel for a man was tolerant, but with Hart, she felt *alive*. She thought of people as puzzles, always trying to pull things out of their shadows, but Hart lacked that darkness she saw in so many others, including herself. And somehow, at some point, her intrigue softened into something warm and sticky, weak and penetrable. It was a feeling she couldn't wash away.

She hated it.

The phone buzzed again. He'd be sent to voice mail if she didn't answer soon. She cleared her throat, and lifted the phone to her ear.

"Hello," she sang, wincing. She never sang.

"How's Cali?"

Lennon scrunched her nose, grateful they weren't FaceTiming.

Missing Page

Nobody who lived here ever called it *Cali*. It was California, and California only.

"Warm." She pressed the speaker button and placed it back onto the marble, smearing lotion on her legs and arms. She eased her pressure along her collarbone, careful over the new ink. "That's all I got so far."

He laughed. "How's the family?"

"Don't know. Haven't seen them yet."

"Where is everybody?"

"Page has school, Dad's at a work meeting. Mom's at the hair salon..." Kaiser whined pitifully at her feet, lifting his nose. Lennon conceded, leaning down to scratch the spot behind his ear. "It's just me and Kaiser right now."

"Talk about a warm welcome," he deadpanned. That made her smile. He echoed her thoughts aloud like that often. She carried the phone with her into the bedroom, opening her suitcases and pulling out a black bikini set.

"What are you doing right now?" she asked, changing the subject.

"About to go to the lake with some friends, make sure they don't get shitfaced and hurt themselves."

"Sounds fun," she kept her tone light. "Hart, be careful out—"

A bout of crowded laughter erupted from his end, drowning out her sentence.

"Sorry, honey, one sec...what are you dumbasses—?" Hart's laughter weaved in with theirs once he saw the cause of commotion. She waited silently, anxiety prickling in her stomach.

They'll be fine. He'll be fine.

"Don't worry, baby," he said, still chuckling. "I'll make sure everyone behaves."

She tugged a pair of gray cotton shorts over her thighs, feeling slightly more at ease. A flock of seagulls passed in formation outside her window then, crying out in an off-beat chorus. The window's frame always turned the views into magnificent, living paintings. It was the closest thing she'd experienced to magic, and her favorite part of the room.

"I have to go," she murmured, watching them until they faded into the sky. "I'm gonna surprise Page, pick her up early."

"She'll be happy to see you, Len."

"Hope so."

She chewed the inside of her cheek. Despite being home, it all still felt like a distant daydream, and would continue to until she saw her sister and could physically wrap her in her arms. Until she knew everything was okay, nothing was.

"Call me when you get back from the lake, if you remember." she said, half-teasing.

"You think I'd forget to call the smartest, wildest, most gorgeous girl I've ever seen in my damn life?" he exclaimed, raising an octave with every adjective. She couldn't help the smile sprouting from her lips. "My *best friend*?"

She thought of all the people who'd claimed him with that title. It made him feel far away, sometimes, and it was nice knowing that she was his.

"Lennon, I swear you have no idea how absolutely fucking crazy about you I—"

She hadn't noticed the warm butterflies his words had procured migrating up into her mouth until after swallowing, and was promptly sent into a coughing fit. It was abrupt enough to cut off his profession, and she had to lift her hand to her mouth to muffle the sound.

"You good over there?"

"Yep," she rasped.

"Am I making you sick?" he asked, amused.

"No," she gasped. "Call me when you get back!"

The call ended before he could say anything else. She tucked the empty suitcases under her canopy bed and descended the stairs, a pre-roll tucked behind her ear and Kaiser at her heels. She tried to ignore the grand piano that stood between her and the sliding door, despite her fingers twitching at the sight of an old friend.

Ten minutes later, she was still rolling the unlit joint between her fingers, deep in thought *Ugh*. Why couldn't she just enjoy the fucking ocean like she wanted to? She *did* care about him—that was the truth. So why did her stomach twist at the thought of something more serious, like she was getting into trouble?

She knew the answer, of course. It boiled down not to fear, but to guilt. If they became official, if she finally validated the feelings that had so far only been hinted at and danced around, it wasn't her that would be getting into trouble—it was him.

What was wrong with her?

The front door opened and closed across the house, summoning Kaiser toward the sound with a bark loud enough to bring her out of her spiral. Lennon tucked the stick behind her ear, hiding her hair over it. She recognized those snippy clicks of heels anywhere.

"Lennon? Are you home?"

Speak of the Cashmanian Devil.

2

"Out back," Lennon called lazily, tilting her chin up to the sun.

Cashmere slipped through the partially open door, taking a stance directly in her line of sun.

"Why are you running the AC if you're gonna leave the door wide open?"

"So Kaiser can—"

"You already double our water bill when you're here. Let's keep the AC to a minimum," Cashmere sneered.

"Right," she sighed. "Because we're desperately low on funds."

Lennon peeked an eye open to see an unamused expression on her mother's face, and quickly changed her tune. Cashmere wasn't one for dry humor. "Good to see you too, Mom."

There were a few ways this moment could have gone. Lennon expected something louder and messier, especially because of how she left on Christmas. Their Cold War ended almost a month ago, after Cash started sending intermittent texts again. That was her version of a white flag, and though it wasn't the most mature, that was Cashmere's way. She'd cross any lines to hurt whoever had angered her, and then freeze them out until she was ready for things to go back to normal. Compared to the tornado of clothes and broken glass she'd left in her wake last time, this was...tolerable.

Cash scoured her daughter's body, checking the damage that college had done to her. She'd gotten a little fuller in the hips, but it was her shoulder that stopped her scan. "You got *another* one?"

Lennon reached for the open book etched just above her collarbone, letting her fingers brush over the newest addition in admiration. "Yeah. For Page."

"Please," Cash scoffed, rolling her eyes and heading back inside. "Don't ruin your body on our account."

Oh, don't worry. I would never get a tattoo of you.

Lennon could say this, and a large part of her wanted to, but she opted for silence—for peace. Cash loved to bitch, and it seemed she had leftover venom from their last talk.

"I have to run out again soon...can you pick your sister up from school?" she called.

"I was planning on it." The chair was starting to burn Lennon's skin anyway, and moisture had begun building beneath her arms. From the kitchen, she could hear Cash's teeth sinking into an apple before the fridge door opened. Lennon heard the pop of a cap, and stiffened like a dog to a whistle. *At least it's past noon.*

Cash took a few more bites before tossing it in the trash, glancing at the deck. A part of her wished she could stay and finish her beer on the deck, soak in the view that sold her on this house so many years ago. The young woman sitting on the lounge chair, however, was tainting her view, serving as a reminder of her life's plentiful imperfections. Despite how well Cash was doing at work, she couldn't seem to get her house under the same control. Between her husband, whom she hadn't fucked in nearly five months, Page's struggles in school, and her eldest's cold return—no doubt an omen to their upcoming summer—Cashmere felt that a beer was the least she deserved.

"Do you remember when you grounded me from dating?" Lennon called.

Cash walked back to the deck, condensation wasting no time forming on the glass and trickling down to her chipping nail polish. She swept freshly bleached, blown-out hair over her shoulder to meet her daughter's amused gaze.

Lennon and Page had inherited their father's dark hair, but they'd gotten their eyes from their mother. Lennon used to wonder if it was the striking sapphire color the women they belonged to that made those eyes so intimidating, until she saw how pure they looked on Page. Pools of crystal blue, like Cash had stolen them from the sea herself.

"You played with them like toys." Cash looked toward the ocean. "The last thing the world needs is more men jaded over their first love."

Lennon propped herself up on her elbows, surprised at her perspective. "I was fifteen, you know. I highly doubt I was their first love."

Cashmere shrugged. "Their first lust, then."

"And their lust was my responsibility?"

Cash lifted the bottle to her lips to take a swig, glowering at Lennon. So much for taking a moment to enjoy her beer. "Why even start a conversation if you just want to be angry? If you want to argue, at least be honest about it, say it with your chest."

"I'm not *angry*, I just—"

"You talk to me like I'm the worst mom in the world. Sitting there, criticizing me from the lounge chair on the deck *I* bought, eating food *I* put in the fridge, using AC *I* paid for...sounds about right."

Lennon lifted her hands to her face, wondering how crazy she'd look if she screamed. What Cash was saying wasn't even true; Stacy paid for the majority of their family expenses. Not that it mattered. God, her mom could be exhausting.

"Sorry. That's not how I meant it," Lennon conceded.

Missing Page

"Speaking of dating, how's Hart? I haven't heard anything about him."

Lennon pushed her sunglasses up the bridge of her glistening nose, trying to keep up with her mother's mood swings. "Still seeing each other."

"Wow," Cash said genuinely, before dipping into a more sarcastic tone. "That might be a personal record. Maybe you've found your soulmate."

Lennon barked out a laugh. 'Soulmate' was a word used in fairytales, or romance novels that used shirtless, flowy-haired men as their cover.

Her mother shook her head, cracking a smile. "Hopeless romantic, just like your mama."

With that, Cashmere took her empty bottle inside and tossed it into the recycling. "Don't wait up for us. We'll be back around eleven."

It'd be twelve at the earliest; her mom always got rowdy at the galas. The times Cash had been carried through that front door were too many to count. Tonight would likely be no different, but at least that meant the girls would have the house to themselves.

"Your hair looks good, by the way!" Lennon called after her, unsure if she could still hear. She wouldn't say thanks even if she had.

Lennon started to reach for her ear when the front door swung shut, pausing to check the time. There was only an hour and a half before it was time to get her sister...as much as she wanted to hear the flick of her lighter and smell the burning of paper, the feeling of getting to see Page was one she didn't want to numb. She lifted herself from the chair, gliding through the house with as much presence as a ghost. She'd fallen back into her old habit of walking on her toes, keeping quiet as possible.

They'd need to stop at the market on the way home, but what to make? *Pizza in the brick oven...shrimp salad...fish tacos, if Dad has any left in the freezer.* Her stomach rumbled in approval. *Everything sounded good now that it wasn't fast food or dining hall.* She'd need

Page to help keep her from going overboard. Lennon tended to do that with things. Once she got going, there was no *off* button.

She replaced her black bikini bottoms with a cotton thong and a pair of loose-fitting jeans, covering her arms with a flowy linen button-up. She noticed two very faint lines trailing delicately up her collarbones and around her neck as she adjusted the collar, peeking in and out of view. It seemed everything about her, down to her tan lines, were afraid of commitment.

She pulled the stick from her ear and tucked it into a pair of crew socks. *I'll be seeing you later*, she promised, before returning to the entry way. She planted a farewell kiss to Kaiser's wet nose, and swiped the keys off the table.

Being the oldest, Lennon never got the luxury of a fun older sibling. She could only leave for appointments or if she was sick; it was impossible to skip class in a town this small. It wasn't ditching that was so important to her though, so much as being anywhere but home. There was slight redemption in being able to extend this sliver of spontaneity to her little sister, though. These kinds of moments were minuscule, but eternally memorable—it's what older sisters were for.

A white Jeep sat at the far end of the three-car garage, top stripped away to welcome May's warm embrace. She made a mental note to thank her dad later; Page didn't have the strength, and Cash wasn't thoughtful enough. Lennon pushed the key into the ignition and twisted, watching in confusion as the gas needle struggled to reach the quarter-tank mark. She frowned, sure she'd filled it up before she left. Lennon gripped the gearshift and pushed it into reverse, squinting against the immediate barrage of sunlight.

The sun illuminated something shiny on the floorboard, causing her eyes to flicker and her foot to ease on the brake. She reached over, lifting it up to inspect. A metal bottle opener engraved with C.B. And, tucked under the seat, an empty Modelo.

The initials confused her a moment, but she was quick to remember. Brockovich, Cashmere's maiden name. Lennon vaguely remembered this hanging in their old house, although she'd forgotten the details of it over the years. Her main concern was that Cash was drinking and driving—she was supposed to be in therapy for this.

Things must be getting bad between her parents. She didn't understand why Cash had to use *her* car until she remembered the new lava red Mercedes that usually sat in the middle of the garage, its glossy coat glinting under the fluorescents. The answer sounded in her head then, clear and obvious. *Of course she did.* Cash's AMG was worth three of Lennon's Jeeps.

Lennon closed one eye and aimed, shooting the empty bottle through the open window into the garbage. The metal opener, however, was stashed in her glove compartment; it'd only be a matter of time before Cash was asking where it was.

Lennon bobbed her head to the music while she cruised down the small streets of Laguna Beach, weaving through the lemon heads —that's what she usually referred to the locals as. She parked a few blocks from the high school at a gelato shop, in a spot that wasn't-technically-a-spot. It wasn't good manners to arrive places empty handed, but was also an excuse to check on her old bosses.

Rich chocolate wafted from within, wetting her tongue with hints of hazelnut and strawberry. Lennon was content to wait outside while the line dwindled, happy to avoid the overpowered AC as long as possible. It was short-lived, taking a meager five minutes for the small store to empty. She finally stepped in and watched as the ink on her arms prickled, clenching her chattering teeth.

The owners were absent, but a kid just a few years older than Page was slouched behind the register, tired from the rush. Despite his posture, he still towered over the counter, tall and broad-shouldered. He looked up once the bell chimed with a knee-jerk smile.

"Welcome to Gelato Para...*oh!*" Once his eyes met hers, recognition lit inside them, and his plastered smile softened into something more genuine.

She recalled that toothy grin from her senior year. He was the younger brother of one of her volleyball teammates, a freshman at the time. She sometimes saw him in the stands cheering, but that was all she remembered. Had it been that long? *What was his name again?*

"S'up, Lennon?" The young man straightened as she approached, clearing any lingering youth from his throat. It was his eyes that gave him away though; they were wide and warm against his dark skin, innocent and child-like. Suddenly, though she was now standing right in front of him, he didn't seem so tall. After all, she'd only meant to get a closer look at his name tag.

"Hey, Theo."

"Did you just get back?"

She nodded. "Few hours ago."

"I just saw Page before I left. She was talking about you, actually...does she know you're back?"

Lennon's nose crinkled. "She's not supposed to." His chatty sister popped into her mind then, eliciting a wince. "And neither is anyone else, so if you wouldn't mind..."

He winked. "Don't worry. I won't tell Taysia."

She smiled relievedly, breaking her eyes away from his unwavering gaze to pour her attention over the flavors. They were memorized of course, burned into her brain after three summers of working here. But she knew Theo's look well, and had no desire to entertain it; she'd seen it on faces of boys and men alike whenever she gave them attention.

"How's college life?" he pressed.

"Fine," she shrugged. "Speaking of, shouldn't you be in school? You're not graduated already, are you?"

His smile faltered at the reminder. "Almost. I work on my half-days, so I've got nights open..."

She nodded, pretending to be interested in the pistachio flavor. Conversations weren't supposed to be games, though to someone as impenetrable as her, they often felt that way.

"You know, I don't think I've ever met another Lennon," he rambled. "Both of you have cool names—"

"You're one to talk." She replied absentmindedly.

"Taysia, maybe, but not me. I'm named after my grandpa," he muttered. "How'd they come up with yours?"

"My dad is a melomaniac, for one." She leaned to get a closer look at a pink gelato bin tucked in the corner. *That's a new one.* "And he's obsessed with the 70's."

"Oh." Theo tilted his head. "So, like...John Lennon?"

Lennon slid her glasses down her nose dramatically. "The very one."

He grinned. "Cool."

"That's why Page's name is spelled without the *i*. You ever heard of Led Zeppelin?"

"Oh, shit! Yeah, of course. Jimmy."

Lennon snapped her finger. "There you go."

"That's pretty sick, actually." He caught her fourth glance at the stack of cones and cups and finally pulled on a pair of plastic gloves, reaching for a scooper. "So, uh...what can I get you?"

Her and her sister's orders were almost identical; one scoop of cookie dough and one of milk chocolate hazelnut, except Page preferred hers in a cup while Lennon opted for a cone. She grabbed a handful of napkins, uttering her thanks after Theo put it on the house, and returned to the car, racing against the heat to deliver them in a semi-unmelted state. She wanted—no, *needed*—this to be perfect.

Lennon parked in the spot closest to the entrance, feeling a new rush of energy as she walked through the gray doors. Mrs. Kylie was sitting behind the desk, wearing thick glasses that magnified an already large set of eyes. Back when she was a student, Lennon worried to breathe too strongly near the woman at risk of breaking her. Since then, she'd somehow gotten even frailer. The woman took her time lifting her head, smiling with a small gasp that moved her entire body once she realized.

"Oh *my*, what a nice surprise!" Mrs. Kylie stretched a sun-spotted hand over the counter, patting Lennon's arm.

She smiled. "It's been a while, huh?"

"Too long, I think. Did you come back for Christmas?"

Lennon blinked, trying to think of an excuse, but thankfully the woman's mind worked much faster than her body. "You've grown again...are you six foot yet?"

"Five eight," Lennon quickly corrected, her shoulders sagging in response. *And a half*, but who was counting? "I haven't grown since tenth grade. I think you might be shrinking."

Mrs. Kylie's laugh was slow, genuine. Lennon liked that she took her time in her old age—the woman deserved a long laugh. "That could very well be true, dear." She brushed back her silver strands and squinted at the computer screen, reaching for the phone. "I'm guessing you didn't come just to chat with an old bat. Let me call your sister down, looks like she's in Miss Johnson's..."

"Wait, my sister goes here?" Lennon's eyebrow rose in surprise.

Mrs. Kylie shook her head with another slow chuckle, punching in a few numbers on the number pad before propping the phone between her ear and shoulder.

Lennon looked over the cork board propped against the wall next to Mrs. Kylie's desk. It was covered in different artwork from what looked like nearly every grade, mostly consisting of jagged collages and single-color portraits. A particular paper was tacked to the top, standing out like a star on a tree. It was painted in gorgeous hues of blue, highlighted and shadowed to look like a glittering ocean washed in sunlight. She recognized her sister's hand anywhere—that kind of talent could only belong to Page. There was a sentence written in the pockets of the clouds, where the sunlight peeked through. *The best years are ahead*, it read.

Lennon had forgotten that Mrs. Kylie announced her retirement a few months ago. Page had texted her as soon as she found out—there wasn't a lot of hot gossip here.

"Good afternoon, Erica. Miss Mayfield is needed in the office... yes, she needs to bring her things, she won't be returning. No, no, everything's fine."

Lennon plopped herself into the closest chair and crossed one leg

Missing Page

over another, her knees bouncing to an erratic tune composed by sober anxiety. It wasn't just seeing Page that made her worry; the office walls were almost entirely glass, visible by any teacher or kid between fourteen and eighteen. The prickly feeling hooked into her shoulders, shrinking her into her seat. She would stay under the radar as long as she could.

For now, there was no obligation or pressure to hang out with non-familial persons. This year the bars would be teeming with newly-legal adults, but Lennon didn't drink, and had given up her other vices months ago. More than that, she didn't want to deal the awkwardness of men who were probably old enough to be her father, or even know him, offering to buy her drinks. No one was safe from the consequences of a lonely, perverse man's actions, but for some reason, it usually ended up being some poor young girl's problem.

Worrying her body heat was melting it faster, Lennon set the cup of gelato to the side, resting her sweaty palm over the arm of the chair. Her nail scratched the wood impatiently—another old habit. She'd sat in this very seat many times, waiting for the guidance counselor or the principal. Lennon had always felt lost, trying to cope with issues no one of that age should even think about. Too many things had happened that weren't supposed to, almost as if she were thrown into an alternate universe. But she was still the same girl, with the same memories, and no answers.

She wished she had more to show for those visits all these years later. Instead, she took her indecision to a bigger, more expensive school. At least she was on scholarship.

Despite being held back in first grade, Lennon thrived in intellect. She was valedictorian in high school—though she refused to make a speech—and passed all her freshmen classes with flying colors. But after two years, the window to choose a major was rapidly closing, and she didn't have the slightest clue where to put her brains. After all the career quizzes, job fairs, and counselor meetings, no career path had yet caught her attention. She hadn't inherited her father's artistic abilities like her sister had. Going into realty had been a consideration for a brief, dark moment, but that would be the ultimate betrayal. Lennon promised herself long ago she'd be nothing like her mom, lest she risk becoming *exactly* like her.

Currently she was leaning toward marine biology, only because she grew up with the ocean at her doorstep. It lacked the mental challenge she craved, though, and Lennon didn't know anybody making a living off studying fish. Some could see this as laziness, lack of preparation, or even entitlement. But the truth was that as long as she could remember, Lennon had felt frozen, unwillingly propelled by time. Every year was a new level she hadn't expected, or necessarily wanted, to reach. Yet here she was, scrambling, trying to improvise her way out of her own trap...again.

In the midst of her spiral, she hadn't heard the door swing open. The small, harmonic voice came before she could even look up.

"I *knew* it!"

3

Page rushed in, wrapping her sister in her long arms. "I *knew* it was you, Lemon!"

Page had used the old nickname as if nothing had changed. Lennon nearly crushed her with the strength of her squeeze, swaying them back and forth. *She's okay*, she thought, closing her eyes in relief.

"Are you surprised?" Lennon asked, pulling away to look over her face. Everything appeared the same, despite how long the past five months had felt. "She didn't tell you I was coming so soon, at least?"

Page pulled away, a dimple sinking deep into one cheek. "Nope. You totally got me."

She drew another gasp of delight at the plastic cup sitting next to Lennon. "Ugh, you're the best...wait, these are hardly melted. How fast were you driving?"

Lennon's lip curled in amusement at Page's motherly tone. She's always had that, even when she was little enough to confuse *n*'s and *m*'s. "Hey, I made it here, that's...what's this?"

She took the painted card in Page's hand, inspecting the talent of her younger sister's hands. "Wow, P. This is *beautiful*."

Page waved dismissively. "Barely had time to make it look good. Thought I'd have a few more—"

"Thank you," Lennon gushed, pressing a kiss to her slightly fluffed hair.

"You're welcome." Page bent over the counter, her frizzy locks falling like a curtain between them. A thick pink strand of her bow tickled her cheek as she scribbled on the sign-out sheet.

"I'm gonna miss you, Mrs. Kylie," Page said softly, lowering the pen. "You'll always be my favorite secretary."

Her words morphed the woman's large eyes into glassy saucers, glistening under the harsh overhead lights.

Mrs. Kylie busied herself with a stack of papers while she regained control. "Can you girls keep a secret?"

The girls nodded in sync, entranced. Mrs. Kylie looked up, lowering her voice to a whisper. "You two are my favorites, too."

Page beamed, and Lennon nodded tightly, struggling to contain her own emotions. Time stopped for no one; not even the innocents were spared. The thought alone had her holding back a wall of tears, and she swallowed them in a lump down her throat. *Don't be such a little bitch*, she scolded herself. Now *that* was some good advice Cash had given. It was during the peak of an argument when Lennon had started crying. It seemed harsh for a twelve-year-old at the time, but she grew to see the truth in it.

The high of being reunited quickly took over once they said goodbye. The summer air was intoxicating, sending the girls into a fit of giggles; Page's voice sounded even more angelic now that her voice wasn't crackling over poor cell service. Lennon hooked an arm around her mini, taking her backpack to hoist it over her own shoulder, and held up a set of jingling keys. "You wanna drive?"

Page gaped as if she'd asked her to smoke heroin. "I'm fourteen, Lennon."

"Yeah?"

"I don't even have my permit yet!"

Missing Page

"I'm aware." She stuck a finger in her sister's open mouth, making her splutter, and Lennon's laugh carried like smoke through the air.

Page wrinkled her nose, but after a moment, she chuckled too. "No. That's such a bad idea."

Lennon pushed her playfully, going around the left side. "You're no *fun*, Jimmy."

Page's brow furrowed at the sight of the Jeep. "You parked in a handicap?"

"Did I?" Lennon asked innocently, settling into the seat. Page grumbled under her breath. It wasn't possible for Lennon and innocent to coexist. She always had intent, a plan, and the curse of over-observance—nothing got past her. Sensing disappointment, Lennon quickly changed the subject as Page tucked her Invisalign into a napkin, eager to dig into her dessert.

"Just gonna be you and me tonight, by the way." Lennon pressed her shoe against the clutch and shifted into first gear while Page pondered. "Any suggestions for dinner? I was thinking fish tacos, or —*hey*, is that my shirt?"

"I can't do dinner tonight," Page said, avoiding her sister's shocked stare. "I'm going to Emery's, we have to finish this project..."

She trailed off at the expression on Lennon's face.

"Emery Felton?" Lennon asked bewilderedly, choosing her next words carefully. It wasn't classy to call a fifteen-year-old 'that bitch,' although the way she'd said her name sounded pretty close. "You two are friends again?"

Her cheeks went pink. "Yeah. We're starting over."

"Page—"

"Lennon," Page interjected, begging her not to start.

"She treats you like shit."

Her little sister fidgeted. Lennon was as stubborn as she was protective; Page should've known better than to think she'd let it go.

"She's been nicer, kind've," Page offered weakly.

"Kind've? What, she's not steamrolling over you in soccer

anymore? Calling you an idiot in front of everyone? You have plenty of other friends you could do that project with!"

Page sucked in her cheek without the dimple, causing the other side to sink in. "She just gets insecure sometimes...she doesn't know how to handle it."

"So? That doesn't mean she gets to make fun of you. You don't have to put up with that, Page, that's the great thing about people who aren't family. You can choose who you keep around, and tell the rest to fuck off."

"You and I both know I won't do well without her," she whined. "She's the smartest kid in our grade, all of her classes are advanced—"

"Well, I'm home now, and I'm smarter than Emery and your friends combined. I'll help you."

Page's lip puffed out in a pout, and she gazed out the window. "Yeah, well, you're not *always* home."

It stung more than she'd meant it to. Lennon's lips formed a hard line, guilt settling between her brows. Page sighed, letting her head fall back against the seat. "It'd be weird to pull out now. She really does have good parts about her...she won't let anyone else be mean to me, she even covered when Mr. Adams caught me cheating off—"

"Caught you *what*?"

Page's nostrils flared, stressing over this sudden confrontation. "It's just one night, Lennon!"

"One night, and then she sucks you in with another guilt trip."

She could see Page's fallen face in her peripheral, silently begging her to let it go. Lennon exhaled, twisted the steering wheel in her hand. She couldn't stand her sister's pain in any shape or form, misdirected or not.

"Just promise me you won't let her humiliate you again. Or I'm gonna have to beat up a minor."

She was joking—mostly. Lennon couldn't stand bullies. It was hard enough having one for a mom and then going to school with more of the same. It left her little tolerance for disrespect anywhere else, and that mouth of hers could be a loose cannon. When it came

Missing Page

to her sister, though, the protective fury was enough to make her fists twitch. It's one of the reasons she resorted to smoking instead of drinking; there was a genetic rage brewing inside of her, waiting for something—or someone—to bring it out.

"Thanks for the gelato." Page raked her fingers through her shiny dark hair, an old nervous tic. "Did you see Theo?"

When did she get so grown-up? Although Page was a mini version of her, Lennon was certain she'd never been that pretty. Page's beauty was magnified by her innocence and compassion, a luxury Lennon could never afford. She wanted the best for everyone, even if it were at her own expense. It was a beautiful tragedy, and that's why Lennon saw her as art—to be admired, not touched, by the dirty hands of passersby who just saw something shiny. Lennon wanted to preserve and protect her as long as she could, give her what she'd been unable to give herself. Woe was the universal story of the eldest daughter.

Then, as if to remind her she was't quite a woman yet, the wind scattered the girl's brunette waves around her scrunched face, forcing her to pluck the loose strands from her mouth.

Lennon smiled briefly, and then turned her attention to the last group of pedestrians crossing the road that separated them from the Pacific Coastal Highway.

"Ugh, can't they wait until June?" Lennon grumbled. The streets were already teeming with tourists, keeping her hostage at each stoplight. Once they were cleared, she weighed her foot over the pedal, sending the Jeep forward with a roar.

"So..." Lennon wet her lips as she searched for a topic, still adjusting to the salty air. "What's new with you? Tell me everything."

Page pursed hers. "Erm...I finally got my math up. I *might* finish with a low B if I did good on finals, but at least I won't have to retake it next year."

"That's great!" Lennon exclaimed, swelling with pride.

Page shrugged, not as impressed. "It's a C."

"School's never been easy for you, you can't control that. You *can* control your work ethic, and look how much effort you've put in. I mean, you stuck with your tutor all semester, without complaint. That says a lot. You should be proud, Page."

She snorted, tucking her chin. "I think Mom would say otherwise. She makes sure to remind me every time I get a report card that you had straight As." Her tone deepened, mimicking their mother's. "*You two have the same genes, figure it out!*"

"Yeah, well, Mom's an asshole." The words shot off Lennon's tongue before she could stop them. Ever the diplomat, Page chewed on her lip silently, not wanting to engage.

"Sorry." Lennon swallowed the last chunk of waffle cone. "I meant to say, it's not fair of her to compare us like that. If it makes you feel better, she always asks me why I can't be as sweet as you."

"Maybe if they had a third kid, it'd be the perfect combination of us," Page suggested, half teasing.

"And she'd be just as miserable." Lennon sighed. "Speaking of, when did you and Emery start being friends again?"

"Few weeks ago." Page answered carefully, scooping another spoonful of gelato into her mouth. "I was eating lunch with Sam, and then she came and sat with us, talked to me like nothing had happened. That's Emery's way of apologizing."

Lennon scoffed. "Sounds familiar."

She eased up off of Page's warning glare. "Isn't Sam the boy who asked you to the dance? What's been going on there?"

Page cheeks flushed with red, crinkling with a wince. "Sam's a girl, so no. That was Zach. And I didn't go, we had a soccer game."

"I thought you liked him."

"I was considering him," Page said politely.

"God, you're just like your big sister." Lennon's lips twisted into a grin. "Did anybody in particular push him out of the picture?"

The teen rolled her eyes, resting her cheeks on her fists. "Nah. I just wanted to focus on school."

Soft, intuitive, diplomatic...Page was everything Lennon wished

Missing Page

she could be, all at the impressive age of fourteen. The girl could forgive as easily as Lennon could forget.

The smell of weed hit both of their faces as they passed a collection of apartments. Page grimaced and Lennon salivated, but she shook the craving out of her head. There would be plenty of time for that; she'd only get a few more uninterrupted hours with her sister before she left, just a few more hours of being Lemon. She turned the corner, pupils swelling as the ocean came into full view.

One of Lennon's favorite parts of driving home was the road wrapping around the rolling emerald hills. Vibrant flowers sprouted out of the mountainside on her right and a view of the ocean glimmered on her left—this speed limit was the only one she followed. Lines of cars parked along the walking trail created a multi-colored horizon along the protective railing, all of which belonged to an array of snorkelers, scuba divers, and surfers.

"You ever wonder why so many beach activities start with S?" Lennon tore herself away from the twinkling water to check on Page, who waited expectantly.

"Is that the beginning of a joke or something?" Page asked finally, cocking a brow.

"No, I'm genuinely asking. Sailing, swimming, surfing, san—"

"Are you high?" Page looked at her strangely, glancing at her hands on the wheel.

Lennon's ears tinged with red. Any part of her that had felt cool before just flew out the window. "No, Jesus! Forget it."

"That was such a stoner thing to..." Page trailed off, something on the road catching her attention.

Lennon turned her head, breath stopping instantly.

She was seeing a ghost hiking up the road. A blonde, tan ghost. Sweat glistened above his brow, and his nose was splashed with fresh freckles.

Page's elbow dug into Lennon's ribs. "Slow down, Len, let's say hi!"

Lennon reluctantly eased her rigid foot onto the brake pedal. She didn't want to stop, as she was still reeling from the five-second heart attack she'd just endured, but it was his eyes and the freckles that brought her out of her building panic. No, it wasn't a ghost like she'd previously thought, but her heart was already miles away.

"Conrad!" Page shouted, waving her hands out the top of the Jeep. The young man lifted his hazel eyes from the road to them, nodding with a small smile.

Conrad Bates was an old family friend, though Lennon hadn't seen or spoken to him since she was a little girl. She'd been closer to his younger brother Wyatt, the boy she'd spent almost every day with in daycare the summer before first grade. Her *first* first grade, anyway.

Her memories of Conrad were less numbered, but just as vivid, and all loud; whether it be shouting after catching them sneaking into his room to play Xbox or booming mischievous laughter after a prank. A memory flickered behind Lennon's lids—the baby-faced version of the man they were driving toward, convincing her that his sandbox was chocolate milk flavored...how his crooked grin pushed up against his chubby cheeks after she swallowed a mouthful. She thought she would die of suffocation, but he found it utterly hilarious. Four years of life experience was no match for a nine-year-old boy's tricks.

Now his cheeks had hollowed out to reveal sharp cheek and jaw bones, and his smile had evened out. His eyes had changed too, less lively than before, but she'd seen that change before he went away. She recognized that dimness—hers looked the same.

It took mere months for the Bates to unravel after tragedy splintered their family. Mrs. Bates stayed, unable to leave the one thing that gave her a sliver of life *before*, but Conrad and his father couldn't bear to stay for the same reason. After they moved, Lennon saw Conrad only during his custodial summer visits, and always in passing; but even that stopped once he turned thirteen. Over time, the Bates had become a bad memory, a distant nightmare.

He'd recently graduated with a civil engineering degree from Stanford, but lack of work placed him back in Laguna for a temporary reset. Seven months ago, Lennon's mom saw Conrad at

Missing Page

the grocery store and stopped to catch up. Cashmere happened to be coming fresh from an argument with Page about her failing grades, and she offered him a tutoring job practically on the spot. Conrad declined at first—Lennon imagined the reminders were too painful—but after a few more weeks of unemployment (and Cash's masterful negotiating skills) he accepted.

Lennon first started seeing him without realizing it during her FaceTime calls to her sister. Back then he was just a pixelated form passing the screen every now and then, a faceless voice politely asking Page to return to her work. It wasn't Conrad, it was just *the tutor*. When she did finally recognize him, it knocked the breath out of her, like shrapnel through her lungs. He was much quieter than she remembered, more grown up. She wondered if he had grown to dislike her even more, what with her being a near-constant interruption in Page's sessions. It was never on purpose, though. Lennon just had impeccable timing for inconvenience.

She thought she'd prepared herself for this moment, but the way her heart pounded said otherwise. *Should've smoked that joint,* she thought regretfully.

"Hey, Page," Conrad called, his voice easily reaching them. He'd kept the same handsome surfer-boy look from his youth, blond hair hanging just above his eyes. But his teenage acne had smoothed over, and his ears didn't seem so big as they once did. *He looked just like him.*

He turned his warm smile onto Lennon as if he'd heard her thoughts, and her stomach plummeted. "Been a minute, Lennon. Good to see you."

She swallowed, still recovering. "You too."

Page reached over and pushed down on her sister's leg, jerking the car to a halt.

"Page, are you crazy?" Lennon hissed. "Don't do that shit again."

Page ignored her. "How's the water?"

He turned to the ocean as if it'd give him the answer. "Pretty good! Snorkeled a little, found some cool fish. Breaking in summer, y'know..." He looked at the Jeep, a hint of longing in his expression. "Just like you two seem to be doing."

"Well, we'll see you around..." Lennon said quickly, her hand tightening around the gear shift. She'd been aching for this slow, scenic drive, and now she couldn't wait to be done with it.

"I'm sure! Hopefully not you." He pointed to Page, who stopped mid-wave, confused. "Nobody should see their tutor on summer break."

Page laughed, and shook her head. "If I see another math problem with a letter in it, I'll rip my eyes out."

Lennon sat a bottle of shaken champagne, buzzing with nervous energy and ready to shoot out of her seat. They'd almost gotten to full stop when she pushed her foot to the pedal, ripping a snarling response from the Jeep. Page spluttered at the hair flying into her mouth as they took, leaving Conrad waving with a confused smile in the background.

"You didn't say bye!" Page hissed.

Unable to bear the confused disappointment in her sister's eyes, she kept her eyes glued to the road. "He'll live."

She should've known better than to come back thinking things could be better, that this would be the time her past magically disappeared. Lennon wished Laguna could be the paradise to her that it was to everyone else, but the mirage had been wiped away long ago. Even paradise was just a place, and no matter how much time passed, no matter who left or who came, she could never rid herself of the memories that lived there, too.

4

Page could read her sister better than anyone. Even with her hair covering most of her face, it was clear something had changed.

"What's wrong?" Lennon didn't answer, but Page had a stubborn streak, too. "Why were you being so weird?"

"I thought he was someone else," Lennon said, purposefully vague. They turned into the driveway, rolling to a stop in front of the garage door.

Page pondered for a moment while they got out of the car until it dawned on her. "Did you think it was Wyatt?"

A cluster of clouds rolled over the sun then, dropping the temperature by a few degrees. Already facing away from her, Lennon let the pain of his name flash over her face for a brief instant before recovering. Of course Lennon she had known it wasn't him—Wyatt was dead. He had been for over a decade.

Page couldn't tell if she had heard her or not, but she was too wary to ask again. The youngest Mayfield followed her sister inside wordlessly, letting her backpack drop to the floor at the door. An oldies rock station played over the house speakers relaxing both of their shoulders; a subtle-but-sure notification of their father's presence.

"Dad?" Lennon called.

"John?" The voice came from down the hall. "Is that you?"

"It's me!" she called again, smiling.

"Ah, shit, let me get the...all right, coming!"

A tall, leather-skinned man grooved down the hall with a film camera in hand, wearing only a pair of camel-colored trousers. His hair was still wet from the shower, sprinkling droplets onto his shoulders and trickling down to a belly that was finally beginning to let loose after many committed years at the gym. Despite his years, the man moved in perfect time with the music, and still kept his youthful humor. He was using his camera to shred an invisible guitar with enough force to shake the rest of the water from his curly salt-and-pepper hair, and the girls couldn't help giggling through their wide grins. He took Lennon into a tight squeeze, and pressed a kiss to the side of her head.

"Hi, baby," he said. "So happy to see you. Welcome home."

In true Stacy Mayfield fashion, he pulled away from the sweet moment to move his hips in an exaggerated circle, unable to resist the raspy screams of Led Zeppelin.

"*Nobody* wants to see that, Dad," Lennon groaned teasingly.

"You heard the man! I gotta roll, can't stand still." He stopped dramatically, lifting his camera up. "Speaking of roll, stay right there... let's see that killer smile—"

"Jeez, Dad, at least put a shirt on." Page laughed.

"And cover up this six pack?" he asked, squinting through the lens. "Thank God your mother isn't here, you'd have to pry her—"

Stacy stopped, tilting his head when he realized the comment came from behind his oldest's tall frame. Page lifted onto her tiptoes to peek her head over Lennon's shoulder, smiling innocently.

"What are you doing home, young lady?" he asked, attempting a stern look.

"That would be courtesy of your trouble child." Lennon lifted her hand. "Wanted to give her the Lennon special."

He checked the silver Rolex glinting on his wrist, and his brows furrowed in response. "You've still got an hour of school—"

"C'mon, Dad, be cool!" Page pleaded.

He scratched his head, but a lenient shrug followed. He took a few steps to hug his youngest, shooting a pointed look at the two of them. "Well...don't make a habit out of this, all right? And nothing's free around here—you two owe me an extra fishing trip next week. With *no* moaning or complaining!"

"Promise!" the teen exclaimed. "Mermaid promise."

Lennon smiled. It'd been a while since she'd heard that. Stacy eyed his eldest, poising a single brow expectantly.

"Mermaid promise," she agreed.

"Alright. Oh, and one more condition...*smile!*" He lifted the camera in a surprise attack, allowing the girls only a moment to pose and grin—though Lennon's felt like more of a grimace—before he clicked the shutter.

"That was a good one!" he exclaimed proudly.

Yeah, right. Lennon would make sure that photo went straight into the trash before it could see the light of day.

"What time are you leaving, Dad?"

"Soon," he sighed, a tinge of regret in his voice. "I gotta run over to the barber and then meet your mom for dinner before the gala."

"She said you guys would be home around eleven...?" Lennon glided over to the kitchen, reaching for a bag of chips. "What do you think?"

"I think that's a load of bologna," Stacy muttered with a chuckle. "I'm gonna try to get her back around midnight. You want us here before then?"

"Nah. You two have fun," Lennon said, grinning.

Stacy scowled. She and her father were alike in many ways; the desire to stay home was no exception. He was kicking himself over this, especially with it being the first night they've all been together this year. But as Led Zeppelin's chorus rounded again, his mood lifted, and he danced back to the bedroom to look for the rest of his outfit.

On the deck, Lennon groaned after the first chip hit her tongue. "Ugh, I missed having food at my fingertips."

Other than the gelato, she hadn't eaten in hours. A content sigh coursed through her, stretching her legs out over the deck chair. Page took a seat on the lounge chair next to her sister, tearing open her bag of chips.

"I'm putting a mini fridge in my dorm if I ever make it into college."

"You're getting into college, Page."

She hated when her sister talked like that, like she didn't have the brightest future of them all. "Even if they don't want to snatch you up the second they see your portfolio, Mom and Dad will take care of it. Nobody's gonna turn down a new art wing."

It was intended as a playful joke, but Page's lips thinned into a worried line. They were quiet for a moment, munching on their chips.

Page was the first to break the silence. "Do you think Mom's gonna get crazy tonight?"

"It's the gala. Crazy's gonna be the nicest way she'll come home." Lennon laughed darkly. She didn't bother to sugarcoat the truth; Page was all too familiar with her mom's drinking habits. If she wasn't getting the brunt of Cash's subsequent behavior, she was watching Lennon endure it.

Page found it all utterly humiliating. A lot of people who attended the gala were parents. It was a small town—gossip traveled among the adults like a plague, trickling down to their children who spread it at school. She was never able to come up with an excuse for her mother's over-the-top intoxication, and refused to brush it off with humor; she wouldn't share a laugh at anyone's expense, especially her family's. Although a lot of people found it funny, none of it was—especially once she got home. Instead, Page pretended she never saw Cash like that, because truly, she wished she didn't.

Her sister's reputation wasn't much better. Lennon wasn't violent, but there were other rumors still whispered amongst the upperclassmen. Everyone wanted the mysterious, unpredictable girl that remained just out of reach, with stories of nights so wild that Page's compassion and quietness came off as boring in comparison.

"I'm glad school's almost over. You're so lucky." Page's words were coated with longing envy, but even envy dripped like honey from her sweet voice. "You only have two years left,. Then you're done forever...you get to start your life."

It should have brought Lennon relief, but it only reminded her of all the decisions she'd have to make soon. She felt like her life was ending, not starting. Her fingers twitched, yearning for the joint hiding upstairs. She turned her hopeless despair to her sister, wondering if she could possibly get an all-solving answer out of her.

"What do you want to be when you grow up, P?"

"Hmmm..." Page thought for a moment, looking out toward the ocean. "Artist, I guess. I can't think of anything else."

So much for that.

They fell into a natural silence, soaking up the sun that had begun its descent. Lennon's thoughts drifted back to Wyatt, trying to imagine what he would be studying. They built a lot of sand castles and Lego sets together...maybe an architect? It was all flippant guesses. Most four and five-year-olds had no idea what they wanted to be when they got older—*Fairy* or *dog* were as viable as vet or teacher.

Well Wyatt, she thought, *at least we're in the same boat.*

A nightmare had begun to creep behind Lennon's eyes when the glass door slid open, yanking her back into reality. Her dad came onto the deck in an old band tee, with a white button-up and suit jacket folded over his arm.

"We probably won't get back before you're in bed." He planted a kiss on her head, squeezing her shoulder. "Where's your sister?"

She swiveled her head to the empty chair. *When had she left?* "She was just here…"

"Well, in case we don't see you, goodnight, sweet dreams, and I love you."

Lennon followed him inside to the entryway, watching him lean over the stairs' white railing. "Page?"

"In my room!" A muffled voice called from below. Lennon crossed her arms, her thumb sweeping absentmindedly over the crook in her elbow.

"I'm heading out, baby girl. Have fun tonight, love you!"

"Bye Daddy, love you too!"

Lennon waited at the door, holding the keys to his prized '73 Bronco in her palm. His father had started restorations years ago, but it was Stacy who finished it. The worn, faded interior was replaced with British tanned leather, and he'd covered the chipped paint with a fresh coat of boxwood green. They'd even installed a brand new sound system.

"Has Mom been using my car?" Lennon asked, dropping the keys into his palm.

"Not recently," he frowned. "Last time I saw her in it was a few months ago."

"Gotcha." Her hardened features betrayed her soft tone.

Stacy chuckled. "Did she leave it a mess?"

Her eyes flitted to his uncomfortably. "No. She left the tank nearly empty, though."

She didn't know why she had omitted the part about her findings. Perhaps she wasn't ready to move into the next phase of Cashmere's cycle just yet; voicing the problem always led to confrontation, and that was Cash's arena, not theirs. If a hurricane was coming either way, she'd stay in the eye as long as she could.

He dug in his pocket and fished out a leather wallet, handing her a wad of twenties. Her gratitude was overpowered by anguish; Cashmere never had to clean her own messes. Lennon let her chest and anger deflate before she looked at him, hoping he only saw her

Missing Page

appreciation. "Thanks, Dad. Oh, and thanks for stripping the Jeep—"

"You know your old man's always got you taken care of." The boxwood green Bronco roared to a start, and he saluted her as he passed. "Don't say I never did nothing for you, John!"

She loved when he called her that. As much as Stacy loved that Bronco, or even photography, John and Jimmy would always be his proudest creations.

Lennon waited until he disappeared to head downstairs, her long legs needing only three strides to get to the royal blue door. She entered her sister's room to find her bent over a paper, her long hair obscuring her work from view.

"Whatcha doing?" Lennon stepped closer to the desk. The page was packed tight with words and artistic designs, but that was all she noticed before it disappeared.

Page jumped, pressing her hand to her chest. "Oh my *God*, you scared me!"

Lennon's brows conjoined, feeling slightly offended. "I live here, dude."

Page folded the paper into a small square, stuffing it into her pocket. "It's just notes for the project."

Lennon turned her attention to the large new addition hanging above the bed. As talented as Stacy was with his camera, Page was able to paint magnificence worlds onto canvas since childhood—it was the best window into what her mind looked like.

A fairy-firefly hybrid took up most of this painting, with a stunning, golden-filtered backdrop of waterfalls and ethereal flowers. The pixie's features were sharp, almost jarring; its chin, cheeks, even nose all came to angular points in just the right places. It looked like Page had seen both heaven and its angels.

"Page...this is incredible. When did you make it?"

"Few months ago." She shrugged, throwing an unimpressed glance in its direction. She clicked the mousepad on her laptop one final time, and shut it gently. "I should probably head out soon—"

"C'mon! First Dad, now you? It's my first day back," Lennon felt childish whining the way she was, but she couldn't help feeling unimportant. "Let's watch a movie, bike around town or something. You can't leave me alone on the first night—"

"You're not alone!" Page gestured to her bed. "You have Kaiser."

Hearing his name, the Shepherd poked his head up from his nap. Once he realized they weren't asking him to get off the bed, he settled back in with a sigh, closing his eyes. Lennon rolled her own beneath furrowed brows, groaning.

"Traitor," Lennon grumbled. She followed her upstairs, trying to think of a way to prolong their time together.

"You want a ride or anything?"

The girl was almost too ready with a counter as she stepped outside. "Nah, I've got my bike."

"You mean *my*—" Lennon cut herself off. She was starting to echo her mother, and even though she'd been joking, it rattled her. She changed her tone, lifting her hands in surrender. "Okay...okay. Fine. But it better be the best damn project I've ever seen."

Page grinned, shaking her head, playfully shoving her sister. "Jeez, you're acting like I'm leaving forever. It's just a few hours..."

"I haven't seen my sister in four months, sue me!" Lennon cried. The breeze picked up, rustling through the loose linen of her blouse.

"Is that a new tattoo?"

An overwhelming sense of love and pride for the young woman swelled in Lennon's chest. This tattoo had immediately become a favorite, even before the artist could wipe the suds off her red skin. "It's you, P."

Though she remained quiet, her face gave her away, lip jutting out just slightly. "Love you," she said in a hushed tone. She hiked a leg over the bike, her muscles slender and strong from soccer season.

"Should be back around ten thirty...ish."

"Love you more. Be safe," Lennon called.

With effort, Page pushed her weight down onto the pedal, urging the bike forward. The blue ribbons sprouting out of the handlebar fluttered into little waves of goodbyes, as did her long, chestnut hair. "See you later!"

She glided down the road with the same grace as an angel to the clouds, floating and effortless. Lennon waited until she turned the corner before allowing her emotion to expel in a breath.

Kaiser met her at the door, nudging Lennon's hand to get her attention. A few hours of solitude after a semester of thin-walled dorm life would be heaven to most college students, and she not only had her own room, but basically an entire apartment to herself upstairs. But she was still dewy eyed once she reached the suite, and yearned to make the time pass quickly.

The solution hit her at the same moment the earthy, slightly skunky smell did. She pulled her dresser drawer open and lifted the stick to the underside of her nose, inhaling deeply. Her quivering fingers closed around a lighter next, and with that she flitted down the stairs for the balcony, stopping only for a quick moment in the kitchen to find a bone for the dog and something for the joint. *No ash trays...* Surprisingly, she was the only smoker in the family; Stacy was trying to set an example, and Cashmere was too worried about wrinkles.

Lennon's scouting eyes settled on a stained-glass bowl sculpted to look like angry, frothing swells. It had burdened the weight of a single apple earlier, but now it was empty—practically begging to be used. As long as she washed it after, there couldn't be any harm done, right?

She took it into her hands and carefully carried it out to the lounge chair, setting it next to her. It was heavier than she'd expected, but at least it was stable. Lennon tossed the bone onto the other chair and twisted the white filter between her fingers as she flicked the lighter. After a few minutes, the air sucked its weight off of her, and her thoughts went fuzzy.

With the stream of consciousness now muted, nature's song sharpened in her ears. She couldn't believe the sounds of her home were now real, tangible. For five months she had to close her eyes to warp the hum of traffic into the familiar song of waves, pretend that car honks were the call of seagulls. On the contrary, the stomping of feet down the halls or sporadic shouting of drunken rage required no twisting of reality. If she had to deal with those either way, she preferred the better view.

Lennon tapped a painted finger three times against the butt of the joint, letting the breeze sweep away its ash in a small dance of smoke and fire. There was something about nature here that could make anything beautiful—even the things that brought pain.

She licked her lips after filling her lungs, hoping for one last taste. The poison kissed her deeply, its smoky tongue traveling through her body like roots of a tree. It was then sleep came to take her from the dying sun's arms, finally silencing the soundtrack of her home.

5

A NEW GRAVITY EVENTUALLY FOUND HER. THE AIR WAS COLDER, drier. Lennon knew it was Hart's arm around her shoulders, having accidentally memorized the weight of him. Ever chivalrous, he had insisted walking her back to her apartment from the his friend's Halloween party.

The two were so close that their hips knocked together like an offbeat Newton's Cradle, his bedazzled pant snagging her dress every other step. Hart was being extra humorous tonight, so much so that she had to pause multiple times in the hall to catch her breath, dizzy with laughter.

With concentrated effort, they found her number and stumbled inside, still giggling at their lack of coordination. Lennon broke away first, plucking the pins from her hair.

"You got a single?" he asked, blinking at the queen bed tucked into the corner.

Lennon shrugged with indifference as she kicked off her last shoe. "Still have the same thin walls as everyone else."

Though the boy behind her had been treated like a king at the costume party moments before, he now felt much smaller. Lennon was surrounded in something powerful—it was both magnetic and impenetrable. He had so many questions, but Lennon *hated* talking about herself, and it wasn't some kind of humility act, either. He'd seen the discomfort spread over her face when he'd asked something too personal, the way her fingers picked at each other until she could throw the question back to him which only drove him further into his maddening curiosity. She was irresistibly enigmatic, and it lit his interest like wildfire.

It turned small things like getting a yes to lunch or studying into huge, earth-shaking wins. The day she asked him to join her on an evening walk, he thought his heart would burst through his chest.

His attention trailed to the pink envelope on her nightstand, momentarily forgetting the unspoken no-questions rule. "What's that?"

"Oh, it's just..." Lennon started dismissively. Once she saw what he was pointing to, her voice lifted in surprise. "Oh, that? It's from my sister."

Sister. She'd never talked about her family before, and he'd certainly never heard that kind of endearing tone in her voice.

Lennon looked up to gauge his sudden silence, feeling her cheeks grow hot off his small, triumphant smile. She'd accidentally opened up. He was too nervous to ask more, but something in his expression made her want to share more.

"She, er—she sends me these care packages every month." Lennon reached underneath her bed to pull out a collection of boxes. Tiny pieces of curled confetti spilled as she removed the lids from each one, littering the floor in multi-colored sparkles. Chip bags, hair-ties, fuzzy socks, and lip balm were some of the most common, but there was a small shop's worth of trinkets and self-care items.

"Wow. She really set you up."

He looked over the collection of goodies in awe. Now she was pulling out a hydrating face mask and...black beard dye. He squinted in confusion.

"What's that for?"

She laughed, and he lit up. "She wants me to match my eyebrows to my hair since I dyed it. She's too nice to say it, but she hates that they're different."

Hart smiled, allowing a small laugh of his own.

"She has a good heart," Lennon continued, returning her treasures to their cardboard chest. "The best, actually."

Hart helped remove her shoes and lifted her into bed, pausing when she nestled into the crook of his arm. She hummed as he ran gentle hands through her hair, carefully breaking up the sticky product.

"I didn't know you could sing like that, back there," she murmured. "You have that classic, old-timey voice."

"Does it make me more attractive?" He grinned.

"Don't tell Hart this, because I know it'll go to his head," she teased. "But yes...a hundred percent." The room was dancing around her, but Hart's caressing fingers kept her grounded.

"Lennon?"

"Mhm?" she murmured.

"Are we dating?"

Her eyes shot open, her smile instantly evaporated. "I don't...do that."

"Date?"

Her metallic eyes held his warm pools with a silent question.

Wasn't it obvious?

His arms did not move, but went cold around her, as if realizing they were unwelcome. "Oh," he uttered.

"I like what we're doing, though. I *really* like it," she assured, mover her hand to his. "I want to keep doing it if you do."

It was as close to the truth as she could manage. How could she explain that she liked him—much more than she was comfortable with, actually—but that these things were so much more complex than a feeling?

He was quiet, but not upset like she expected him to be. She thought she saw the corners of his lips lift ever so slightly, though it was too dark to tell.

"Will you sing one more song?" She lowered her voice to a whisper. "A private show? For me."

"Hmm..."

"For me," she repeated, a slight beg in her voice.

He chuckled. "Okay. Let me think of a good one."

She held up a finger. "It has to be Elvis."

"All right, all right." he groaned teasingly, catching her wrist before it poked him in the eye. Somehow, having her as an audience felt much more nerve-wracking than the dozens he'd performed to earlier.

After a moment, Hart cleared his throat and flattened her hand over his heart. She felt the deep lull of his voice rumble the first few lines of Love Me Tender into her palm and cheek, and immediately her eyes grew heavy.

That was the moment Lennon had fallen in love with him. Falling would be a euphemism—it felt more like being thrown headfirst into it, like her heart was being ripped with this all-consuming feeling. And yet, somehow, it wasn't painful. Her heart wasn't breaking, it was *stretching,* making room to accommodate this new person taking residency. It verged on scary more than romantic, but she was pretty sure the feeling would be gone once the chemicals faded away.

So she remained, still spiraling behind closed lids while struggling to stay above the waves of unconsciousness, expending all of this effort just to to keep listening to the man next to her. Ugh, she really *was* in love, and though the moment probably should have felt sweet and made her want to cuddle closer to him, she instead imagined rolling under him and letting him fuck her however he wanted.

That's how she knew she was twisted. Her idea of love was letting someone use her, fulfilling their darkest fantasies with her body. Deep down, every man had them. Hart couldn't be any

Missing Page

different; he just had a better facade.

Hart's gaze drifted to the bare window next to her headboard, trailing off in his song. After a beat, Lennon's eyes fluttered open, realizing the memory was turning into something foreign. She caught the blank, frightening expression that had taken over his face too late, and saw why his muscles had contorted underneath her. This happy memory was meshing with one much more sinister.

When he reached for the strings that held the blinds up, she saw that Hart's warm brown eyes had transformed into someone else's. They were cold, dark and beady; it wasn't him anymore. Her heart pounded as she reached up to stop him, unable to move fast enough. "No, wait, stop! Don't shut those—!"

The room warped around her the second his hand tugged them loose, sucking her like a vacuum out of Hart's arms and into something else entirely.

Wherever she was, her eyes were stuck closed. She could feel her tiny body swaying back and forth in someone's arms; she was being carried. It was the same place she'd gone to on the plane, and almost every night before then. This was another memory— one of her first.

Her breath skipped, and eyelids that once protected her from the outside world now trapped her like a helpless animal. She wanted to squirm, make a noise, let whoever was holding her know she was awake. But her body remained paralyzed, feeling hot breath spread over her face from above.

The light of the sun warmed her eyelids, which meant she was safe. But she was being moved, and if the light went away, bad things would happen.

The arms holding her suddenly lowered, releasing Lennon onto a scratchy material. She listened to footsteps tread quietly around her, casting shadows over her lids. Fear pressed down on her shrunken bladder, forcing her breath out in small bursts. *It's going to get dark soon.* With all her strength, she worked to wiggle the tips of her toes, her fingertips, and finally, her eyelids. Her lashes left each other's fearful embrace enough for Lennon to see out of them, a fuzzy vision of her small, bare arms coming into view...

WHOOSH

She gasped, grabbing on to the rigorous hands pulling her out of her nightmare. Whiskey-ladened breath hit Lennon's face like a ton of bricks, and her mother's face appeared once her eyes shot open.

"*There* she is!" Cash righted herself, lifting a nearly-empty Fireball shooter to her lips. "Wakey—"

Something tripped her, nearly throwing her into Lennon before she caught herself. Cashmere glowered, her happiness twisting into anger instantaneously after finding the culprit.

"Tell me—you did not use—*this*—*bowl*!"

Lennon was still reeling under the star-filled sky, trying to figure out where she was. Only when she found the tattoos on her arm was she able to suck in a breath, her croaky speech finally returning. "What time is it?"

"Cashmere, honey...Cash!" Stacy ran out to the deck, trying to distract his wife. "We gotta get you dressed for bed, c'mon—"

Cashmere started to rant again, but Lennon was quick to tune her out, patting around for her phone. Once she felt the rubber case against her palm, she retracted it into her chest, looking down—thirty minutes past midnight. Her focus changed stations again, tuning back to her parents, and Cash's words finally sharpened into something comprehensible.

"Stacy, your daughter is getting *stoned* on the deck, using a six-hundred-dollar bowl as an *ashtray*. Do you have anything to say about this? Either of you?"

"She's twenty-one, Cash—"

"Why do we have a six-hundred-dollar fruit bowl?" Lennon asked.

Flames of fury were beginning to claw their way out of Cashmere's mouth. She diverted it to her hands, throwing the empty shooter down at their feet. "Forget it! None of you give a shit about this house, *or* this family. You're assholes, both of you!" Her dress swished behind her as she stormed inside.

The air that had been holding the world off of Lennon now trembled under the tension, unable to hold the guilt and shame bearing down. Most of it belonged to Cash, Lennon knew that, but her mom had taken cover inside. Her dad lifted his hand to his temple in attempt to ease the pounding, using the other to tug the tie loose from his neck.

She wanted to ask him why he let her drink that much, but she knew the answer to that, too. Instead, she she opted for humor. "Looks like it was a good night."

Not even a smile. He was stone-faced, clearly processing his own night of horrors. That couldn't have been a fun drive home.

"At least she didn't go full Cashmanian?" Lennon tried again, blinking moisture back into her bloodshot eyes.

Her father didn't laugh, signaling they were too far to recover. He was the best temperature gauge for her mom, and it wasn't looking good. She wondered if she could have avoided this if she'd mentioned the bottle she'd found earlier, but supposed it was neither here nor there now. The damage had been done.

"Where's your sister?" he asked quietly.

Lennon carried the heavy glass bowl to the sink while her dad went downstairs. She twisted the faucet handle, listening as water traveled through the pipes. There was a time when she was young and imaginative enough to think it was little crabs carrying buckets back and forth, though that was long, long ago.

Downstairs, Stacy peeked his head into the royal-blue colored room, first looking at the bed. There was no one, only a slightly rumpled blanket. The room felt cold, like it'd been empty for hours. Even her bathroom light was off, which she usually kept on as a nightlight. His fingers traveled over his graying whiskers in thought before he turned to climb the stairs, a little faster than he had descended them.

Lennon was on her own path upstairs when he took her wrist gently in his hand. "Hey. Did you *see* Page go to bed?"

She blinked again, slow to process. "Is she not there?"

Lennon dug for her phone, pulling up her sister's contact, then location, a frown appearing on her face. "She must be at Emery's still..."

"Let me see." He took her phone, zooming in to the map. "Yeah, that's the Felton's. What's she doing over there?"

Lennon began to type up a text, telling her to come home. "They're doing a project...she probably lost track of time."

He turned away, walking slowly, pensively. She expected him to go down the hall, but he took a seat on the couch, pulling the tie fully off his neck, and his suit jacket after.

"What are you doing?"

Stacy didn't answer right away. He shimmied his shoulders into the cushions, crossed one leg over the other on the coffee table, and rested his hands on his lap. His chin tilted toward the ceiling and a deep inhale followed, shutting himself in his head with closed lids.

"If she doesn't text you back or come home in the next fifteen minutes, we're going over there."

Lennon's fingers found the skin around her cuticles. "You think something's wrong?"

"C'mon, Len. Of all people, *you* should have been the first to pick up on this."

Lennon's brow furrowed defensively, waiting for him to explain.

"She's got two days of school left," he continued. "Her grades are finalized. That was amateur teen bullshit she gave you."

Lennon's stomach dropped. It seemed obvious now that he pointed it out, but Page had never—*never*—lied to her before. *What was she doing?*

"Page isn't like that," she said with loyal confidence. "She's good."

"She is good, and she's also fourteen. She's not a little kid anymore."

Missing Page

Lennon shook her head. She couldn't let his memories of her teens taint his image of Page. "She's not like me."

His eyes opened to find hers. "And what are you like, Lennon?"

The silence was deafening, filling the house like a scream.

Her dad's next words reached her ears like a distant hug. "You know, you're good, too. You can be a good person who sometimes does bad things."

She *hmph'd*. *You can be a bad person who sometimes does good things, too.*

All she wanted to hear were the wheels of a bike crackling over small rocks on the concrete and for Page to walk through that door. The seconds ticked into minutes; first a few, then six. She prepared herself for how Page might return. Angry? No, not likely—sad was more probable. But Lennon was most fearful that she'd return hurt. She considered herself a strong person, but that strength evaporated at the sound of her sister's meek cries. Despite the walls she'd built over two decades, the sound of Page's pain could crumble her to dust in seconds.

Lennon needed her home *now*. For ten minutes her thoughts wheeled, screeching in burnout after burnout. Once the thirteenth minute passed, she strode to the entryway table, yanking the drawer open to grab the Bronco keys with her dad following right behind her.

She couldn't stop her knees from bouncing in the passenger seat, digging her nails into the flesh of her palms to exert the extra energy. *She just fell asleep, that's it.*

A pulsing path of streetlamps shone down through the windshield, illuminating the black vein traveling down the inside of her arm in quick bursts of light.

The Bronco took the Felton's driveway with ease, headlights illuminating a humble little home. The area was quiet, with a park across the street instead of neighbors. It was thick with trees that traversed over an entire acre, a winding dirt path surrounded by colorful, native growth. Their house was the kind where the entrance was on the top floor instead of the bottom, though this style was usually reserved for tight-knit neighborhoods. Most importantly, the lights were off, and Lennon's theory that Page had fallen asleep solidified in her chest.

She followed her dad to the creaky stairs, stopping at the bottom as he ascended. Adrenaline sharpened her senses enough that she could make out the dark shapes tucked beneath the shadow of the patio—dusty storage boxes and rusted junk, all lined against a rough gray wall. Stacy knocked again, but nobody answered. Not even a light flickered in response. Lennon lifted her phone to her ear as she tried Page's phone, still searching. *Ring...*

There was a set of stairs on the back side. She took them to the second floor, stopping at a window. The dark room was partially visible, lit softly by the overhead moon. Lennon leaned so close her nose brushed against the cold glass, searching for any sign of life. *Ring...*

"You see anything, Lennon?" Stacy called from around the corner.

Her bloodshot eyes squinted, trying to bring something —*anything*—into view.

Hi, you've reached Page....

She'd rested her hand against the glass to steady herself, but it popped open with a small intake of air, shooting a shiver down her spine.

"Page!" Lennon yelled, lowering her head to the opening. Stacy joined her at the window, cupping his hands over his brows and squinting.

"What do we do?" Lennon pressed, impatient for the next move. The air was thick with uncertainty, prickling the hairs on her arm the same way an incoming storm would.

He lowered his head to the opening, circling his hands around his mouth. "Page!"

After a moment of silence, Stacy's lips tightened. "Well, she's not here. At least not anymore."

Missing Page

He took slow steps toward the edge of the patio, lifting his phone to his ear. Lennon followed, frustrated with his ambiguousness.

"Who are you calling? You have her parents number?"

He muttered something, but she was sure she misheard. Lennon shook her head, as if that could get the high haze out of her ears. "What? Did you say—"

"I did." He gripped the railing, his hand twisting around the metal. "Emery's parents should still be there."

6

Across town in a small, wooden bar, a phone bellowed at a platinum-haired bartender who looked ready to kill. She shot a glare at the bleating receiver, already swamped with sixteen drink orders and a large crowd fresh from the gala. It rang six times before finally ceasing. Oh well... she was overloaded enough as is without that annoying—

She groaned out loud when it came again, yanking the corded phone from its carrier and tucking it between her ear and shoulder.

"Seadog's," she barked. "Can you hold?"

"It's urgent. I need you to get Kelly Felton on the phone."

She went back and forth for a moment in her head, letting the caller ID make the final decision. The name instantly changed her tone, draining the color from her face. "All right, give me a sec...it's just me tonight, might take a second to find him."

She lifted herself onto her toes, checking the dance floor. She found Mrs. Felton first, a brown-skinned woman with one hand in the air and the other clutching her shimmery dress as she moved to the rhythm. Despite the gathering male crowd, Mr. Felton's eyes seemed to be the only ones missing from the group. As the bartender lowered her heels back onto the ground, the petite woman realized she needn't look any further than her bar. Kelly Felton sat unbothered and content, a whiskey neat traveling through lips covered in the overgrowth of his mustache.

She handed the corded phone to him, beads of sweat glistening above her bleached brows. "It's for you." She nodded.

He raised an eyebrow. A little strange, getting called at a bar, but his interest was piqued. He took the phone, slightly amused.

"Kelly," a familiar voice sputtered through the phone's speaker.

Kelly glanced to the bartender, who mouthed two syllables in an exaggerated form. *MAY-FIELD*.

"Stacy Mayfield," Kelly drawled. "I thought you'd be in bed by now! How's Cash? She seemed to be really enjoying herself—"

"Kelly, listen to me. My daughter's, she's..."

"What?" Kelly shouted, plugging his ear with his finger.

"We can't find Page!" Stacy shouted into the phone.

"Oh. I'm sorry, have you called her?"

"She's not answering," he said impatiently.

Kelly reached for his collar, pulling it off his sticky neck for the hundredth time. "Well, I'm sure Emery can—"

"Kelly, do you know where *your* daughter is?"

"Home," he said, his tone hardening at the accusation. *Where else would she be?*

"I'm standing on your porch right now. She's not here."

Kelly took a beat, the alcohol in his system slowing his processors. "Let me get Paola."

From the lounge chair on the Felton's deck, Lennon was leaning forward, trying to listen despite her many distractions. Her hands felt strange on the wicker, as if they were melting into it. Besides the nervous adrenaline short-circuiting her memory, sativa still coursed through her, distorting her reality into something almost cartoonish and impossible to think in. She ripped her hands from her wooden captors and opened her sister location, paling when nothing showed up. It had gone offline.

"Should we call Mom?" Lennon whispered.

"She wouldn't be able to help. Let her sleep."

"Dad..." Fear shook her voice, betraying her lip.

Stacy reached out, gripping her hand tightly in his. She wondered if he had that same terrible feeling in his gut, the one she'd been trying to deny the past forty-five minutes.

"It's fine," he coaxed. "She's okay, don't freak yourself out."

Lennon clenched her teeth, trying to stop them from chattering. She wanted to believe him, but he wouldn't even look at her—he just kept looking out at the park.

"Well I'll be damned..." he squinted. Lennon straightened, trying to follow his line of sight.

A person was running down the trail, barreling straight toward them. Her body flashed underneath each lamp in quick streaks, the speed whipping her black ponytail against her glistening face.

"*That bitch,*" Lennon seethed. She stormed past her father, meeting the winded girl downstairs.

"Where's my sister?"

Emery panted, glazed eyes scouring for something—or someone. "Are my parents here?"

"Answer me!"

"I haven't...how would I know where she is?" Emery struggled to catch her breath, much less form a thought.

Lennon analyzed every move with overly observant eyes, noticing her slow, glassy stare. *What was up with this girl?* Stacy met them at the bottom, wedging between them.

"We're looking for Page. If you know where she is, *please,* I need you to tell us now."

Emery frowned. "I haven't seen her since—"

"What were you coming from? Is she on her way?" Lennon's voice raised with each question. "Why were you running?"

Emery's response came quick and venomous. "It's perfectly legal to take a jog, *thank you.* And I told you, I haven't seen her."

Missing Page

Lennon snapped. "We tracked her location here, so cut the bullshit!"

"What?" she squeaked.

"You're not in trouble, Emery," Stacy interjected. "And neither is she. We just want to know where our girl is, we're worried about her."

Emery crossed her arms. "I'm telling you, I have *no idea* where she is."

"You're lying," Lennon snarled.

The girl rolled her eyes. "I don't have to explain myself to you, you're not my mom!"

Lennon's fury rose to a boil. *She's fifteen,* she reminded her twitching fingers. Headlights appeared in the distance then, blinding them.

"Fine then, we'll make you tell *everyone*," Lennon hissed after her father walked away. "And you can explain that smell on your breath while you're at it."

Emery's eyes swelled, the blood draining from her face. Lennon left to walk with her father, stopping in front of the old Mercedes parked in the driveway. Paola got out before it fully stopped, rushing right past them to her daughter and murmuring angrily in Spanish. Kelly came next, shaking Stacy's hand as they all came together.

"Emery's saying she hasn't seen her, but—"

"Page told me she was coming here earlier," Lennon interrupted. "We tracked her location."

Kelly looked at his daughter expectantly.

"She never—" Emery winced as Paola's hands tightened around Emery's shoulders, shifting uncomfortably. "*Aye.* Okay, yeah, she—she stopped by."

Paola's nails sank deeper into Emery's shirt. "You had someone over without asking?"

"She didn't even come inside, Mama." Emery shrank from a snarky teen into a scolded child. "It was all a surprise, I didn't know! It was so quick, and then she biked off into the park...she could be anywhere now."

"Yeah, she could be." Stacy put a hand to his forehead. "Look, Kelly, I'm trying real hard—*not*—to lose my shit right now."

"If we knew what Emery was doing out there—" Lennon gestured, trying to bring order to the chaos. "I think that would answer a lot of our questions." Her tone didn't match her eyes, glaring murderously at the intoxicated teen.

Paola looked to her, and then her father. He was supposed to be the one they were discussing with, so why was the twenty-something doing all the talking? Her maternal hackles rose at the girl's clenched fists, stepping protectively in front of her cub.

"Go inside, Emery."

"But Mama—"

"Go!" she repeated.

Emery was more afraid of her mom than Lennon, though only by a slight margin. She glanced back every dozen steps, clearly torn.

Paola glowered. "If I didn't know any better, I'd think you were blaming my daughter for Page's disappearance."

"If she knew anything about where Page was going, don't you think she'd say something?" Kelly added.

"I don't know," Lennon growled. "You just sent her off before we could get an answer!"

"It's past midnight. Emery is fifteen, she's a *child*," Paola snapped.

"So is my sister, and she's *missing*." Lennon retorted. "It's great your kid is safe, but I need to make sure my sister is, too."

Paola's eyes narrowed—she might as well have been talking to Cash, except that this one was whip-smart. She used her dagger of a tongue with technique instead of brute force like her mother.

Kelly came in again, trying to ease the tension. "I understand you're upset. We all want the same thing, and we're going to help you find Page. But I think you're pointing fingers in the wrong direction."

"Your daughter is a bully," Lennon spat. "She's been nothing but hateful to my sister. The only reason Page even went here today was because they...were..." She trailed off. *There was no project.* What

Missing Page

had Page been doing? It didn't matter—she had been here, that was certain.

"Emery is not a bully." Kelly looked at Lennon firmly, then Stacy. "Strong headed, I'll be the first to admit it. But she's not *mean*. And she's certainly not the reason you can't find her."

Lennon would roll her eyes if she wasn't so anxious. "We don't have time for this."

Stacy agreed. He'd stayed much longer than he'd wanted to; Page wasn't here. That's all that mattered. "We have to keep looking, Kelly. If you hear or see *anything*..."

"I got your number from the bartender." He nodded solemnly, placing an arm around his wife. "You'll be the first one I call."

They could never convince Lennon that Emery, the girl with a history of humiliating Page, who was green with envy, was not worthy of suspecting. She'd lied to them, for God's sake! Lennon stormed back to the car, waiting until the Bronco was speeding down the street to let her anger spew.

"Why didn't you stop her? You know Kelly wouldn't make her talk, she *knew* something!"

"Her parents were the ones trying to get her inside, Lennon. They wanted to talk less than she did." Stacy lifted his phone to his ear, lips hardening into a thin line. "Nobody wants to be involved in a missing child case."

The words rocked through her like a tsunami wave. "Who are you calling now?" Lennon asked, exasperated.

"The police."

Her nausea was coming to a peak. She'd been so sure this would have ended at Emery's house—she thought Page would be in the back seat by now. Where *was* she? Was she hurt? Did Emery do something so terrible that Page was hiding, or trapped somewhere? There were so many questions, and the only person who could have answered them was hiding safe inside her home.

She wished she could get her car to cover more ground, but her vision was still swimming. Though she was much more sober than she'd been an hour ago, she didn't want to add 'driving under the influence' to her dad's stress.

They covered every inch of Laguna while Stacy talked to the police. Lennon navigated, directing him to every hidden spot she knew of, every hideout she'd sworn to keep secret. She even texted her old classmates asking for help looking, though most of their phones were on Do Not Disturb.

After the fourth failed attempt, Stacy pulled into a gas station, leaving Lennon alone in the car. She curled up in the seat, trembling with fear. It was getting harder and harder to breathe—her stomach and mouth had completely dried, and the chips she had earlier were threatening to leave her. Her mind was buzzing, desperation reaching spiritual levels.

God, I know you know I don't really believe in you. And if I did, I'd be pissed at you, because what the fuck? She took a breath, trying to calm herself. *In case you are real...I have never asked you for anything*—anything—*and I never will again. But God, if you are even slightly real, I need your help. We're already losing our minds. So please—*

Her icy eyes melted, hot tears threatening to spill over the edge.

Please, bring her back.

Despite her chest rising, it felt as though no air could make it down her closing throat. Her body was convulsing, suffocating. She reached out, feeling for the door handle, and swung forward after it opened abruptly. She tumbled, and a loud crack shot through her spine as her body hit the concrete, all prayers erased by excruciating pain. But from that, she had automatically sucked in, and oxygen pushed forcefully back into her lungs.

Stacy rushed to her aid her as she gasped with short, pained breaths. "You okay, honey?" he grunted, helping her stand. She didn't answer, detaching more and more from this unwanted reality, robotically shutting herself off from the pain.

He hugged her tightly, trying to hold her together. "We're gonna find her, okay? I promise." The gas pump clicked, and he

Missing Page

lifted her into the passenger seat, pulling the seatbelt over her torso.

"It's almost three. I'm taking you home, and then meeting Kelly and some guys back at his house. They're gonna help search."

"What, I'm supposed to go home and *sleep*?"

"That's exactly what you're going to do."

She took one fall, and he was already sending her back? "Dad, I'm *fine*—"

"I'll wake you up as soon as we find her. Or she will, and you can rip her a new one yourself. You're in no shape for this, Len. You gotta go home."

Lennon stifled her guilty sobs, trembling all the way to her bruised tailbone. She hated that he was right. Her eyes remained closed the entire ride, but she recognized familiar bumps once they turned onto their street. They shared one final look after the car shuddered to a stop.

"I'm sorry, Dad."

"Don't, Lennon. Call me if she comes home. I'm sure you'll be the first one she wants to talk to."

She wrapped her arms around her chest as she walked toward the door, listening to his tires roll down the driveway. Kaiser barked from inside, but she stood frozen at the threshold. No step seemed like the right one.

Her dad's words echoed in her head. She had to believe that whatever he was doing or instructed would be best for Page. She put one foot in front of the other until she found herself under the heavy pressure of her shower head, and only then did she let herself cry, digging her nails into her arms until red lines marred the black ink.

Her phone buzzed from the bedroom—a message from Hart, letting her know he'd returned safely. That strange, gut feeling she'd had earlier on their phone call came back to her; he hadn't been the one she needed to worry about, after all.

Lennon didn't realize how exhausted she was until her body settled into the mattress, tailbone complaining. Her bones felt like boulders; anxiety had tightened all of her muscles for the past three hours, pulverizing them into jelly. Lennon's head was going in circles, but she could only come back to one thing–this was her fault.

Sleep settled over the room, melting her emotions into a dull buzz. That floating state felt like an eternity. It was the first time she'd dreamt of something she hadn't experienced, though the flashes were mostly indiscernible. She caught glimpses of open water, heard the distant sound of bell-like laughter, and a strange, out-of-place mirror, but none of it made sense, and it didn't matter. She wouldn't remember any of it once she woke up.

∽

The change in the air was immediate once she regained consciousness. The end of her mattress held her father's weight, but he sat like a stranger, his face obscured by blankets. Every time it seemed like he was about to speak, he took another shallow breath. Though he said nothing, the stillness was loud.

It took a few minutes for her to gain enough courage to peek her head above the covers. The room was filled with sunlight, and the clock next to her read ten.

Ten? Her eyes traveled to her dad, stomach twisting at the sight. His face was pale, aged twenty years overnight. Shades of purple pooled under his tired eyes, and his lips were now set in a permanent frown. Even half-asleep she was laser-focused, her mind sharp as ever. He couldn't keep anything from her.

She sat up slowly, worried she'd crack him if she moved too fast. "Where is she?"

"We found her earlier this morning. In the cove."

Lennon's eyes flashed. *So why isn't she here?* He said 'the cove' as if she should know...did he mean the one they'd visited as children? It couldn't be...nothing was making sense.

"They have her now, the police," Stacy uttered, his voice tight.

Lennon wracked her brain for any sense of reason. *Catalina Cove?* They hadn't been there in years. "Is...is she okay?"

Stacy remained frighteningly statuesque. He had prepared this talk the entire ride home, and now that she asked, was at a loss. Stillness was his only strength.

Again, Lennon's intelligence answered her questions before he could. "How bad is it?" Her lip gave way after a beat, and her voice rose an octave. "Why aren't you saying anything?"

Her father's breath came out staggered. "Because I don't want to tell you, Lennon. I don't want to say it."

Tears streamed down her cheeks, but she stayed silent, waiting. She'd been strong enough to wake up, to ask the questions. It was his turn. With another struggling breath, he turned, finally meeting her eyes.

"She was dead when they found her. She's gone."

7

THE SOUND THAT CAME FROM HER WAS GUTTURAL, ALMOST inhuman. Stacy had braced for a gut-wrenching reaction, but his resolve crumbled as he held his grieving daughter. Her sobs were strong enough to shake them both, coming out in pants bordering hysteria.

She needed answers. The different scenes playing in her mind were torturing her, each more gruesome than the last. "How...what—?"

"They're figuring that out right now. But they need our help." He pushed himself to his feet, pulling her with him. She was surprised she could stand at all; her body was taking over while she wailed, like it knew she would die if it didn't.

"I know, baby. I need you to get ready so we can go to the station. They want to talk to you."

Lennon's brow furrowed, a brief moment of clarity breaking through her grief. "What about Emery?"

"They got what they could from her. She didn't know much."

Of course she didn't. Shock was a temporary buffer to her grief, but it was less effective toward her anguish. The only thing she knew

Missing Page

for sure was that she needed to make it to the police and tell them everything she could remember before Emery could be removed from the equation. *Page was gone.* It would feel real for a few seconds, and then her brain would shut down again.

Kaiser waited for them at the foot of the stairs, head burrowed between his paws. Even he could sense the change in the house, the heaviness in the air. Lennon slipped a hat over her head and began to reach for her keys, but her dad covered her hand with his.

"I'll drive."

She flinched at his touch, pulling away. "I need to be by myself for a bit." She swallowed. "I'll follow you."

Stacy left first, allowing her a few moments to recoup. The metal grooves of the keys dug into her palm, leaving jagged indentations. She didn't want to talk, she needed to *think*. What were the facts?

One, Page's location had been at Emery's before it turned off, and still had yet to be found. Two, Emery was sprinting from where Page had supposedly gone to, dodging nearly every question they asked her, and lying about the rest. And third, Emery was the last person to see Page alive. It all pointed to the very question Emery had evaded last night:

What did she know about Page's disappearance, and how much of it was she responsible for?

The ding of a low gas tank brought her out of her spiral, informing her she only had twenty miles left in her tank. *The cherry on top of a very shitty sundae.* Tears pooled in her eyes, but she gritted her teeth, swallowed them down, and jerked the gearshift into reverse. Tears wouldn't help her now.

The station's waiting room would have felt cold even if it wasn't sixty-seven degrees. The walls were drab gray, same as the linoleum floors. She'd half-expected seashells and paintings to line the walls, but she supposed this place wasn't meant to incite happiness.

Lennon's mother was already there, sitting with her head in her hands. Dark circles exposed her lack of sleep, her hands trembling as she took hold of her daughter and squeezed tightly. Lennon was so confused she couldn't decide whether to stiffen or lean into her. Instead she stood like a mannequin, claiming neutrality. After Cash pulled away, the last Mayfield daughter sat, folding her hands in her lap. She stared at the ink poking out the edges of her sleeve rather than her surroundings, keeping her exterior hard so that nothing could be absorbed.

Her phone buzzed in her pocket, the heartbeat vibrations instantly recognizable. She didn't know how long she could push Hart away for, but how was she supposed to explain this to him when nobody had yet explained it to her? She clicked the lock button twice, sending him to voicemail.

The clock hands' ticking filled the room, counting out seven minutes before she lost count. Though it was silent, she could feel a conversation happening between her parents' fidgeting, their sighs. Cashmere pinched the bridge of her nose to try to stop the tears streaming down her face, Stacy checked his phone every few minutes for the time. They both wanted to escape—Stacy to the ocean with a fishing rod, Cashmere to the closest liquor store. They hadn't found comfort in each other for a long time. Lennon was suddenly filled with an overwhelming, blood-boiling anger at life. THC normally cushioned these kinds of emotions, but nothing could stop the storm clouding her nervous system, twisting her insides into a vicious tornado. She gripped the edge of her seat with white-knuckled fingers, trying to weather it.

Another heartbeat-patterned text came through. Lennon swallowed, paling. "I think I'm gonna..."

The door swung open, revealing a clean-cut man in a white button-up. There was a subtle empathy hiding behind an otherwise professional manner. He had the kind of smile that still ended up being a frown. "Lennon?"

She opened her mouth to greet him, but instead, the entire contents of her stomach emptied onto the linoleum, the sound echoing off the bare walls.

Missing Page

The detective froze, and Stacy rushed to action, rubbing her back comfortingly.

"Oh, God, Lennon..." Cashmere pinched her nose in disgust. She had a thing about vomit.

"That's all right, that's...erm–" the detective stuttered. "Here, let me get..."

He trailed off, disappearing behind the door he came through. Moments later, he returned with a cup of water and a handful of crumpled paper towels. She took a swig from the cup, pressing the scratchy napkin to her lips.

"Sorry," she breathed.

"No need to apologize. You've been through a lot."

"Don't worry about this, we'll get it cleaned up," Stacy murmured, brushing her sweaty hair out of her face. He seemed to have lost every sense of himself over the night, all parts except *Dad*.

"Lennon," the detective continued with practiced professionalism. "If you could follow me, I'd like to ask you a few questions about Page and what you remember from yesterday, if that's okay."

Her mouth was dry, and now a little bitter. The next gulp took its time, making sure nothing else came up with it.

"Yes." Lennon nodded, eager to finally be helpful.

The room the detective placed her in was cold, eerie, and gray. It was as unwelcoming as it was unsettling; she could feel it sucking the soul from her the second she walked in.

She couldn't tell if the smell was from the carpet, walls, or her. There'd been no time to shower this morning; she'd barely been able to brush her teeth or wash her face. Not that hygiene was much of a priority at the moment; as far as she was concerned, her sister's murderer was still out there, roaming free.

The detective extended his hand, gesturing for her to sit in what could potentially be the world's most uncomfortable chair. She wondered how many had sat in it before her—more than she'd thought, based on the sinking middle and tired leather. What had they done? Did they hurt someone, were they the ones hurt? Once she took her seat—the middle swallowing her as she predicted—she felt so small, so helpless; almost as if by design.

He started a recorder, leaning forward. "This is Detective Shultz, the date is May 26th, 2018. I'm currently here with..."

He looked up, waiting for her to answer. She was staring at the recorder, numb.

"It's Lennon, right? Last name Mayfield?" he asked, tapping his pen against the table. She nodded, and he continued. "How old are you?"

"Twenty-one," she croaked, watching him scribble. She wanted to ask him the same thing. What qualified him to investigate the mysterious death of little girls? He couldn't be more than early thirties, and he didn't look like a superhero; he was just a man. The cup crinkled in her palm, and he looked up to her.

"Did you want more?"

"No." She wanted him to start already, so she could see what questions he had for her—if his suspicions matched hers.

"All right," he sighed. "Well, firstly, I'm extremely sorry for your loss. Your father told me you two were very close."

She remained frozen, her shock dulling the pain of his past-tense words. What was she supposed to say? *Thank you?* It was already feeling like an uphill battle, and they hadn't even started yet.

"Now, if you can, I'd like to hear your version of how things happened yesterday. You were with Page for a good amount of time, right?"

She swallowed tightly, nodding.

"Okay. Then let's start from the beginning."

A fly flew close to the fluorescent light, wings buzzing at a particularly annoying frequency in a desperate attempt to reach the source. *Careful, Icarus,* she thought.

She lifted the crushed plastic cup to her lips, shaking the last few droplets onto her tongue while the detective pulled out a yellow notepad and a pen from his pocket. Had he introduced himself? Her eyes fell to his name tag: Shultz. She was feeling more hopeless by the second. How qualified was the Laguna Beach PD to investigate a death of this caliber? The worst thing to happen here were tourists stealing from a gift shop, or when Cash got kicked out of Seadog's for fighting a few years ago.

"Page was with you yesterday, correct?"

She nodded again.

"What can you tell me about your time with her?"

"I picked her up from school..." Lennon watched his pen return to the paper, and clasped her hands around the cup to keep from picking nervously. "I just came home from college—"

"Welcome back," he mumbled, inserting compassion wherever he could.

"And I wanted to surprise her. We ate gelato, went home, and talked for a while. Then she went to Emery Felton's to work on a project. But there was no project."

"We'll get to that, don't worry. But I'm curious, what did you talk about? Did you notice anything off when you two spoke? Anything troubling or out of character?"

Lennon's eyes closed in focus, ignoring the confusion his questions brought. "Uh...no, not that I can think of. We were catching up. About her, mostly. She's doing better—*was* doing better in school. Then she told me she was going to Emery's...I tried telling her she shouldn't."

"Why?"

"Emery isn't—*wasn't* her friend. She's always been jealous."

The detective nodded, pen tapping against the pad like a metronome. "Keep-your-friends-close kind of situation, huh?"

Lennon nodded, her hopes jumping a level.

"What time did Page leave for Emery's?" he continued.

"It was right around sunset...six, maybe seven?" She fidgeted with the cup between her fingers, nervous about her accuracy.

"And you didn't see or talk to her after that." Shultz said it more as a confirmation than a question, and she closed her eyes in guilt.

"No. I fell asleep."

The look Shultz gave her was knowing. Cash probably gave him the details. "Did she say anything about going to the beach, to a cove?"

Lennon shook her head. "Nothing."

He stared down at his page, dragging his teeth across his lower lip. She could tell he was running out of questions. *Why wasn't he asking more about Emery?*

"We went to that cove when we were kids," Lennon continued. "We'd pack sandwiches and do 'mermaid picnics.' She loved it. But we stopped going a few years ago."

"Pretty secluded spot. I'm only asking because, as I'm sure you know, that's where we found her. They've already started the autopsy, and we don't know for sure, but we believe there was a pretty large amount of alcohol involved."

Lennon blinked. "She was drinking?"

"We found some empty shooters next to the site."

She thought of the one her mom had thrown at her last night. Cashmere had scared both of them away from alcohol; Page was almost annoyingly anti-drugs, complaining any time she so much as smelled it on Lennon's clothes. Shultz's revelation didn't compute. Emery's glassy eyes suddenly flitted behind Lennon's eyes, the smell of her potent breath still in her nose. She remembered how the girl had sprinted back to the house, as if running against time.

Lennon didn't want to accuse Emery outright and risk sounding crazy; she was a young, grieving woman—credibility was not in her favor. She had to make this seem like his idea.

"She..." Lennon faltered, trying to think of the right words. "Page doesn't drink."

The detective looked up from his paper, looking at her with sympathetic understanding. "Your dad told us how close you two were. I understand how jarring this all might be."

"We were *very* close. Page doesn't...didn't...drink." Lennon repeated.

Missing Page

"We were all teenagers once—"

"You *have* talked to Emery, haven't you?" Off the officer's confused expression, the words spilled out of her. "Emery Felton. The last person she was with before she was found dead."

The look he wore was not a surprised one. Someone must have warned him she'd bring this up.

"She was one of the first people we spoke to. She's very upset about the news. We're investigating her involvement, but she *is* a minor, so these things are a bit—"

"She was the last one with Page before she went missing. Before she *died.*" The word rang through her like a bell, sharp and full sounding. "Why isn't she here?"

"We can't just arrest her, Miss Mayfield. That's not how the law works. I agree that some of her actions are certainly questionable, but questionable does not equate to guilt. We have to follow due process."

Lennon took a deep breath, trying to keep her impatience contained. "We—my dad and I—went to her house last night. Page's location was there before it went offline, have you looked into that? They were both gone when we got there. Emery was the only who came home, *sprinting,* might I add. Out of the park *she* said Page disappeared in."

He was still taking notes, but she noticed there were less details than the previous ones. She grit her teeth in frustration. "She was drunk. Did you know that?"

His analytical eyes darted to the plastic crying under her grip, and then to her glower.

"Emery told us everything," he said. "Page stopped by unexpectedly. They talked for a while, trying to work their issues out. It didn't end well—Page left, Emery became upset and started drinking. She claims to have no idea about Page's phone. They allowed us to search, and we couldn't find it anywhere. She also informed us of an open window to her room, which was apparently closed when she left."

Lennon took account of his narrowing eyes, her mouth drying at his words. "I don't have it, if that's what you're asking."

She was losing him. He had said most of the right things, but was concerned about the wrong parts. Maybe she never had him to begin with. Her fingers had found each other, picking furiously.

"Emery bullied Page," she blurted in a desperate last effort. "Severely. *That* was their 'issue.' You can ask the kids at her school, it's been going on for months. Emery's the smartest kid in their grade, sir. She's not just some dumb teenage girl, she knows *something*," Lennon insisted, throat tight with conviction. "Or at least more than she's claiming. I'm not even saying it was on purpose. It could've all been an accident, maybe she was scared to get in trouble. But I *know* my sister. This was—" She broke off again, cursing her wavering voice. "Something's not right."

She held his gaze with siren-like intensity, willing him to listen.

A hint of a smile touched the corner of his lip. "You're asking good questions, Miss Mayfield. You ever think about becoming a detective?"

Her hackles raised. This was *not* the time for small talk. Shultz raised his brows at her sudden hostility, unsure of when he'd offended her, and quickly backpedaled. "Lennon, I can't imagine what you must be going through right now. You want answers, I get that."

He glanced at the door for a moment before leaning in, crossing his arms on the table. "But we have no evidence that Emery hurt her, no indication she was even at that cave, or near it. *Nothing*, nada." His lip pulled to the side. "With Page being that drunk, it's much more likely she got caught in the high tide. There was an abrasion on her head that matches a spot on the wall. We think she fell and hit her head on it."

"Or someone pushed her," Lennon snarled.

He shook his head sympathetically. "I know this must be incredibly difficult, and I'm truly sorry for your loss. But we can't let our grief take us on a witch hunt."

Missing Page

The Icarus fly whizzed past her ear as her teeth clenched. These people weren't going to help her.

He took another long look at the notepad. "I think that's all. Do you have any questions for me?"

Can you do your fucking job?

"That's it, then?" Her words caught in her throat, frustrated tears threatening to take any credibility she had left.

"Unless you have any questions, I think so."

She shoved herself away from the table, finding her own way out of the room and down the hall. She passed her parents without even a look in their direction, feeling like her insides were combusting.

Lennon made it to the Jeep before bending over at the waist, sucking air deep into her stomach.

"What happened?" Cash asked incredulously.

Lennon shook her head, a dark laugh pushing through her nostrils. "You heard what their story is for this?" She paced back and forth, her thumbnail tucked between her teeth.

"Yes." Cash's voice was tight. "I'm very...*very* disappointed in her."

Lennon stilled, blinking at her mother. "Don't tell me you actually *believe* that cowshit. You can't—"

"Yes. I can." Cash did a once-over of her daughter, a flurry of sleepless nights playing behind her swollen eyes.

The buzzing that filled Lennon's ears was loud enough to block out the birds singing, even the sound of her own heart. It felt like the fly was still there, circling her.

"No. No, you can't do that!" Lennon cried. "You *know* we're different. Page isn't—she wasn't like that!"

"No, she wasn't!" Cash snapped, lip quivering. She lifted a hand to her mouth, turning away for a moment before whipping around with a pointed finger. "I told you, Lennon, I *told* you...she was *always* watching you!"

"Cashmere..." Stacy's voice came then, low and warning.

"You think this is my fault?" Lennon whispered in disbelief. She leaned against the warm metal of the Jeep for stability, her view swirling.

"No, we don't," Stacy said. He looked to Cashmere to echo his words, but she stood simmering, glowering at her daughter through blurry tears.

Lennon's mouth opened, itching to let her sword of a tongue cut her mother. She wanted to unleash a bomb strong enough to shatter bones, to tear flesh. She was confident the truth could do that. But instead, her lips sealed over the words like a martyr, feeling them quake against the roof of her mouth in a mushroom cloud. *That* was the difference between her and Cash; she didn't want to inflict the same painful guilt that was ripping through her onto others.

She couldn't allow Page's innocence and justice to be clouded by her own past. It was crippling, an unbearable pain.

No. She wouldn't allow it.

Her posture straightened, eyes hardening with a new, reinforced wall. Lennon had an obligation to get the truth, more than anyone. And she *would* get it, no matter who she lost in the process. Page had been her purpose, and she would remain that way even in death. There had never been less to lose, but there was everything to gain.

"Lennon." Cash uttered, noticing the change. Her eyes widened, as if she were coming to. "Of course...of course I don't blame you."

"I'm going now." Lennon's voice was robotic, void of emotion by design. Her body was meant for this; the detachment came almost too easily. Almost as if all this time, it knew...

"Sweetheart—" Stacy started.

"I'm *going*," she said. The finality in her tone was inarguable.

Cash crossed her arms over her chest, watching as her daughter sped away. She couldn't even lean into her husband for comfort, who now felt colder than ice next to her. There was no relief in her surroundings; only a deep, pulsing grief, as if she'd lost both children instead of one.

8

Nature was trying desperately to apologize. Wind ran its wispy fingers through Lennon's hair during the drive with a gentle force, and the sun planted petal pink kisses across her pale nose and cheeks, warming her cold skin.

The fire-hydrant red gas station Lennon was driving to was hard to miss. It sat just off the beach, a tiny thing, but it was always stocked with fresh turkey sandwiches. Despite having only eaten a bag of chips in the past seventeen hours, there was not a single pang of hunger that hit her when she cut the engine. She couldn't imagine ever feeling hungry again, not when her stomach was so full with agony.

She'd popped the console to toss her keys when greeted with an old weed pen waiting at the bottom. There wasn't even time to think; it was between her lips in an instant, glowing bright as smoke entered her lungs. Waiting until she was a fraction less miserable than she was before, she stepped out to swipe her card and let the gas guzzle. Tight muscles started to relax, and by the time the screen hit the three-gallon mark, her emotions had become fuzzy.

A text bubble popped onto her lock screen, from Michaela True.

Lennon didn't know a bigger gossip than her; she checked social media first thing in the morning like an old man reading the paper. But Lennon herself had just found out—surely Michaela couldn't...

> Holy shit. So sorry to hear about Page.
>
> Me, Macy, and the gang would love to take you out tomorrow if you're up for it. Take your mind off everything for an evening? Xo

How? Michaela had contact with a young police officer she dated for a few months, but Lennon hadn't seen him in the office. What surprised Lennon more was Michaela's suggestion of a night out, as if this were an ex she was trying to forget instead of her baby sister.

Lennon attempted a calming breath, letting her hands loosen around the pump handle. Michaela's solution was always parties or chemicals that could melt feelings into mush. She didn't understand real hardship; her strifes consisted of out-of-stock makeup products and not being able to squeeze a Botox session in before leaving for vacation. She'd never experienced a quarter of what Lennon was currently enduring—she was incapable. Michaela and those like her wouldn't know real if it slapped them in the face.

Her pen glowed with another inhale, only halfway through when a voice cut through.

"Lennon?"

Fuck. Whoever was behind her, fuck them in particular. Clearly she was going through it, and apparently most of the town already knew why. *What could this nosy piece of shit want to talk about?* She tugged the brim of her hat low over her brow to cover her red eyes and cleared her throat as she turned, ready to strike.

The face disarmed her in a single instant, snapping her narrowed eyes open with a surge of adrenaline. The blond's surprised expression matched hers, looking almost as disheveled.

"Conrad...hi."

The short sleeves of his yellow button-up hugged his muscled arms, likely built by the surfboard tied to the top of his fossil of a truck. She guessed the model was from sometime in the early nineties by the rugged state of it, though there was a bit of charm left in the Toyota's camel paint.

His eyes were heavy with exhaustion, his skin papery. The fresh freckles that she'd seen yesterday were now grayed and dull against his nose. "I er—I heard, about..." His eyes couldn't hold hers for long. "I heard."

"Wow," she sneered. "You guys are quick. Is there a group chat I'm missing?"

"No, no, that's not—" He paused. "Your dad asked me to help..."

The end of that sentence would have certainly pushed her over her limit, but it didn't look like he had the strength to finish it. It suddenly clicked in her mind, all the diving gear scattered in the truck bed. Of course he'd helped search; Conrad didn't know any of her 'friends.' It was silly to even think.

"I'm so sorry," he uttered. "This is...I can't believe it."

He was talking to the concrete, but she wished he'd look at her again. Maybe it was selfish, but it felt like she was looking at Wyatt, even if it was just pieces of him. Of all people, Conrad probably was the best person Lennon could've run into. He understood better than most. He didn't even ask her how she was—he knew.

"I don't know how you did it," she said quietly. "I feel like I'm dying. I think this might actually kill me."

She was tiptoeing over her words. This was worse than death. Her muscles were sore as if she'd been run over by a semi, like her brain had maxed out on grief and dumped the rest into her body. The pain was *everywhere.*

Conrad nodded slowly, unable to provide any comfort.

"How are you...how did you..." Lennon struggled for words.

"Survive?"

It sounded dramatic, but it felt the most right. She waited helplessly, desperately in need of guidance. He dipped his chin, his honey waves falling over his eyes.

"I think being a kid helped. I was only ten when he..." He trailed off, staring at the sparkling ocean to their left. It'd been almost seventeen years, and he still couldn't say it. "It still hurt though. A lot."

Conrad's stony face grew even more solemn. Lennon waited, hoping her silence would urge him to say more. It was the first time they'd ever talked about it.

"I'm—I *was* the big brother," he continued. "I felt responsible for a long time, still kinda do."

"Why?"

"I should've gone back with him. Dad couldn't guide Mom and watch you kids at the same time."

"You were a kid, too," she said softly. Lennon was grateful her eyes had the cover of her cap as the haunting memory overtook them both.

He shrugged. "I guess I got over it because I had to. There wasn't a lot of time to be sad. There was work to be done, people to take care of, so that's what I did. But that doesn't mean I don't think about him all the time. I do. Every day."

"Me too."

A small light came back into his eyes. "You do?"

Her breath came out in a quick exhale. "Of course I do. You guys were family."

Family. She rolled the word on her tongue as she looked out toward the ocean, trying to imagine what had happened in that cove. Would he think she was crazy if she told him her theory? Did family hold the same weight as trust?

"They said it was an *accident*," she blurted. The gas pump click pierced the following silence. She could sense his eyes burning into her from beneath her hat and crossed her arms over her chest, feeling more exposed than before.

"You don't think it was?"

"Are these things ever *just* an accident?"

Conrad remained silent, but his raised eyebrows exposed his curiosity.

Missing Page

Lennon sighed. "She was with this girl, Emery..."

Recognition broke through, rippling his previously empty face. "Felton, yeah. I remember her."

Lennon swallowed. She'd forgotten that Conrad couldn't be qualified only as the brother of her dead friend anymore; he'd also been Page's tutor for the past six months. He'd been with her more than Lennon had this year.

"Did you ever meet her?" Lennon asked.

He shook his head. "No, she never came over...I just know they didn't get along very well. At first I thought she was being sensitive, figured it was just catty teenage shit, but eventually she told me some of the stuff Emery was doing and saying to her. Pretty nasty stuff."

Lennon grimaced. "She was the last person Page was with."

Conrad finally caught her eyes. "You think she hurt her?"

She hated the way it sounded coming from him. "I know it sounds crazy, thinking a fifteen-year-old girl could be capable of that. And maybe it is, I'm not saying I know anything for sure." She took another drag to slow her rising heart rate. "Not yet. But I will...that I'm sure of."

His eyes turned pitiful, knowing too well the pain of losing a younger sibling. The sight made Lennon's walls shoot back up instantaneously; her shrug was expertly nonchalant, and her hands crept casually into her jacket pockets to ease the tension. He began to step forward, but she flinched away before he could give any kind of comfort. It wasn't likely she'd ever be able to let him get that close. Not when he looked so much like *him*.

"Sorry," she whispered.

His forgiveness came easily. "It's okay," he said, letting his arm fall. "No apology necessary."

She stared at the hand he dropped, marred with thin scratches that ran along his fingers, over the bone in his wrist. Some were scabbed over, a few fresh. He flicked his wrist to see what her eyes were bulging at.

"The ocean beats the shit out of me," he explained sheepishly. "But I still love her. Kinda toxic, I know."

She knew he'd gotten those from searching, but appreciated his vagueness. "Nah. I get it." she said. She was looking out at the twinkling water, but her mind was far away.

After a moment, Lennon shifted, angling toward her car. "I should get going."

"Wait," he called. Conrad pulled out his phone, handing it to her. "If you ever need anything—*anything*—please, don't hesitate to ask."

Her nod was numb as she took it from him, typing in her number.

"And I know you won't ask, so I'll be checking in on you." He offered a grim smile. "Feel free to tell me to fuck off, or whatever."

She returned the phone, muttering her thanks.

"By the way..." His voice softened. "I didn't know her for too long, so I hope I'm not overstepping. I just wanted to say that it's really a shame, all of this. You never see that kind of sensitivity anymore. She was really special."

Lennon sucked in her cheeks, swallowing the sudden wave rolling down her throat like sour medicine. In her autopilot state, her arms almost reached to hug him, and she had to fight it so hard that it sent a shiver through her. It could have been anyone in that moment; the little girl in her was just desperate for comfort. But it could never, *ever* be Conrad. She nodded curtly, wishing her Jeep was covered as she entered it. He could see through her enough as is.

Conrad turned and jiggled the nozzle in his tank, extracting the truck key from his pocket with a hollow sigh. It felt like an inverted mirror—two people who had gone from *eldest* to *only*.

Lennon drove ten under the speed limit to prolong her arrival. She had to go home at some point, though that word felt like a shell of what it once was. Page had been Lennon's home—where could she go now?

The door shut shortly after the melodic beep, locking her in with her mother's wails coming from down the hall. She could feel Page's

Missing Page

room waiting below with a newfound heaviness, and breathed shakily under its weight.

Kaiser was the only one to greet her, his wet nose tickling her fingertips with cautious confusion. There were already piles of food covered in tinfoil and cards scattered in the kitchen, vases of flowers covering the entirety of their entry table. *Flowers.* Like it was someone's fucking birthday.

Lennon couldn't bear to read any of the condolences; she needed something that looked and felt the same as before her sister was taken from her. Lennon ran upstairs to the loft, feeling her heart return once Cash's cries were out of earshot. She dug through her suitcase, pulling out the fuzzy joint she'd saved for a special occasion. These would be have to be saved for bad days, she decided, when she wanted to be so numb she couldn't remember her own name. The sound of the lighter flicking wetted her tongue, preparing her inhale. She paced back and forth as she released the plume of smoke, hoping the movement would speed up its effects.

Her phone sent a heartbeat pulse through her thigh—*Hart,* she remembered with a gasp.

To answer or decline both felt like the wrong decision. She'd have to tell him eventually...wouldn't it be better to rip off the Band-Aid now? After sliding his name out of view, she saw five missed texts and three calls. Hart wasn't the clingy type; he was genuinely worried. That's what happened when you shared your soul with another person. They saw your good and your bad. Lennon cursed, and finally answered the call, preparing to give him her first ugly.

"Hart," she started, already choking.

"Oh, thank God. Are you okay?" he demanded, voice thick with concern.

What could she say? *No, my sister just died, and it wasn't an accident even though everyone thinks it was, but no one will listen to me.*

He was raspier than usual. She'd forgotten all about his lake day.

Her radio silence had probably worried him sick and ruined his night, and now she was about to dump even more bad news on him.

"Where are you?" she asked warily. "I'm not on speaker or anything?"

"No, of course not. I'm at home. What's going on, are you safe?"

"It's my...Hart, something *terrible* hap—" She couldn't finish, her body already betraying her. She held her grief between her brows, the pain of it condensing behind her eyes.

"I'll get you the first flight out of there, baby, okay? We knew it might've been too soon for you to see your mom, I'm so sorry."

She was biting down on her thumb nail, shaking with nerves. He was getting the wrong idea; she *had* to tell him. She had to say the words that Conrad couldn't even after seventeen years, within less than twenty-four hours of it happening. But it seemed, as many things were with her, that the only way out was through.

"My sister...Page, she...she died this morning."

She could hear quiet exhales as his brain worked through her words for a long, silent moment. She didn't know how he would respond, but hoped he wouldn't ask her to repeat it. She wouldn't be strong enough to.

"Honey," he uttered, finally gaining control over his tongue.

She could feel some kind of break coming. She squeezed her lids shut before the tears could escape, but words came pouring out instead. "They found her in the cove we used to go to when we were kids. I don't know how, or *why*...why she was there. All of it feels so wrong."

"What can I do?"

She looked up to the ceiling, hearing Conrad's words replaying in her mind. He'd been right; she'd rather shove splinters under her nails than ask someone to share her burden. Unless they could bring her sister back, it was no use.

"I think I just need time. And space."

He went quiet again. She imagined him trying to decipher the hidden meaning under her words, as there often was. "You shouldn't be alone right now, Len. I can get a flight and be there by tomorrow morning—"

"I know you can," she said reassuringly, hoping he heard her conviction. "But I need time to think, to figure things out."

"Figure what out?" The phone creaked under his anxious grip.

Maybe she should have said *to grieve* instead—*that* would make sense. She fidgeted, debating. "I don't think it was an accident."

"What do you mean? You think someone...did this? To her?"

She pinched her fingers against the bridge of her nose. This is exactly why she wanted to avoid this conversation; Lennon had nothing but a gut feeling so far, and she understood that wouldn't be enough for most.

"I don't know, Hart. But nothing they were saying made sense. I was with her most of the day, nothing seemed out of the ordinary, she didn't seem sad. They said she was drinking, but she doesn't—she didn't...you know how she felt about that."

"Baby," he said, "I can't imagine how hard this must be. Things don't need to make sense right now, though. You just need to try and take it easy, and take care of yourself."

She knew Hart was desperate to find any words of comfort to give her. That was his way. But it only reminded her of the detective at the station, and she soured further. Couldn't they see? She didn't need comforting, she didn't *want* to feel better—her anger was what would drive her forward.

Lennon was unique in that she saw her vulnerability as a weapon, one that could hurt only her. To show weakness was to press her chest against the tip of the sword and wrap the other's hand around the hilt, letting them decide whether to push or pull.

"Can we talk later?" she asked.

"Y...Yeah. I'll check up on you in a bit," he uttered. "But you can call me whenever–"

She'd already hung up. She was doing it again—pushing everyone and everything good away, hurting herself before they could.

An angry scream bellowed from deep within, rattling all four corners of her room. She hurled her phone against the opposite wall, leaving a dent in the textured paint before it thudded against the ground. Despite its protective case, a long crack traveled down the front of the screen. She interlocked her shaking fingers, squeezing tightly until the fury faded.

∼

Her eyes peeled open after the sun had slipped away, unsure of when she'd fallen asleep. The moon and stars were covered by clouds, making her room appear much darker. Without light, the four walls felt more like a cage than a safe haven.

She left her bed to slip on a pair of old running shoes, treading silently down the stairs. The house was dark, but not at all quiet. Kaiser waited for her at the bottom, tail wagging hopefully. Lennon's hand ruffled the soft fur between his ears after clipping on his leash, wincing at a loud wail erupting through the halls. She took off before another could come, eager to escape her hollow home.

Blood tightened her calves as she jogged down the street, her heart pounding in her ears not five minutes in. Kaiser bounded none the wiser at her heels, expecting the varsity endurance she once had.

The Shepherd barked once after Lennon stopped at the end of the road, his feet pattering in an excited dance from the rush of exercise. She reached to calm him while she regained her breath, squinting through the dark for her target. The cove was visible in the near distance now, long strands of yellow tape whipping angrily in the sea's violent breeze. Lennon couldn't help imagining what it had looked like with all the police in there, taking pictures, placing numbered cards around the scene. The innocence of what used to be a family's hidden picnic spot, forever tarnished.

"Come out," Lennon whispered, willing her sister to emerge. "Come *out*, Page."

It was unbearably painful to picture, but she couldn't stop. Different scenes played behind her eyes like a horror movie, raising

Missing Page

question after question. Did Emery deliver the fatal blow, or was it the cove walls that committed the final act? Was Page left to suffer? Did she fight back? Did she call out for her parents, for Lennon? *Did she scream?*

Emery was capable. Not only was she the smartest in her school, but she was one of the best on the soccer team—broad-shouldered, strong. Page was sensitive, soft, sweet; she never stood a chance of protecting herself.

Women have always been smarter than their male counterparts could ever give them credit for. It was almost impressive how Emery used her youth and the men's ego to her advantage. The police would never want to admit that they had been deceived by a fifteen-year-old girl. It was up to Lennon to figure out just how much Emery hated Page, and if she was in that cave with her or not.

Most, if not all of these answers could be found at the Felton house. But she couldn't go now, at risk of scaring them off permanently. Lennon had brains, too, and had a few extra years of experience on her side. She had to play the game better than Emery, find her tracks and predict her next steps before she made them.

Fire melted ice. Motivation felt better than her grief.

"C'mon, Kaiser," she growled.

She noticed the entry light was on when they returned. A shadow passed behind the door, and she swallowed, on edge from her earlier thoughts. Her shoulders relaxed when she saw her father, but the relief was premature. He was clearly upset, arms crossed and lips thinned into an angry line. She'd barely gotten through the door when he snapped at her.

"Where were you?"

She reached down to unhook Kaiser's leash. "Couldn't sleep."

"Lennon, for God's sake, you can't just leave and not tell anyone where you're going!"

She nodded guiltily. "I didn't think...I just went down the road, I didn't want to wake you. I'm sorry."

She kept her eyes to the floor while she hung up the leash, but when she finally met his eyes, he enveloped her in a tight hug.

"I need you to be *safe*. And I need to know where you are." He pulled away, gripping her shoulders. "Understand?"

She nodded, her strength deteriorating by the second. Stacy lifted a thumb, letting it hover over a tear before brushing it away. It had made her look so young, but the pain swimming in her eyes aged her again. "What are you thinking about, baby girl?"

Her lip quivered, keeping her voice just above a whisper. "That it should have been me."

His hazel irises darkened, and he hugged her again, even tighter. "I don't want to hear that from you ever again, Lennon. Do you hear me?"

She was thankful her face was crumpled against his chest, concealing her streaming tears.

"We should get some rest," he continued. "Mom and I gotta start planning the funeral tomorrow."

"Already?" Lennon breathed. He rubbed her back comfortingly, until she was collected enough to trek up the stairs.

She lay restlessly in bed, devising her investigation into Emery and trying to plan a way into her house. It seemed impossible, but those were her favorite kinds of puzzles. She's broken them before—she could do it again. Minutes trickled into hours, until the sun teased its arrival over the horizon. She finally sunk into her mattress, conquered by exhaustion.

The sun had warmed the room by noon, but the layer of sweat perspiring over her body and her violent waking had nothing to do with the heat.

Shhh...go back to sleep.

She didn't think it would ever be possible to prefer being trapped in her nightmares instead of real life. But once she remembered, she ached to crawl back into that hellscape just so she didn't have to feel this unbearable anguish. It spread like poison through her veins; even the tattoo trailing along the inside of her arm pulsed, throbbing with the infection of grief.

Even though she was awake, traces of that whispered, breathy voice still lingered in her ear, raising the hair on the back of her neck. After years of practice, she could usually wake up just before the monster yanked the curtains shut and avoid those soulless, beady eyes. But it still wasn't enough—she knew what happened next.

The window on the opposite side gave her a beautiful view of the coast; the clouds filtered golden light over the waves, crashing against the shoreline like cymbals. It came off spiteful to her; how could it continue so beautifully, like tragedy hadn't struck the town and her life the day before?

Lennon rushed through her shower and went downstairs, ignoring the growing piles of tin-foiled food packages with a wrinkled nose. Her parents had already left.

Despite her father's lecture about knowing her whereabouts, there was no way she could tell him about her plans. But she was an adult—Stacy didn't need to know *everything*. Anyway, she needed something to distract from the new waves of heartache that had filled her upon waking.

Well, Lennon supposed. *Now's as good a time as any.*

9

From where Lennon stood, Emery's home appeared the same as it had a few days ago. There was no trace of tragedy, no wretched wailing coming from within.

Must be nice, Lennon thought with a scowl.

There weren't any cars in the driveway; 3she wouldn't have to worry about parents, at least. She'd walked a mile and a half here to keep the element of surprise; one look at the Jeep would shut their windows and lock their doors. She crossed from the pavement onto the grassy yard, pausing at the red paint sprayed in large letters over their lawn.

MURDERER.

Her gaze drifted up, noticing the mess half-hidden under their balcony. Most of the storage boxes had been opened, their contents strewn about in a chaotic mess. It'd been dark her first time here, but she was sure it wasn't like that before.

Not exactly the same, then.

Her pace quickened over the yard, ascending the creaky steps two at a time. She wasn't one hundred percent happy with the plan, but nothing better had come to mind on her way over. Her nose crinkled with disgust thinking about the faux sympathy card she was about to play, but after a few steadying breaths, she lifted her knuckles to the door and knocked three times.

Something creaked down the hall. Lennon could hear a pair of feet padding across the noisy wooden floor, dried from years of salty air. It was a short walk to the door, and then there was silence. Lennon smoothed her expression and held her breath, suddenly feeling watched.

Emery yanked the door open with a guarded look. Her dark hair was dripping wet, soaking into her T-shirt and curling around her full cheeks.

"Hey, Emery." Lennon cleared her throat, remembering the gentle tone she'd practiced.

"Hi," she responded cautiously. "My, uh—my parents aren't here."

"That's okay." Lennon stuffed her hands into the pocket of her hoodie. "You're the one I wanted to see, anyway."

"My dad said I'm not supposed to talk to you guys." The girl's eyes darted every few words as if a squadron would jump out of the trees any moment.

Lennon forcefully relaxed her shoulders, trying to ease Emery's tension. "I just wanted to come by and say I'm...I'm sorry for how I treated you the other night. I was worried about my sister—I'm very protective over her."

"Oh," Emery uttered, shifting her weight to her other foot. "Yeah. No worries."

"How have you been?"

The girl hardly looked like she was experiencing anything close to grief—though a little puffy, her eyes were still relatively light.

Emery hesitated, her thick brows furrowing. "I mean...pretty terrible."

"How so?"

Emery raised a calculating eyebrow, but Lennon waited in silence.

"Everyone already hated me," she scowled. "I was used to my locker getting messed with...but now they're coming to our house."

Lennon nodded. "People are pretty upset."

"So? I am, too. Doesn't mean I get to vandalize people's property."

"I mean, you two weren't *really* friends, though. You haven't been for a while," Lennon mused.

"It's still awful." Emery pulled her hair behind her shoulders. "It's hard enough without everybody messing with our house."

Lennon nodded idly, hoping her silence would make Emery want to fill it.

"They're all saying it's my fault," she continued. "Because we ended on a bad note—"

"Bad note? What does that mean?"

The girl faltered, growing fidgety. "We, uh...we were going down different paths."

Lennon's focus drew her another step forward.

"She basically broke up with me," Emery mumbled, tinged with red. "As a friend. And then she said she had to go, and biked off into the park..."

"You didn't try to stop her, talk it out? Why would she go in there?"

"It was over, there was nothing left to say," Emery spat darkly. "And I've seen her walking through there for months, it didn't seem out of the ordinary..."

"It just doesn't make sense." Lennon's thumbnail paced over her bottom lip. "Apparently she'd been drinking. Did she seem drunk when she came over?"

"No." Emery shook her head quickly. "She was sober when I talked to her."

"*You* were drunk, though. I remember."

"I drank on my own, *after* she left," Emery retorted defensively, saying it as if she'd rehearsed it. "Look, I know you think Page was a goody-two shoes, and that I was the bad influence, the bully. But she

Missing Page

came, we talked for a second, and then she went. I don't know anything that happened after."

"How convenient," Lennon muttered under her breath. "Why did she end the friendship?"

"We were both pretty mad at each other. She stole the one job I was offered, I took her starting spot on the team. I realized she only really talked to me when she needed help with school. But even then, even after knowing she was *using* me, I still wanted to be friends. She's the only—she *was* the only friend I had. I guess she didn't feel the same."

Lennon could hear the bias in her voice, sour with jealousy. *Stealing, using*...those words weren't even in Page's nature.

"If she was so terrible to you, why would you want her as a friend? Why even open your window?"

"I just told you why." Emery snapped. "I don't have friends. Page is popular. In my head, if she was my friend, that meant everyone else would be too. Whether she knew it or not, they were *assholes* to me—unless she and I were cool. And even though I can't *stand* her sometimes..." Emery twisted her lips, her eyes clouding with something unreadable. "I needed her. So she came in, and we talked. That's all."

"You said she never came in."

She blinked. "What?"

"The night Page went missing," Lennon repeated. "You told your mom she never even came in, that she just stopped by."

The red that had filled Emery's cheeks before had now drained from her face. Lennon's fury erased her previous strategy, and she pushed further. "Who did you lie to, her or me?"

"N-Nobody. I misspoke."

Lennon leaned forward, her eyes piercing. "What else are you not telling the truth about, Emery?"

Emery stammered, frightened by her rigid calmness. "I..."

"She drank at your house, didn't she?"

Emery swallowed. Lennon's jaw flitted, but she kept her voice calm, speaking each word slowly. "I need you to listen very, very carefully. From this point on I want the truth, and the truth *only*. If you can do that, we can keep this between you and me. But if you don't, I *will* be taking you back to the police. I will *drag* you there, and I will make sure everyone is watching."

Lennon's eyes darkened into something sinister. "You see, Emery, I don't care if people think I'm crazy—in fact, I prefer them to. Your mom was smart to hide you from me."

She drew back. "Those are your choices," Lennon said, picking at her nails, as if she were bored. "You'll be in a lot more trouble with them, though. Lot longer, too."

Emery eyes were vexed with darkness, like a cornered animal debating its next move. She glanced back into the living room, debating, before closing the door, speaking in a hushed tone. "We gotta go to the other side. There's a camera in the living room, they can't hear any of this."

Lennon nodded silently, following her to the spot near her bedroom window. Emery's eyes flitted around, double-checking they were alone.

"I think I caught her right as she changed her mind about coming. I heard footsteps on the deck, but she was going down them like she was leaving. I invited her in so we could really talk about things. She was being really short about everything, and eventually she said it was probably best that we weren't friends. Page was the one who suggested the first shot, actually. As a no-hard-feelings kind of thing."

Off Lennon's glare, Emery shriveled. "I asked her to do a second, but that was it, I swear. I thought she was going to stay and hang out, but as soon as we took it she said she had to go."

Slowly but surely, with every piece of information Lennon revealed she knew, Emery unraveled. She was getting close.

"They found alcohol shooters next to the cove," Lennon said. "Seemed like more than two shots' worth."

"Those weren't me."

Missing Page

"How convenient that you disappear right before the trouble starts," Her eyes narrowed. "What were you doing in the park?"

"I'm a runner," she answered, crossing her arms. "I was upset about how things ended, that's how I clear my mind."

Lennon's teeth sank into her cheek. "You're smart, Emery, but I'm smarter. Everyone else might be letting you off the hook, but—"

"*Nobody's* letting me off the hook," Emery growled. "You have no idea how much trouble I'm in, I can't get away from it! At school, my classmates, my *parents*. Everyone hates me or is scared of me! I'm already grounded forever just for sneaking her in. If they found out we were drinking...?" The thought hung like an ominous shadow over her.

"I told you, this can stay between us if you tell the truth."

"I've told you everything, I swear."

"Then you have nothing to worry about." Lennon turned away. "Stay safe, Emery."

She turned to descend the back set of stairs, turning to amble around the front of the house. The storm of chaos that had gone through here was in full view now; picture frames shattered, holiday decorations spilling like guts out of their storage boxes. This must have been the work of the kids Emery spoke of earlier.

Lennon heard a creak and looked up, catching Emery's scowl as she flew down the stairs, trembling with rage. "Look, you can't just threaten me like that. I know she's gone, but Page wasn't this perfect little—"

"Shut up, Emery," Lennon warned, still walking.

"I let you talk," she snapped. "It's my turn. If you're gonna..."

She trailed off. Both girls had become distracted by a bicycle propped against the wall. It stood out from the rest, with blue ribbons hanging limply from the periwinkle handlebars, and a familiar, dainty basket adorning the front. Lennon couldn't believe it at first, expecting it to disappear when she blinked, but it remained.

It was Lennon's bike.

Page's bike.

Emery paled just as Lennon whipped around, her entire body vibrating with adrenaline and blind rage.

"I—I don't know how that got here, r-really." Emery stammered, lifting her hands protectively.

"Stop bullshitting me!" she bellowed, surging forward. "Tell me how the hell my sister's bike is at your house!"

Emery shook her head helplessly. Her mouth opened, but shock had stolen her voice.

"Both of you disappeared that night. *You* were the only one who came back." Lennon's lip curled. "I told you what would happen if you lied to me again."

"You're insane," Emery cried, shoving her away. "I didn't kill her, I have no idea how that got here! Leave us alone or else I'll call the police, you *psycho!*"

She turned, sprinting up the stairs. The door slammed and locked behind her, leaving Lennon alone under the patio.

Call the police. With shaking fingers, she sifted through her shoulder bag for the card the detective had given her. Lennon fumbled and dropped it, cursing and squinting through the dirt stains to decipher the number. After dialing, she pushed the bike away from Emery's house and toward the street.

His voice came after the third ring. "Shultz."

"This is Lennon Mayfield, we spoke yesterday. I just found my sister's bike at Emery Felton's house, how fast can you get here?"

There was a beat on the phone. "Miss Mayfield, did you say you're at the Felton residence?"

"Yes," she said impatiently.

"I...you...well, don't touch anything or go in the house, all right? I'll be there soon, but do me a favor and go wait on the curb. I'd hate to have to charge you with trespassing."

That's what he's worried about? "Detective, I don't think you heard me. *Page's bike* is under *Emery's* porch."

"I assure you, my ears work perfectly fine, ma'am." Shultz's voice hardened. "But you can't just go walking wherever you please. Now, I should be able to get there in about thirty minutes..."

"The station's a ten-minute drive!" she snapped.

"If you need to go somewhere, just leave it, and we'll take care of it."

"What, and then Emery gets another chance to get rid of it for good?"

"Miss Mayfield, that bike is evidence. If you could just—"

She cursed her phone and the detective as she hung up. The bike creaked as she urged it forward, injured from whatever it had gone through two nights prior.

The ride to the police station gave her time to calm down, but the look on Shultz's face when he came out ignited her all over again.

"She told me Page was drinking at her house. She admitted it."

His eyes remained on the bike, his pacing painfully slow.

"What?" she asked defensively.

"I told you not to touch it." He shook his head, sighing with frustration. "Your fingerprints are gonna be all over this—"

"I couldn't just *leave* it there. What if she hid it somewhere else?" Lennon seethed. "Did you even hear what I said?"

"Yes, Miss Mayfield. Page drank at Emery's house...did she admit to murdering her, too, or are we just charging her for the misdemeanor?"

His words paused her, bringing brief clarity in her red haze. Detective Shultz slid a pair of gloves over his hands, gingerly taking the complaining bike. "I'll take it from here. Do you have a ride back?"

"I'll walk," she said lowly, almost mumbling. He nodded solemnly.

"I'll get this back to you soon, then. Listen, Lennon..." His use of her first name jarred her. "I understand what you're trying to do, I do...but you have to let us do our job."

"You know she did this," Lennon whispered, angry tears stinging her eyes.

"It's suspicious. No one's denying that. But in the eyes of the law, which is what we're going by, this isn't proof of anything. And *if* she had anything to do with this, we have to go about it the right way to avoid any kind of mistrial. None of us want that, right? So, please, try not to make this *more* difficult in the name of helping, okay?"

She nodded tightly. Shultz wheeled the bike around the building, and her breath whisked away with him. The chime of her phone startled her, a text lighting up the screen.

MICHAELA
Where are u?

Shit. Lennon had completely forgotten. Now that her fury was simmering, she was able to think more clearly, and a new idea sprung into mind. She was sure she'd lost the police's trust with this, but if anyone else had heard or seen anything, Michaela True would know about it.

10

"Lennon, what're you doing over there? You look like a creep!"

Lennon had been standing at the edge of Sea Dog's parking lot, trying to decipher the different tracks in the dirt. Animals, boots, tires, and now Lennon's sneakers, adding their own personal marring.

She blinked herself out of her stupor to focus on the group waving in the distance, particularly the pair of identical girls. One was rubbing her rib where her twin had just elbowed her. Lennon stepped forward, crossing the parking lot in long, slow strides.

Michaela was the first to greet her, squeezing her in an awkward hug. Macy was waiting next to her, breathing a puff of smoke into Lennon's face as she wrapped her arms around her. Lennon gave them quick once-over, checking for any crystal or pill-filled baggies that she'd been hoping for, but none were visible. She swallowed the disappointment and forced a smile—half of her plan was ruined, but there was still a chance Michaela knew something helpful.

The two had matching auburn waves and big brown eyes, but Michaela had some work done in the past year, making her cheeks more prominent, her lips fuller.

"Ugh, it's been too *long*," Macy groaned, pressing her cheek against Lennon's. Rowan waited behind to give her a hug, a little warmer than the girls'. Trick's was the tightest of them all, and the most awkward.

They'd dated for three weeks her junior year, but it would have been less if Cash hadn't demanded she give the boy a proper chance. He'd been her first official kiss, and it was so jarringly unemotional, she was sure she was gay. She'd shared a short moment with Michaela the next night, which was equally apathetic. She guessed it was just another thing wrong with her, that she was too guarded to feel anything...that was, until she met Hart.

Despite becoming another one of her emotional victims, Trick took the breakup better than most would, and they managed to maintain some sort of deformed, distant acquaintanceship once his ego healed.

Why did I come to this again? She groaned mentally. Page's bike appearing under Emery's balcony was the only thing on her mind, but no answers had formed from her overthinking. She needed a break, or information. But she had to play the game first—she couldn't start off with an interrogation

"C'mon, let's get you a drink." Trick smiled, an old inside joke between them.

The four took seats on either side of her at the bar. Her only escape was forward, which led her to a platinum-haired bartender who stared like she was seeing a ghost. Lennon's brows furrowed, and the blonde fidgeted, returning to her ticket.

Something caused the group to go into a fit of laughter, and Lennon pulled her eyes away, trying to figure out what she missed in her pondering.

"What?" she asked absentmindedly. That made them laugh again, and she felt heat rush to her cheeks.

"Don't be embarrassed, Len, it was cute," Trick said, sporting a grin.

She frowned. If she was going to be the butt of their joke, she should at least be in on it. Lennon quickly averted his amused gaze to look back at the bartender, whose eyes were full of nervous anticipation. She was leaning away, as if Lennon would spontaneously combust. *What was her problem?*

"What's going on here?" Michaela leaned forward, crossing her arms under her full, unnaturally perky chest. "You two know each other?"

A small smile crept across her swollen lips, full of mischief. Michaela was a master instigator, and loved putting Lennon up to bat.

The blonde blinked. "Well...no, but—aren't you Lennon Mayfield?"

It finally clicked. This must have been the girl who answered the phone the other night, or maybe she'd overheard; Lennon was sure the gossip spread fast amongst the employees. In a split second, that night came back to her in a disorientating, paralyzing wave of panic. *Think about something else...* But what else could she focus on? There was the fact that every time the group laughed, Trick's hand would somehow find her shoulder or her leg, for however brief a moment—his eyes lingered even longer.

She felt an underlying sense of irritation, but wasn't surprised. It's what men did. They'd look, sometimes they'd touch; it was a game of ever-moving goalposts. And there was nothing they loved more than a wounded doe. Of course, if she were to speak too soon, it was easy to play off as overthinking, even narcissism. *Relax, I didn't even think about it like that, it's nothing!* were common phrases, sometimes conjoined into one big manipulation tactic. Another common defense was to try to humiliate her for even *considering* they were flirting with her, as if *she* were coming on to *them*. It was a game women could never win.

The twins only made it through half of their semester at Pepperdine's recap before their speech began to slur.

"You and Jake broke up?" Lennon interrupted, confused. "When did that happen?"

"Long time ago," Michaela waved dismissively. "Right before Christmas."

Rowan shook their head. "I still can't believe it. You seemed like you were ready to marry that guy."

"I was, until he asked if we could have a threesome." Michaela wrinkled her nose at the memory, lifting her straw to her pouty, Juvéderm filled lips.

"You guys *did* have a threesome." Rowan said flatly, lifting his brow.

"That was with a stranger, who *I* chose. *He* suggested Macy."

Rowan's face morphed into a bemusing mix of horror and disgust.

"On behalf of straight men, I apologize." Trick bowed his head.

"I do not claim the straights, but I do claim men. Partially. So I also apologize." Rowan lifted their beer and took a swig, wiping the foam from their lip. "Our audacity will never not disappoint me."

Lennon was preoccupied with the grooves in the bar, following them with her finger as they spread out like branches of a tree. She found it interesting how everything was smaller versions of themselves.

"Are you still seeing that guy, Len? His name's Hart, right?" Macy lifted her vape to her lips, trying to bring Lennon back into the center of the conversation.

Trick scoffed. "Heart? Like..." He drew the shape over his chest with his finger, raising his eyebrows with a mocking grin.

"H-A-R-T, but yeah. And I wouldn't be laughing so hard, *Trick*." Lennon rolled her eyes, continuing her pathing along the wood. "And to answer your question, Mace, yes—I am."

All were intrigued except for Trick, his jocular expression replaced with disappointment. This revelation was not just a rare feat —it was unprecedented.

"Is he hot?" Macy asked, her glassy, small-town eyes gazing through her full lashes.

"He's got a horse cock, doesn't he?" Michaela breathed.

"I stalked his Instagram, this man *screams* big dick! This bitch hit the jackpot." Rowan exclaimed, fawning.

Lennon frowned. There was no way they could tell his size based on his pictures—he was a from-the-waist-up kind of guy. "How'd you find him?"

She'd never posted him before. She didn't post, period—she only had social media to keep up with her sister and her dad's photography.

"That Halloween picture he tagged you in! After that, I had to see this man from *every* angle. His captions are funny, which means he's smart. He used to play baseball, but he still has the body and the ass from it. This man is *hot*." Rowan fanned themself. "You got the Holy Trinity. And here I thought you could only pick two!"

"You can't, unless you're Lennon F'ing Mayfield. Look straight for a second, Rowan," Macy teased. "She's hot!"

Trick nodded, glancing at her metallic eyes and tattoos with a shrug. "It's true."

"Seriously," Michaela nodded. "Did I ever tell you I showed a picture of you to my surgeon when I got my tits done?"

Lennon's eyes widened. "You what?"

"You do have an objectively unreal bod," Rowan relented. "God definitely picks favorites."

"*And* she's mysterious." Michaela pointed her straw at Lennon. "What else could a girl need?"

"You didn't include funny," Trick noted.

"Or smart," Rowan interrupted. "She *was* valedictorian, Mic."

"Of course she's fuckin' smart." Michaela rolled her eyes, wishing they'd keep up. "But guys hate that. Men want to be the smartest person in the room—need to be, in fact. It literally drives them crazy when they're not, and *not* in the good way. In a raging, I'm-thinking-about-murdering-you way."

Lennon's brows lifted in surprise; it appeared they finally agreed on something. Perhaps Michaela was a little more observant than she'd given her credit for.

"You still haven't said she's funny," Trick lilted. Michaela shot daggers his way, and he put his hands up innocently. "I'm just saying! Sometimes she comes in with the one-liners."

"Lennon doesn't need humor. She's jaded, that's her appeal." Rowan lifted their emptied beer to catch the bartender's attention, tapping their finger against the glass. "And Hart's the sweet, gentle giant. It's kind of perfect."

Their praise made her skin crawl; it felt like confirmation that she was fucked up. Hart *was* all those things and more—he only ever wanted to help, because that was how he loved. Which was exactly why she couldn't let him.

Lennon knew that four-letter word was a spring trap, waiting for her to wander close enough before clamping its metal teeth into her tender flesh. That word wanted to snap her in two, expose the darkness spreading like disease through her. It would reveal her for what she was—spoiled meat.

"He's amazing," Lennon agreed, extending her arms to push her sweaty glass away. "I miss him."

"Why isn't he here? We'd love to meet him," Macy gushed.

"That was my choice," Lennon answered, her tone cold.

"Why?" Her brows shot up in surprise.

"Have you always been this nosy?"

Macy lowered her eyes submissively, not as brave as her twin.

Michaela watched the smoke waft from her lips to Lennon with a bored glaze over her eyes, pouring over the tattoos that disappeared into her tight black racerback.

"You got more," she coughed, changing the subject. Lennon nodded, rubbing her hand along her bicep.

"They look badass," Rowan said between drinks. "Are you gonna do a whole sleeve?"

"Maybe."

This was a bad idea. Paranoia was setting in; it felt like everyone

Missing Page

was watching, treating her like a time bomb, and her social battery was draining by the second. Her eyes flitted to the dance floor, and she cursed wordlessly at the pairs of eyes confirming her intuition. She had yet to find a good moment to ask Michaela if she'd heard anything, anxiously circling her finger back and forth over the groove.

"Ouch!" she hissed suddenly, retracting the wounded appendage to her chest. Squeezing was the only way to alleviate the sting of the splinter that had slid underneath her skin, summoning a thick drop of blood to the surface. She stole a napkin from Rowan's drink and pressed it against the wound with a wince.

Michaela nudged her sister, jerking her head toward their friend. "Lennon, we're gonna go smoke real quick. You coming?"

Lennon nodded, standing from her stool to follow them outside.

Macy flipped the lid of her Marlboro pack, offering to Lennon. Michaela had her lighter ready the moment her twin propped her own between her lips, perfectly in sync.

Lennon broke away to look down at her opened hand, noticing a small white pill enclosed with the cigarette. "What's this?"

Michaela wiggled her eyebrows. "You know what it is."

The glands in her mouth swelled with saliva. It'd been almost a year since she'd sworn off pills, and seven months since she'd ingested one.

"You need a break." Michaela nodded encouragingly. Her cheeks hollowed until the end of her cigarette glowed, casting a subtle red over her face. "One won't kill you."

It felt heavy in her hand. She couldn't pretend a small part of her hadn't been hoping for this the whole time; Lennon hadn't slept the past few days, and weed was a sick joke against her monster's wrath.

Just one. It sounded so innocent, like a slice of chocolate cake.

Just one, she promised herself, meaning it this time. Lennon's neck tipped back along with the pill, and she swallowed, chasing it with a drag of her cigarette.

Though the girls' mouths were moving, Lennon could only make out every few words. With no food to wait behind, the chemicals began to dissolve in less than twenty minutes, and the world's volume turned into a quiet murmur. She nodded at the right beats, interjecting a *yeah* or *totally* when they looked to her for validation. Michaela got extra excited after one in particular.

"You will?" she squealed.

"Will what?" Lennon's pupils had become large saucers, glinting under the security light.

Macy laugh rang out like wind chimes. "Come out with us more!"

"Oh. Sure, yeah." She'd go with them anywhere, as long as she got to feel like this. Whatever took the pain away.

"We miss you." Michaela's smile seemed a little too wide. Lennon blinked, trying to force it back into a normal size. "And you need to stay busy."

Macy shook her head. "I couldn't be alone if I were you. Ugh, I can't imagine..."

Off her expression, it seemed like they had imagined all too well. Lennon was willing to bet the first thing they did was picture their twin's face instead of Page's. Head down in the sand, pruned and lifeless. Not that she blamed them; Lennon had found out her mom was pregnant just days before Wyatt's passing. She'd had to listen to all kinds of stories circulating the school. First graders had crazy imaginations.

He was chopped up in the propeller!

No, he just hit his head on it.

Well, my dad said he fell off and drowned...

In every version, she imagined her baby sister instead. Lennon had her first anxiety attack on the lake the next summer, when they'd brought Page. Lennon sat next to her mother the entire time, making sure she was holding her sister tight enough. Whenever her mom removed a hand to eat or drink, she was right there to replace the support, too grown for her meager five years.

"What've you heard?" Lennon's shoulders shifted against the brick.

Missing Page

The girls looked at each other uncomfortably. It was the first time Lennon had ever seen Michaela reluctant to share gossip.

"You can tell me," she pushed, nodding for emphasis.

Macy deferred to her sister. If anyone was going to say it, it'd be Michaela.

"Just about what happened, how she went. We're all heartbroken. They're talking about that Emery girl, obviously."

"Yeah?" Lennon asked, ears perking.

"Ricky said she's shunned. Nobody will talk to her," Macy answered. "Sounds like she was already a shitty friend—"

"They weren't friends," Lennon corrected.

Michaela paused, noting the venom in her tone. "He told us about how mean she was to Page, too."

Macy fidgeted. "You don't really think she *killed her*, do you, Lennon?"

"I don't know," she answered quietly

The twins shifted, sensing her tension.

"It was negligent, for sure," Macy continued carefully. "We can all agree on that."

Negligent. Lennon rolled the word around on her tongue. No, it didn't feel strong enough for what Emery did—or let—happen. She flicked her cigarette onto the ground, twisting her shoe over it.

"Did Ricky say anything else?"

Michaela shook her head. "Nah. Did you, uh...did you ever find her stuff?"

Lennon paused, debating whether to tell her the truth. Whatever she said would be in everyone's ear by the next day. But maybe if people watched Emery more closely, something else would come to the surface.

"Her bike was under Emery's porch. Just found it today."

The girls sucked in matching breaths, leaning into each other for stability.

She should've known information from the Trues would be worthless. They wanted information from her as much as she did.

Ricky and Page had known *of* each other, but Page had never paid him any attention. She'd never been a fan of the youngest True; he was an asshole in his own regard. Only with Michaela's level of embellishing could he be called a friend.

She thought about Theo then, how warmly he'd greeted her at the gelato shop. He lacked that maliciousness the Trues all seemed to possess, which she knew Page would have appreciated. Maybe he'd become an older-sibling figure to Page, one that could be there in a way Lennon couldn't. *Had she confided in him instead?*

Michaela mistook Lennon's pension for sadness, and she took her and Macy's hands. "I don't know about you bitches, but I need another drink. You coming, Len?"

Lennon ached to go home, but she hadn't even been here an hour.

"Yeah. I can stay for a bit," Lennon conceded. The twins pulled her inside, lifting a few fingers over the growing crowd to order shots. The loud chatter in the bar tickled her ears, bassy sound waves dancing on her hot skin.

"Holy fuck, that bartender's *hot*." Michaela's eyes turned sultry.

Lennon rolled hers. Michaela had things for bartenders, especially ones who gave out free drinks. She'd made it a game years ago to flirt at least one into her hand before changing locations, and was usually successful.

Leaving her to it, Lennon nudged Trick, who had been laughing at Rowan on the dance floor. "How have you been?" she asked, attempting conversation.

Trick licked his lips while he thought, clearly taken by surprise. She wasn't known for her sociability. "I've been...good." It took only seconds for him to buckle under her icy stare. "I'm happy to see you, don't get me wrong. I just didn't think you were gonna come."

"Me neither," she agreed, looking around. "I don't really know what the fuck I'm doing."

"How have *you* been?" he asked warily, unable to look at her head-on. After her silence, he rushed to recover. "Right. I'll shut up if you don't want to talk about it, but I'm really sorry about your sister.

And I'm sorry about the casserole...my mom thinks food is the answer for everything. I couldn't think of anything better—"

"You're fine," Lennon said quickly. *No Page talk when I'm rolling*, she decided.

"So, were you guys, like...really close?"

"Patrick," her voice warned. "Not here. Not now."

There was no way in hell she was allowing him to use her sister's death as an *in*.

"Sorry." He coughed nervously, scrambling for a new subject. "Er...why isn't Hart here, again?"

He must not have heard her warning to Macy. Luckily for him, she was desperate to change subjects.

"I didn't want him to come." She shrugged, her walls feeling a little less concrete. "It'd be a lot for anyone to handle, and we haven't even made it to a year, so...I don't know. He shouldn't have his summer ruined over someone else's problem."

"You say that like that 'someone else' is a stranger. You're his girlfriend. If he loves you, I'm sure he wouldn't see it like that."

"Maybe." She interlocked her fingers, her attention fading. He noticed she detached whenever feelings got discussed, and Trick almost only ever talked about his feelings. He'd never felt more boring than those few weeks they dated.

"Would you go for him?"

She looked up, taken aback by his question. *Would I?* Her teeth mashed into her lip while she thought, dented with two small lines by the time she thought of an answer.

"I think I would. If he wanted me to."

His eyebrows were creasing, trying to understand. "But you don't. Want him here, that is."

"I can barely take care of myself right now."

Unable to argue, Trick patted her shoulder sympathetically. He'd known Lennon—as much as anyone could—for a long time, and watched from from afar even longer. She wondered if he could see any of the fragility she hid underneath her steely exterior. Did anybody see her for what she was, a sheep in wolves' clothing?

A shot glass slid past her at dangerous speeds. Trick's hand finally dropped from her shoulder to stop it before it spilled into his lap, shooting a look down the bar. Lennon swiveled her head to see who had saved her, only to find an equally perplexed pair of hazel eyes, lingering on the space Trick's hand had just left.

11

"I didn't order this," Trick frowned.

"On the house," Conrad called, unsmiling. He kept his eyes trained on Lennon from behind the bar, shaking a tin with one arm and gunning soda into a glass with the other. The white shirt hugging his arms was surprisingly unstained; he must have just gotten here. Was it him vibrating, or was that the drugs?

"I...what are you doing here?" Lennon asked, suddenly feeling naked. She didn't like the look on his face, like he was judging her for being out so soon after her sister's death.

"I work here," he shouted over the chatter and music. "What... what are *you* doing here?"

She tried to think of an answer, but eventually dropped her shoulders in defeat. "I don't know."

His eyes bore through hers, intense enough to make her curl inward. Those eyes could read her better than anyone else here.

"Do you *want* to be here?"

Anxiety and obligation had kept her chained to her barstool, but his question rattled through her, simplifying something that had previously felt too complex. She gave a quick shake of her head, and he glanced at the group, plotting with a subtle nod.

"Five minutes," he mouthed to her.

She watched the clock with waning patience, relaxing her shoulders once the time was up. He tossed his strainer and rag into his pockets like smoking pistols into gun belts, circled around the bar and waved his hand for her to follow while the group was still downing their free rounds. Michaela's attention was fixed onto him as he passed, hearts practically leaping out of her eyes, but her excitement fizzled when he approached Lennon.

"Typical," she grumbled under her breath. She scowled and turned, sucking down the rest of her cocktail.

Once they made it outside, Conrad pulled out his phone, typing in his password. "Were those your friends back there?"

"Uh—kind've...not really. Not my best idea, I know."

"As long as you know they're shitty fucking friends," Conrad shook his head, glowering. "Are you even ready to do all this? You know there's no rush, you can take all the time you need. You don't have to bounce back..."

She had stopped listening, focusing in on the address he was typing into the rideshare. "Don't call that. I'm walking."

He looked up, landing on something across the lot. "To your house? That's two miles from here."

"It'll be fine."

"You can't just be walking around alone, in the dark—"

"Right. All the serial killers," she deadpanned, nodding seriously.

He glowered at her. "I need you to be safe, okay? Please, Lennon. Drop the stubborn act."

It was rare she was shocked out of a witty response. Knowing her as long as he did, Conrad didn't care to sugarcoat things, or tread lightly around her. She'd expected the attitude, but it had always come in the form of a jeer or prank before. She didn't know how to argue against concern for her wellbeing.

"Conrad," she tried again, more genuine. "I've lived here my whole life. I'll be okay, I promise."

"Weren't you drinking?"

"I don't drink," She said matter-of-factly.

"There's plenty of other things that can impair your senses." He said, clocking her bottomless pupils.

She grinned. "You sound like a D.A.R.E cop."

Frustration creased his tan forehead. "Lennon... "

"I'm *fine*, Conrad," A hint of annoyance tinged her tone. The fun was over. "Really."

Conrad's nose twitched, unconvinced. But he knew that expression; he'd seen it long ago on a four-year-old version, begging to keep playing after injuries. That stubborn set of her lip meant there would be no changing her mind. "Can I walk you out of the lot, at least?"

She stared at him for a moment. As much as she wanted to turn him down, it didn't look like he would take no for an answer, either. She sighed through her nose, letting him lead the way across the parking lot. Something about the action stirred something warm in her, and which only urged her to freeze it out in defense.

She jerked her head for him to follow, but refused to look at him while they walked. "This doesn't make us friends."

It didn't sound cruel, just factual. She was taking protective measures, for the both of them. Lennon wasn't looking to make friends with anyone, especially one of the Bates. There was too much history with the family, too many painful memories to forget. Surely he had to understand that.

His lip quivered, fighting off a smile. "You're a real California Dream, Len, you know that?"

She shrugged unapologetically, still keeping her eyes on the cluster of trees they were walking toward. She was being unfair, she knew that. Sure, he'd been an ornery, conniving kid, but that was years ago. He'd been nothing but nice since the day she passed him in her Jeep, and here she was freezing him out without rhyme or reason.

Well, there *was* reason—a few of them, actually, though none of them were his fault.

"You still livin' with your mom?" She asked casually, crossing her arms.

"No, I got my own place a while ago. She's here, though. Dad still lives up north."

Her skin prickled at the mention of his father, but she blamed the breeze, forcing herself to stay in the present. They stopped at the line where pavement met dirt; bugs screamed from the brush, high-pitched and relentless. *Those have to be the loudest things in America,* she thought hazily.

"Are you, uh...are you doing okay?" she murmured. "With all that?"

He snorted. "I thought we weren't friends."

"We're not."

His smile finally broke through, but he only allowed it to touch the corners of his mouth. Taking the hint, she averted her gaze, glancing at the tattered bar door. "I didn't know you bartended."

"Something to do over the summer, while I figure my life out. It's good money." He seemed embarrassed, but Lennon held no judgment over him. She knew that lost feeling well.

"I bet." Her listening brain had turned on auto-pilot, watching silhouettes pass through the porthole windows. An uninhibited thought weaseled its way into her mouth, blurting out before she could stop it.

"Why do you think your dad moved?"

It was innocent enough, but her heart was pounding in her ears.

He blinked, taken off guard. "Er...I guess it was too painful to stay. He never really said."

Lennon nodded slowly, looking to the trees. Something about them—maybe the screaming insects—gave her the heebie-jeebies. "I should go," she said quietly.

"Seriously, Lennon. Get home safe." He started to lift a hand to wave, but realizing she was already walking away, quickly bent his arm to scratch the back of his neck.

Lennon took the long way home so she could stop by the old gelato shop, jogging to make up for the time. A sigh of relief inserted itself between her panting at the sight of the lights still on inside. She was even happier when she spotted the tall boy she'd been hoping to find leaning over the counter with a spray bottle and rag. Easing into a walk, she mustered one stiff leg in front of the other, weak after the unexpected exercise.

A bell chimed upon her entrance, and she was greeted with a familiar teeth-clenching blast of cold air.

"Sorry, we're cl–" He looked up, stopping when he recognized her. "Oh."

She took a few steps, closing the distance between her and the counter. "Hey, Theo."

"Hey. Sorry, I just cleaned everything out…"

She waved away his apology. "I didn't come for gelato. I was wondering if I could talk to you, actually. About my sister."

No way out but through. He nodded slowly, and she chewed the inside of her cheek.

"I figured since you and Page worked together, you guys might've talked…I know how boring it gets when it's slow." Lennon had plenty of her own memories here, though she imagined her ideas of passing time were much more troublesome. She fiddled with the pen chained to the pay screen. "I've never questioned how close she and I really were until she died. I've been trying to make sense of everything… figure out what's true, what's rumors."

Her slender fingers released their anxious hold on the pen. "That led me here. She seemed to like you. I thought I could get the truth— or at least some of it—from you."

"We never hung out besides school or here," he said, almost regretfully. "But I felt very protective of her. I trained her, she felt like a little sister to me."

Lennon swallowed, feeling her heart tighten. It was so easy to love her.

He mistook her pain for nerves. "I know a little about her and Emery, if that's what you wanted to ask about."

The name stiffened her, turned her ears hot. "Know what?"

"She spent a little time here. She started a lot of arguments with Page. That girl could get mad like *that*," he snapped his finger.

Lennon felt a surge of adrenaline course through her. "I didn't know she worked here."

Theo shook his head. "She barely made it through trial week. We couldn't take them both, it was too catty. Page was easier to get along with, and she lived closer, so she got it." he sighed, eyes losing focus. "That's what caused the big fight."

"What big fight?" Lennon demanded. *How had she not known about this?*

The air grew heavy, and she instinctively leaned closer, waiting expectantly. Theo's lips tightened, torn between telling her or not. He glanced out the window as the memory unfolded, watching a pair of ghosts only he could see.

"I think it was Page's first or second official day. I was still training her. Emery showed up towards the end of the shift screaming about unfairness and other bullshit...I guess she'd just found out. She couldn't give Page any credit, blamed it all on you and said it was a grandfathering thing.

"Emery demanded that Page quit because she needed the money more. Customers started staring, so Page went outside with her to talk. They were just by this window." Theo pointed. "And after a minute, I heard a thud against the wall." His hand hit the counter to recreate the sound, drawing a wince from Lennon.

"I ran out and saw Page rubbing her head, wasn't hard to put two and two together. I didn't *see it,* and we don't have cameras outside, but I knew. I knew what she did."

Goosebumps lit up Lennon's body. Scalding fury bubbled inside

Missing Page

her, eating the chemicals that the pill had given her. Theo noticed her stillness, but continued.

"I made Emery go home and tried to help Page. But she wouldn't let me check her head, kept saying nothing happened."

How many times had Page heard Lennon say after a fight with their mother? Having to comfort her older sister while pretending she hadn't heard screaming upstairs, or a slap down the hall. What had Lennon been protecting her from all this time, what kind of silence had she taught her?

Theo shook his head sadly. "She protected Emery. I still don't know why."

Lennon looked out the window, glad she couldn't see the same scene he did. She would kill before she allowed someone touch her sister that way. "Because she's good. Page saw the best in people to a fault. There was never judgement with her, never ego...she just loved."

Embarrassment flushed her cheeks with red. Theo was a kid, not a therapist—he didn't need any of this, and he certainly couldn't understand any of it. And yet, he looked at her with eyes as sad as Lennon felt. Maybe, to some extent, he did.

"She made everybody want to be better," he agreed, struggling to keep his composure.

Lennon sucked in her lip, nervous to ask her last question. "Did you ever see her partying, drinking? Anything like that?"

His response was immediate, without a second thought. "Nah. That's not...that wasn't her thing."

Her quiet exhale was filled with relief. Of course she knew that already; she felt terrible even having to ask.

"Thanks, Theodore. Sorry to bother, I'll leave you to it."

Lennon broke into a jog once she reached the street, gritting her teeth against the pain pumping through her legs. She kept pace with the rhythmic sound of the ocean, sizzling like tv static.

The drugs and exercise had whittled her into a zombie by the time she reached her entry door, dark eye circles and all. She ambled until she found herself in the shower, keeping the water hot enough to stay awake.

Page had seen so many dumb, reckless decisions Lennon had made throughout her adolescence, but she thought she'd kept her safely outside of them. She wished she had told Page that not everyone had the ability to retain their chaos in one singular body.

The guilt she felt pushed her over her limit. She wasn't sure if she felt more physically or emotionally exhausted, but the answer came as soon as her head hit the pillow.

Her dream placed her back into the shower. A hand swept over her shoulder and up her neck, pulling her hair back to place a kiss on the tender skin just beneath her jaw. She closed her eyes, instantly recognizing Hart's warmth.

His hands lifted, massaging shampoo against her scalp. She winced, gently leaning forward. "Hart, you know I don't like that—"

He yanked her back suddenly, knotting his fingers in her hair as she gasped. He'd never hurt her before...

This couldn't be him. Her eyes opened wide, but she was held hostage by his hands, unable to move away.

"*Shhh...*" The whispered hiss slithered into her ear, raising the hackles on her neck. She saw a head of wet, blond curls standing behind her in the mirror and blanched. The hands, eyes, and hair all belonged to different men, combined into one terrifying creature. She herself looked different, now a young, chubby-cheeked girl, peering into her own eyes with terror, defenseless against the monster behind her. Her mouth opened in a silent scream at at the beady, unfeeling brown eyes that stared back at her.

"*Go back to sleep.*"

The moment she reached to defend herself, her body jolted awake. Lennon's skin was damp and her breath heavy, as if she'd been running in her sleep. She ripped the duvet off, letting the waking sun wash over her bare stomach. A cry escaped as she stood on her stiff legs, lactic acid shooting painfully through her muscles. She placed a hand on her nightstand to ease her weight, waddling towards the bathroom with a pinched expression. She rinsed cool water over her forehead, taking a deep breath and letting her hair fall to curtain her from the world.

It's not real. It's not real.

The effect it continued to have on her, though, *that* was real. Even though she was safe, she could still see those eyes in her mind.

The sound of her parents' voices below were quiet, muffled under the terracotta floor. Not yet ready to interact with the world, she padded back to her room, pulling her computer out of her suitcase to check emails. There'd be least one from her advisor, which she would avoid like the plague.

The computer's black screen reflected an unrecognizable face. Lennon moved her fingers tiredly to the power button, cursing at the red battery symbol flashing. She flipped the laptop next to her on the bed with a sigh, and maneuvered around an extra chipper Kaiser to trot downstairs, still half-asleep.

She pushed the royal blue door open, expecting to see Page's hair peeking through the duvet, or sitting in front of her mirror with her makeup spilled around her. The emptiness hit her like a truck, and reality came after to finish the blow.

It was like she died all over again.

It took a while for Lennon to gain enough strength to stand. *Emails. Focus on the emails.* She found the cool metal of Page's laptop, unplugging the cord from the side to move to her bed. The password was easy to guess: 0711. She shook her head at Page's predictability, but a small smile exposed her fondness. The structuring was neat; only her most important shortcuts were displayed on the desktop, each placed symmetrically. She was a one-tab-at-a-time kind of girl...another way the two were opposite.

Lennon opened the browser, and then her inbox. In her rush to delete spam, she accidentally sent herself to one of the sites. She went back within seconds, but pop ups wasted no time appearing on the side of her screen.

Great, she grumbled, blowing her hair out of her face. She opened another tab, frustration making her fingers extra clumsy.

How to get rid of computer virus, she'd started to write. But she had only typed in *How to* before Page's previous searches stopped her. She leaned forward, squinting.

how to password protect word doc
how to hide location
how to erase search history tabs

She clearly hadn't figured out the last one.

Everything else forgotten, Lennon opened Word and clicked into Page's files. What could she be hiding, and why did she need to hide at all? Her breath hitched at the three documents displayed, each coupled with a lock symbol next to it.

Journal 12/31
Journal 3/13
Journal 5/25

What had Page done that she needed to keep secret? Or, on the likelier side, what secret was she hiding for someone else? Lennon was torn between respecting her privacy and finding answers.

After each number Lennon pressed, a knife dug further into her heart. She started with the most obvious—Page's birthday. Four circles sat on the screen, and she took a deep breath, pressing enter. After a moment, the code box shook, signaling a wrong attempt.

Damn.

She tried a few more—her own birthday, *Kaiser,* even *password.* After the fourth attempt, Lennon pressed her fingers against her eyelids, trying to think. What the hell was in here, and what would she use to keep her deepest secrets safe?

An image of their pinkies wrapped around each other floated behind her eyes, and her fingers found the keys to input *mermaidpromise* into the bar. She was scared to press enter, not knowing how many attempts she was allowed before being locked out. But nothing better came to mind, and Lennon was desperate.

Missing Page

Her teeth bit down on the flesh of her lip as she hit enter, tasting blood when a file opened before her.

She shoved the screen down, not yet ready to read the words her sister had written in confidence. Was she really going to do this? If Page were here, would she be able to forgive her?

That's what gave Lennon her answer. Page *wasn't* here.

Before lifting the screen, Lennon swore that nothing she might read would change her perception of her sister, even if it was a side she hadn't known about. She'd skim everything unless it was important. *Mermaid promise, Jimmy.*

She sucked in a breath and lifted the screen.

12/31

It's embarrassing how paranoid I'm being about this, I know. But I swear Mom's been reading my journal. The day after I wrote about having a D in math, somehow she knew and chewed me out.

Speaking of, Mom completely freaked out on Dad last night. She was wasted, obviously, and brought up Lennon. He was kind of taking Len's side, and she lost it. I think she's extra on edge since Christmas, she thought Lennon would've come back by now. We all did.

I miss her like crazy. I hope she's not upset I told her to go…I only said it because I thought she'd be happier away, not because I wanted her gone. But now we're barely talking.

School's been a bit better. I'm not scared for break to end anymore, even though I don't know how I'm going to feel seeing Emery. She's cool when we hang out alone, but whenever we're around people she starts making fun of me. Anytime I struggle with a problem she makes such a big deal out of it and calls me retarded, which I don't even think people are allowed to say anymore. At our soccer banquet she said God made me pretty because I don't have anything else going for me, and everyone laughed. Lennon told me I need to have stronger boundaries, but when I try Em just says that I'm used to people kissing my ass.

I think she just needs more time to feel safe. People only give her attention when we're together, and I guess she thinks putting me down is the way to keep it.

I just need to prove her wrong, and I think tutoring is gonna help. We've only had a few sessions so far, but Conrad's good about making everything simple, and he's patient even when I'm doing really bad. Apparently he used to be even worse than me. He said he had almost all D's freshman year, but once he found a way that worked for him it changed everything. Who knows, he might've just said that to make me feel better. Another plus is that Mom acts better when he's here.

What else? Oh, Dad surprised me with a mermaid lunch today. We ate on top of the mountain where that little lookout is instead of the cave. We sang Beautiful Boy, but it just felt sad this time. It made me realize we're all growing up, getting older. I think he felt it too.

I hope Lennon comes back soon.

Lennon shut the screen, pressing her fingers to her eyes to stop the stream of guilty tears. Her sobs grew stronger as the memory played behind her eyes, realizing that the terrible Christmas Page had written about would end up being her last.

Page was too kind to say it, even in her most private thoughts. Lennon always seen it as escaping instead of abandoning, but now it seemed obvious. It made her feel like everything her mother claimed about her—her selfishness, her recklessness—was true. Her body shook.

Oh god, oh god...

12

On the night of December 25th, just past ten p.m., Lennon and her mother were lounging on the deck of her home. Family holidays were no exception to Cash's drinking habits, but she tended to get more sentimental. The woman had been lost in a slurring rant for an impressive fifteen minutes, but only a few days into her return, Lennon held more patience than usual. She'd started quite the game for herself, trying to guess when her mom's animated hands would spill the spiked eggnog sloshing in her glass.

"You know I love you, though. We have this bond, you can feel it." Cash's gaze rolled to her daughter.

Lennon nodded, only half-listening. "You're my mom. Moms and their kids always have that bond." Though, depending on the family, that bond could look like a beautiful, winding dance of DNA strands, or cancer clinging to your cells.

Cashmere stared out at the black ocean, resting her freshly filled lip on her glass as she pondered her next sentence. "That didn't happen with Page, you know."

Lennon swiveled her head, sure she'd misheard. "What do you mean?"

Cash kept her eyes trained on the view in front of her. She had buried this particular shame deep within—she wasn't sure what about this night or this moment was bringing it to light. But it was spilling out of her, and she couldn't stop it; it felt too good letting someone else carry it for a moment.

"I barely got to hold her when she first came out. We were both exhausted after fourteen hours of labor...you can't imagine. That euphoria I got with you wasn't there. I thought it was the exhaustion. They took her, got her cleaned up...and when she came back to me..."

Lennon waited, trying to keep her face blank. It was important not to show judgment or fear of what was to come if she wanted to avoid conflict.

Tears welled up in her mother's eyes. "There was nothing. I felt...*nothing*. I was sure they had switched her. I mean, of course I *tried* to love her—"

"Mom." Lennon couldn't hear any more. Page, the girl she was convinced was an angel sent to give their lives a sliver of light, was the one her mother couldn't love?

"She really started getting a personality around four or five. And she was so *good*, down to her soul. That's when I loved her. And of course, she *had* to be mine, you two look so similar..." She trailed off, downing another gulp of eggnog.

Lennon was frozen in place, trying to collect herself. Cashmere finally took notice of Lennon's stillness and sat up straighter, her eyes focusing. "Lennon, look at me."

She swallowed, meeting her mother's glazed-over expression. A tear spilled before she could stop it, and it was too late by the time she wiped it. It was that break in Lennon's walls made Cash snap back to the present, realizing what she'd done. She recoiled, tightening her fingers around her glass.

"You can never, *ever* tell Page that. No matter what. You *swear* to me."

The hardness in Lennon's tone was impossible to hide. "You

Missing Page

think I would ever tell my sister that you had to *decide* to love her? That it didn't come naturally?"

Cash stared at her, apathetic. She needed to know she could count on Lennon's silence.

"Why would you tell me that?" Lennon's voice broke.

"For fuck's sake, Lennon, you're nearly twenty-one. I thought we could talk about things like adults."

"She's perfect. She's always been perfect." Lennon stood. "But that wasn't good enough. You want someone broken like *you*. So you don't have to wallow in your own misery."

Lennon left Cashmere there, locking herself in her room to process. She couldn't think, couldn't make a plan. She needed help, and though the first person she thought to call wasn't even in the same state, she called him anyway.

It was the first time she cried to Hart. It was only for a moment, equally mortifying and terrifying, but he held her vulnerability with care. He'd shown up for her as he always did, calming her down while finding the quickest flight out. She remembered him asking if noon was early enough, and not knowing how to let go of her shame and accept. The question ended being more a formality, anyway–she had a flight itinerary to Utah in her email before she could say yes.

She didn't come out until the next morning when Page knocked on her door for breakfast.

"Why are you packing?" Page asked, her eyes widening at the open suitcase on Lennon's bed. Lennon stepped to cover it from view, gently turning her sister around and throwing an arm around her shoulder.

Page stared while Lennon forked eggs into her mouth, keeping her eyes glued to her plate. Too scared to ask out loud, she texted her dad to ask for a ride to the airport. She had no idea his iMessage was attached to the tablet Cashmere used for work.

That was the match that struck fire—burning through the dining room, up the stairs and engulfing the suite in Cash's flames. "You can't just run away every time someone hurts your feelings. You're going to end up alone if you keep this up!"

Lennon remained silent, stuffing her toiletries into her bag.

"You know what? *Fine*. You'll last a day before his parents see your true colors, and don't bother coming back." Cash seethed. "You can manipulate your boyfriend or whatever friends you have left, but you *won't* do it to me! I'm done, Lennon, *done!*"

She knew better than to think Cash was done so soon. Her mother wouldn't stop until she guilted her into staying, or somehow convinced herself that this was Lennon's fault and not her own.

"You manipulate so much you even have yourself convinced I'm the bad guy! You're being delusional, Lennon. I mean, seriously, do we need to admit you? You've painted yourself as the victim, *again*, after we just had an amazing holiday as a family. Why are you acting like this?"

"I need you to leave my room, please." Lennon said through her teeth. "I don't want to talk to you when you're like this."

She thought her words would be water over fire, but she'd thrown gasoline instead. Cash's flames burned hot through her room, spewing clothes from her closet and dresser.

"Fine, then, I'll help you. We don't want you here, get the hell out!"

That's when Page stepped in. Seeing Lennon wordlessly pack the mess Cash was creating away into her suitcase, stuffing down tears as their mother screeched, sent her into a desperate attempt to help.

"C'mon Len..." she whispered. "Can't you just stay for a few more days?"

Lennon sucked in a shallow breath, the guilt sinking into her stomach. She hugged her sister to her chest, pressing her lips to her hair. "I'm sorry. I have to go."

"You're *ruining* Christmas!" Cash shrieked.

"*I'm* ruining Christmas?" Lennon hissed, her eyes sharpening into daggers. Her tone stopped Cashmere in her place, bringing back a recollection of the previous night that sucked the air out of the room, and the firestorm with it.

Stacy's feet pounded noisily up the stairs, warning his arrival before he came in. Cash hated that he stood at the door instead of uniting with her as a front; she was constantly fighting for her husband's support, and in this moment, she'd never felt more alone.

"I'm leaving, Mom," Lennon said. "You're getting exactly what you want."

Lennon's cursed memory would make sure that she never forgot what her own mother, the woman she was born from, responded with. It would live with her day after day, no matter how many drugs she took to try and forget. There were a few things that had that effect on Lennon–Wyatt's death, the summer preceding it, when her mother had screamed that she hated her after a piano recital, and this.

"*Perfect.* You're dead to me, anyway."

Lennon's brows raised, her face becoming much younger than before. Normally she could detach, but the way Cash spit those words at her left her paralyzed in place. Lennon felt the truth of them, even if it was only in that moment.

Page started pulling on her mom, trying to get her out of the room —that's when hands started flying. Stacy and Lennon got to them within seconds, but Cash caught her youngest's temple during the separation. Page sank into a ball as stars swirled behind her eyes, shaking with sobs while Stacy took his belligerent wife downstairs. All Lennon could do was rub her back in hopeless circles, apologizing over and over.

One of the hardest things Lennon had ever done was leave her shattered family that morning. She was only able to do it because she thought they'd be better off without her, and because Page seemed to agree.

It might help things, she'd said. *You and Mom just need a break.* Lennon remembered Page's strained smile and the pain she felt from it.

Cash was right about one thing. Lennon had been running away since she could remember; through getaways, her 'friend's' houses, and then college. But on this flight to Utah, she realized the issue had never been in getting away. Lennon could never escape her life or her memories. Wherever she went, her mind followed.

It was a culture shock, leaving a broken home for one where she was immediately showered in love.

Hart's house looked like the ones in snow globes. Its roof held a few feet of pearlescent powder, and icicles hung from the gutters like a runny nose. The inside was lit in warm yellows of candles and fire, and behind the frosted windows a silhouette grew into the shape of a human as it approached the door.

Fresh food wafted into Lennon's nose before she fully stepped through—Hart's dad took her bags downstairs, and his mom rushed from the table she was setting to wrap her in a tight hug.

"Lennon, how lovely to meet you! I'm Carrie, and this is—well, that speedy devil was Paul, my husband. We're so happy you're here, honey."

She began removing her shoes, still taking in the house. "Thank you for having me. I know it was such late notice, I'm sorry to interrupt your holiday—"

"No, nonsense! You should have seen me when Hart told us you were coming. We usually have two more, but they're with the in-laws this year. Come in, dear, come in...do you like tacos?"

Lennon nodded, reaching to slip off her shoes. She looked down at her socks, realizing too late they didn't match. One was pink and polka-dotted—Page's, no doubt—and the other was white, with the words *no nonsense* written across the seam. A flicker of a smile touched her lips.

In some crazy way, despite having met them for the first time, her place at their table felt natural. The three shared stories about Hart and his older siblings, Cooper and Peyton, which incited deep, genuine belly laughs from the whole table. Never once did they ask her to talk about the situation she'd come from.

She noticed the ice-waters sitting in front of them, their clear speech. Hart held her hand under the table, brushing his thumb over her cold knuckles. Mrs. Rogers—who insisted on being called Carrie, or Mom—had set up Peyton's room for Lennon. There was a basket of hair care products, creams and oils, as well as a handwritten note letting her know she was welcome to anything in her daughter's bathroom or the house. There was a P.S. in smaller letters, noting that the pantry was included in that offer. It reminded her of the care packages her sister had sent her every month in college, changed only by a mother's love instead of a sister's.

Lennon showered a little longer than usual, basking in the citrus scent of her new body wash. Her phone buzzed with a heartbeat-patterned text in the middle of her night routine.

> **HART**
> Sleep over?

A minute later, Lennon was tucked into Hart's bed, nestling her head over his chest. He fell asleep within minutes, leaving her in a calm silence while her head bobbed with his deep breaths. She stared above at the ceiling, her ears filling with the salty tears that leaked from her eyes. The Rogers' had welcomed her into their home like she was one of their kids, but she still felt like she was watching them from outside the globe. All by her own doing, of course. It was painful to let people love her in this way, knowing it wasn't really hers to enjoy—knowing she had a return date.

The next morning, Lennon was surprised with a second Christmas, gifted with presents they'd originally planned to send back with Hart.

"Now we get to see you open them, how lovely!" Carrie exclaimed cheerfully, clapping her hands together.

There was a charm bracelet, a few dorm accessories. Lennon apologized over having nothing to give back, but they were insistent that her presence was enough. She couldn't make sense of it; her own mother couldn't find something to love in her. How could these people love all of her before they'd even met her?

Unable to think of another way to thank them, Lennon cooked the entire week, whipping up her best recipes. She made sure her room was neat and tidy, that the kitchen was always cleaned before they could get to it. Her mother's words hung over her head like an ever-present cloud; the need to prove herself, to avoid giving any reason to believe her mom might treat her that way for a reason, never left.

Each day was laid-back, and much quieter than Lennon was used to. The four went errand running, took morning and afternoon walks, and always ate dinner together. Carrie would often brush a strand of hair out of her face or rub her arms to give her warmth without a second thought. And every night, she gave her a hug before they went to bed. Lennon stiffened every time, unsure of how to react. She couldn't remember the last time Cashmere had touched her with a loving hand instead of an angry one. She didn't know how to carry this much love.

Though these moments were technically insignificant, she knew she'd remember them forever simply because of how she *felt*. It was the safest comfort she'd ever known—she'd even started to let herself imagine coming back here, that this wasn't a random stroke of luck. But her dreams were always lurking in the night, waiting to remind her of what she'd left behind. Hart and his family were beautiful in every sense, and it was exactly why she couldn't let them get close. She was a weed that had somehow snuck into their garden; if she stayed too long, everything would rot.

The second to last day of her break, she'd gotten an onslaught of drunken texts from her mother after realizing Lennon was not returning. She'd immediately texted Page to check in, worried her sister was getting the brunt of Cash's anger. After seeing the read receipts and no response, she'd spiraled into a full-blown panic attack, eventually excusing herself from the dinner table.

"You're *sure* you're okay?" Lennon's voice asked in a hushed tone, hidden under the pantry's shadows. She watched each of the Rogers

Missing Page

throw down their cards onto the table, crying out in either frustration or victory.

"Yeah, things are fine." Page's voice crackled, struggling through the poor signal.

"Fine?" Lennon repeated, unconvinced.

"Good, I mean. They're good."

Lennon turned away from the family, resting her forehead against the wall. "I miss you. So, so much."

"We miss you too. Dad's asking every five minutes if I've heard from you."

Lennon made a mental note to call him in the morning. "I'm good. You guys don't have to stress, okay? I gotta go, but I love you, I love you guys."

She collected herself once the line cut, making sure her face was smooth before moving on. She pulled a loaf of sourdough from the shelf, balancing it in her hand as she fished an array of cheeses and fresh tomatoes from the fridge. Lennon saved her famous fancy grilled cheese and tomato bisque for their last night.

After his third serving, Hart and Lennon went down to get ready for bed, which mostly consisted of a long, shared shower. He combed her hair like he always did, planting kisses beneath her ear between brush strokes.

"This week has been really nice." she said softly.

"You're always welcome here, you know. They like you a lot."

Guilt overpowered her gratitude. She felt like an imposter. Surely, if she spent enough time here, they'd see her flaws, too.

"Wanna go back up for a little?" she asked, turning to him.

Hand in hand, the two returned and joined his parents for a few more poker rounds. After Hart's final sweep, they all retired to the two couches, soaking up warmth from the kindling fire.

"We've heard raving reviews about your piano playing, Lennon." Mr. Rogers—*Paul*, she corrected herself—said innocently, tapping his fingers together.

She glanced at Hart with narrowed, accusing eyes, but kept her smile innocent. She'd told him she *used* to play, hadn't she? He had no way of knowing if she were actually good or not.

"We have this old thing." Mrs.—*Carrie*, gestured to the lightly dusted Yamaha, as if it wasn't the first thing Lennon noticed when she arrived. "Normally we have Cooper play, Hart sing, and Peyton dance."

"That sounds fun," Lennon chuckled. Hart's face changed suddenly, with a new understanding she did not yet have. It locked his jaw, tightened his eyes in unspoken warning, and he shook his head as subtly as he could manage.

But Carrie hadn't noticed. "We were hoping you'd give it some use?"

The room raised a few degrees, now a bit too warm for comfort. Blood rushed to her cheeks. "Oh. I mean, it's been a *long* time, I—"

"We're not expecting Beethoven, hon. We just to make sure it works," Paul teased, his smile bringing out his son's resemblance.

Lennon swallowed, glancing at Hart.

"It's late, guys...." He argued weakly. They ignored him, looking to her hopefully. She couldn't bring herself to say no to the people who had given her the best week of her life, to decline the first request they've made since she arrived. She sat up awkwardly, ambling over to the bench.

Cashmere had ruined this hobby of Lennon's years ago. It wasn't hard to guess how; she'd showed up wasted to her tenth grade recital and caused a scene in front of all of her fellow students and their families. She'd never apologized, and in turn had left an open wound. Lennon hadn't touched a piano since.

Lennon jumped when a note played accidentally, laughing nervously. His parents joined in, none the wiser.

She began with a simple melody, hoping her memory wouldn't fail her. The notes came out quiet, unsure. She tried to remember that this family was not the same, that the mother sitting in front of her was not like her own. With her full, round cheeks and twinkling eyes, Carrie was incapable of cruelty. Lennon watched as Mr.

Rogers' thumb brushed over his wife's knuckle, the same way Hart's had over hers their first night.

Her eyes flickered to their son, who was watching her with an encouraging smile. *Was it possible?* she wondered. Had she found one of the good ones? Maybe he truly had no master plan; if Hart had been raised in a home like this, it was no wonder he was able to paint every room in shades of love, to coat every action in it.

The next song came stronger, with more confidence. She was shocked at how her fingers remembered even when her mind didn't; they danced across the keys like they had their own individual consciousness. She went through her favorites: Tchaikovsky, Ludovico, and an intricate movie theme she'd learned just before quitting. By the time she finished, she'd almost forgotten her audience, and waited for their response with bated breath.

They gushed.

"I think it's time to come out of retirement!" Paul said, whistling.

"Oh, honey, that was incredible," Carrie beamed.

"*That's* what you've been hiding from me?" Hart exclaimed with astonishment.

She couldn't believe that those melodies still lived inside of her, and how much they'd flourished in this space. Is that what love did?

It wasn't long after that yawns stretched Mr. and Mrs. Roger's mouths. They thanked Lennon again, kissing her and their son's heads before departing for bed, leaving them to their own.

She peered over at Hart, only to see that he was looking back at her with a matched burning. It felt so intense and so filling that she could feel the emotion rolling into words over her tongue, aching to be released. She'd felt this same wave earlier in the shower, but blamed it on good sex.

"I love you," she almost sighed.

"What're you thinking about?" Hart grinned.

Oops. Her teeth released their hold on her bottom lip, her voice low. "I'm thinking about how we're supposed to be on a plane in six hours."

"Must be a sexy plane." He took a seat next to her on the bench, his thumb brushing absentmindedly over the bee etched into the nape of her neck. She shivered from his gentle touch, and a victorious smile rippled through his curved lips. He liked knowing he had some sort of effect over her, especially since she could unravel him with a single touch.

"You remember when I was singing Elvis to you in your room? After the Halloween party?" he murmured.

Of course she did. She thought about it more than she cared to admit. "Mhm."

Hart lifted a hand to tuck a strand of hair behind her ear, gazing affectionately. "Play something for me."

"I just did," she chuckled.

"No, no. A *private* show," he whispered teasingly. "For me."

She wanted to play something that sounded as happy as he'd made her feel all week, but the one song that kept returning was a melody she promised she'd never play. It was the song she listened to countless times with her sister, when their dad would take them to explore a hidden grotto on the beach—*that's* how happy Hart made her. The way he was looking at her made her sure he felt the same way.

She played a few keys, focusing on her fingers to avoid his expression. He rubbed his stubbled chin, lips spreading as recognition hit. He pressed warm lips to her temple and hummed along, tickling her nose with his musky cologne.

"You know this?" she asked shakily, unfamiliar with this new, untouched vulnerability.

His deep voice rumbled through his chest. "Beautiful, beautiful, beautiful...."

Her fingers lifted from the piano, touching his cheek. She finally met his eyes, the emotion in her chest nearly too much to bear.

He cupped her cheeks carefully in his hands, kissing her with a sensitivity that melted every thought, every fear she'd ever had.

Beautiful Boy.

13

THE LAPTOP WAS SEARING AGAINST HER LAP, ITS FAN DROWNING out the sound of Cash descending the stairs. Lennon's fingers were frozen mid-scroll on the mousepad, her eyes deep in memory.

"There's a delivery for you upstairs," Cash said, interrupting Lennon's absentminded humming.

She finally looked up, brows knitting in confusion. "For me?"

Tension draped over the room, heavier on Lennon's side. Now that Christmas was fresh in her mind again, it was hard to separate that woman from the one standing in front of her.

The wear of the last few days morphed Cashmere into something almost unrecognizable. Even Botox struggled under the constant attack of her stress and grief, and the extra booze was deepening her creases, flushing her cheeks. In that moment, Cashmere looked more like a person trying to survive than her mother. It was something Lennon could find familiarity in. Sometimes, they really weren't so different. Lennon's anger faded, and compassion took its place.

She followed her mother upstairs to the kitchen, met with two bouquets of flowers. One vase was filled with deep purple poppies, the other with lavender hydrangeas accompanied by a plush yellow bumblebee. The latter had to be from Hart, but the poppies... something struck in her, but wasn't quite close enough to grasp.

"We need more help around here, Len." Cash's voice pierced her ear like a drill. "There's so much to do with the funeral, having to tell everyone, God knows how many showings I have to reschedule. You've hardly been home. I didn't even see you last night."

"The twins invited me out."

"I thought you scared them off after the Vegas trip."

Hardly. They still loved telling that story over a year later.

"They're just trying to be supportive. I needed a breather."

Cash pursed her lips, deflecting the excuses. "What about us? You still have a family, Lennon. It feels like you're running away—"

"I'm not running away. I'm here, right now." Lennon's voice hardened. "This doesn't have to be a fight, Mom. Just tell me what you need help with."

Only Cash could find something in that to be annoyed with. "Do you really have to ask? Look around. Errands need ran, the cars need gas, we have to organize all this food, respond to letters. Kaiser's been stuck inside, he's getting antsy—"

"Okay," Lennon breathed. "I'll do those today. See? We can get to a resolution without all the jabs."

Cash grit her teeth. Before she could retort, her phone chimed from the counter. Whatever the name read sent a loud sigh through her, but her annoyance was quickly wiped away with a plastered smile and her signature work voice. She shot a final glare at her daughter and snatched her sweaty, half-empty Corona off the piano, her heels clicking down the hall.

Lennon turned to the counter, holding the bee to her chest as she read Hart's note. She could feel the ghost of his thumb brushing over the nape of her neck, and imagined the sound of his family's laughter filling the room. Thinking back on that week she spent with him and his family, she couldn't believe how much her feelings had changed since then. She pushed people away when things felt too good, thinking she was getting ahead of the inevitable disaster. Though the strong feelings she had for him couldn't be erased, she would continue to push them down, and keep their warm fingers from wrapping around her frostbitten heart.

The poppies gently caught her attention, sprouting shades of muted and polite violets. A note was tucked deep into the bundle, folded tightly as if it wasn't sure it wanted to be seen.

It was thin notebook paper rather than the thick kind printed from the shop. It sliced through her finger when she picked it up, eliciting a hiss. A small drop of blood kissed the edge of the open note, reading only three words.

Deepest condolences-
Conrad

The memory she couldn't catch before floated back to her. She had given the same kind to his family after Wyatt's accident—they'd been his favorite. She supposed they could have been been Conrad's, first; children loved to steal traits from their older siblings. She folded it again, tucking the letter into the pocket of her hoodie and her injured finger into her mouth.

Her father's frustrated grumblings tickled her ear from the deck. She turned just in time to see him enter from the balcony, rubbing the lines in his forehead as he mumbled into the phone apologetically. *Who was he talking to?*

His eyes flew to hers as if he'd heard her. She fidgeted uncomfortably at the new expression that darkened his face—whatever it was about, she was involved.

"All right. Ok, yeah...all right. We'll make sure it doesn't happen again, Kelly."

Kelly. Either Emery had tattled, or the camera had caught her after all. Lennon should've never left that spot; at least then they'd have Emery's true account of events recorded. It would be her word against Emery's, now. *That smart little shit...*

He lowered the phone, eyes burning through her. "You went back?"

"I just needed to ask her a few questions..."

"Jesus *Christ!*" His hand dragged down his face, resting over his silver whiskers. Though she was all too familiar with being a disappointment, it hurt more when it was her dad.

"Lennon," His tone deepened, demanding her attention. "Look, kid, I know you're convinced Emery had something to do with this—"

"Page's bike was at her house, Dad."

"I know. Detective Shultz called me to pick it up this morning, they're running fingerprints as we speak."

He expected her to interrupt, but she was silent. Her eyes were frozen over, resolute in her theory.

"If you listen to one thing your old dad tells you, please, let it be this," He set his phone on the piano, meeting her eyes with a simmering intensity. "Emery *did not* do this."

"How can you say that?" Lennon shook her head in disbelief. "We saw her running that night. She admitted she lied about giving Page alcohol!"

"I believe you, but c'mon, Len. They checked the tires for sand and couldn't find a speck, not one. We didn't look under there that night, maybe Page left it before she went to the cove..."

Lennon shook her head, refusing to listen.

"The girl's only fifteen—"

"You know what I was doing at fifteen? I knew how to sneak out with house alarms set, how to manipulate my location. I can't tell you how many times you thought I was at a friend's house when I was out of town, two hours away. I made sure neither of you had a *clue* the things I was doing, or what I was capable of, until I wanted you to."

"I'm sure you were running circles around us." He grimaced, as if her words physically stung him. "But I'm curious, who do you think who was watching you do all those things?"

She faltered, unable to counter.

"It wasn't Emery, I'll tell you that."

Missing Page

Despite her preparation, his words still rocked through her like a punch to the gut.

"I don't blame you for what happened," he repeated. "But if anybody was a mastermind in this situation, Lennon, it was your sister. She just didn't have the same luck to pull it off."

The crashing of glass down the hall broke their silence, followed with an anguished wail.

"Don't go back to that house, Lennon." he commanded. "I mean it."

She was unable to nod her head, expending all of her energy to hold her quivering lip tight. Once he closed the door behind him, she made a dash for the door, desperate to get out. Page's bike waited for her on the porch, and she escaped without a sound under the cover of strong winds.

The perfume of early summer swirled around her in sweet florals and salty notes as she pedaled down the street, squinting through the early morning fog. Her dad had told her even thirty minutes ago to not go back, and technically, she wasn't. She was going to the park with plans of retracing Page's steps, hoping to find something the police missed. After all, Emery lived in a location perfect for obscurity.

Wet grass tickled her ankles once she stepped off the bike, ushering her to a dirt path that flowed into a cluster of trees. She reached into her pocket, and the smell of lighter fluid soon percolated in the air, followed with something more pungent and earthy. By the time she reached the clearing, her eyes were a soft red, and she could breathe normally again.

A small group of high-schoolers occupied the small area. Three girls swished paint brushes over canvases, and two boys launched a foam football to each other over the green dewy sea. A third barreled through wispy fog with a second pigskin, holding it high in victory.

Lennon didn't think much of it when they all stared her, except that they looked like they'd seen a ghost. She waved away the smoke traveling from her nostrils, thinking that was the focus of their ogling.

Laguna was a health nut of a town—smoking and fast food were borderline sins.

The tall, deep-skinned boy lifted an unsure hand. "...Lennon?"

"Theo?" she squinted. A second plume of smoke filled her chest as he jogged towards her, with his buddy following close behind. She tightened her arms over her chest, trying to ignore the way the nameless boy gazed at her,.

"I thought you...it took me a second to realize who you were." Theo breathed.

It was the first time she looked forward to the funeral. These kids deserved some form of closure. "Sorry. Didn't mean to scare you."

"How...er–how've you been?" Theo asked awkwardly.

"We're managing." Lennon shrugged. "I miss her. A lot."

"So do we." Theo jerked his head back to his friends. "We held a memorial for her after school on the field. Pretty sure everyone was there."

"Yeah, everyone except the Guest of Dishonor." The boy next to him couldn't hide the disgust in his face. "We would have run her off, anyway."

Lennon turned to him. "Are you talking about Emery?"

His red curls bounced as he nodded, nose and cheeks covered in freckles. She fidgeted uncomfortably at his lingering once over—she was in a hoodie, for Christ's sake!

"She's can't move away, they don't have the money. I can't believe they're making us go to school with a mur–"

"Dude," Theo growled. "This is her sister, have some respect."

"Were you friends with Page?" Lennon asked the redhead.

"We were friend...ly, but never really got the chance to get close. She's kinda shy, y'know? Especially those last few months. Her nose was buried in her phone...but when we would talk–"

"What do you mean?"

"The pen pal," Theo clarified, as if that explained things.

Lennon stared at them, waiting for more. It took a moment for

Theo to process her look, his brows knitting once it clicked. "You didn't know?"

Curls jumped back in. "She was obsessed. How'd you not notice?"

"I was at school," Lennon said, her exterior hardening.

"She was kinda crazy about it. She wouldn't even say it was a guy or a chick."

"*Dude.*" Theo let his head fall back. "Pretty sure it was because they were nonbinary. That's why she was always saying 'they.'"

"I don't think so, bro," Curls groaned. "And I know what nonbinary is, shit-brain. But why else would she hold her phone like *this*," He made a show of holding something tight against his chest, "Every time she checked a message?"

"You think everything's a conspiracy. You're fully convinced Emery, a fifteen-year-old *girl*, *killed*–"

"You don't think she did?" the boy challenged.

Theo glanced between them a few times before he gave a defeated shrug, finding something in the woods to busy his attention with.

"Where'd she meet this person?" Lennon asked.

Curls deferred to Theo, who sighed. "Online. I asked who it was, but she only called them Twofor2, never by name. That's the most information I ever got out of her about it. But seriously, Lennon, don't listen to him. He's making a way bigger deal out of it—"

"Am not!" he exclaimed, his cheeks flushing.

She nodded slowly, trying to absorb all of this new information. Page hadn't even *mentioned* this Twofor2...

"Damn," the redhead sighed. "You think they know why she's not responding anymore?"

Lennon needed that phone more than ever. But she needed to finish her original plan, first.

"It was good to see you, Theo." She reached out her hand for a fist bump. His knuckles met hers, nodding once before jogging back with the football in hand.

"What's your name again?" Lennon asked the other.

"Wyatt," he chirped. He fist bumped her and bounded in the opposite direction, leaving Lennon to amble alone, slightly paler than before. They said something brief to the girls before continuing their game. Were they relaying what they'd just talked about, or explaining who she was? Off the girls' wary stares, she opted for the latter.

The clearing thickened into a forest of trees after another fifty feet, providing a nice shade from the overbearing sun. Beads of sweat had swelled enough under the brim of her hat to trickle down her temples when she finally reached the end, marked by a large, rusted, electric box. Dozens of shoe and tire tracks surrounded it, marring each other's tread patterns. It'd be impossible to match one to Page's tire tread.

The lock hung broken on the metal door, inviting her to peek in. A few wads of trash littered the inside, along with two empty shooters tucked into the bottom. Her fingers twitched.

It was a small town; secret hiding spots like this were passed down amongst siblings and friends. Those bottles could belong to any one of these kids, but it *could* have been Page's. Maybe this had been a stop along the way, a stop to finish her stash before embarking on what was supposed to be a fun night. Their dad was right—Lennon's luck ratio didn't make sense. She'd always relayed her stories with wonder instead of exhilaration, in disbelief over some of the things she recalled doing. Page had listened with careful curiosity, dipping her toes in by listening to the stories, but she'd never partaken in them. When did that change?

This question stayed with her as she circled back around. It propelled her forward on her bike, drove her toward the cove. She used her elbows to steer while she picked at her cuticles, a nervous, idle habit. Page would be so mad if she were here—Lennon could hear it clear as day. *That's so dangerous!* she'd lecture. It'd be even worse if she happened to see the blood shot eyes Lennon hid behind her sunglasses.

Those phantom criticisms brought Lennon's hands back to the

handlebars, the sleeve of her hoodie pulling just enough to tease the tattoo that traveled along the vein inside her arm. Her wicked streak.

She thought of the curly headed boy who shared a name with her friend, forever frozen at four-years-old. The chubby cheeks thinned and morphed into a higher set of cheekbones, the eyes lightening into a melted bronze.

Goddamnit. Lennon swallowed, braking to pull out the folded note in her pocket.

She set her foot down to stop the bike, typed Conrad's name into her phone and held it to her ear. The rusted railing spread on either side of her like metal wings. The cove would be in view soon, once the fog dissipated enough. After four rings, she was sent to voice mail, and an impatient puff left her. *So much for reaching out whenever.*

It wasn't Conrad who she'd really wanted to call, anyway. She missed Hart above all else. Before she dialed, she promised herself that no matter what, she'd keep herself and her feelings under control.

He picked up before the first tone finished.

"Hi," she mumbled, scolding the relief that filled her. "I, uh...I got your flowers. Thank you."

"Wish I could do more."

Lennon struggled to swallow the lump in her throat. "I'm really sorry for how distant I've been. If you want me to leave you alone—"

"Don't say that. You don't need to apologize for anything, okay? All I care about is making sure *you're* being taken care of. We're all worried sick about you over here."

"You shouldn't." Guilt wracked her ribs. "Please don't. That's the last thing I want."

"Mom said if you want to talk, she's here for you, too. You have her number, right?"

A sad smile broke through the pain in her face. "I do."

But she wouldn't. She wouldn't dare burden that happy home with her own dysfunction. Lennon stared out at the ocean, watching the fog creep back in slow retreat.

A figure appeared through the wispy clouds for just a moment, shiny and black. She would have dismissed it as a high hallucination, except that there was a splash and ripples coursing through the spot it disappeared into.

"Lennon?"

"Sorry, what'd you say?"

"Nevermind." Hart was desperate for any inkling of what she might be feeling. Her aloofness wasn't out of character, but it was usually more endearing.

"Can you tell me about what's been going on with you guys?" Lennon asked, angling her bike around. "I wanna hear about you. Your siblings are home now, right?"

"Yeah, they are. Peyton's kind've the star right now, because of the engagement..."

The feeling of being watched came over her, and s. A tall figure stood at the window, the same size and shape as her father. She lifted a hand up in a half-wave, Hart's voice fading into the background. The figure waited a moment, debating, before lifting a returning wave.

She refocused once she started pedaling, keeping close to the railing. "

"...she was totally surprised. He was waiting at the lake house with all these rose petals and candles. There were these big light-up letters, and Peyton freaked over the ring. I mean, he really went all out."

"That's sweet." Lennon murmured, gasping softly as the cove peeked through. She let her bike fall to the ground as she jumped off, squinting for a better look. Water was flooding from its mouth from high tide, wild and dangerous. Wince-inducing images flitted behind her eyes, and she had to grip the cool, wet metal under her fingers to stay upright. There was one final string of caution tape whipping angrily from the entrance, reaching out in a desperate attempt to escape. What horrors had it seen that first morning?

"Are you at the beach? Those waves sound huge."

"Mhm." She watched the tangled piece of tape reach out like an extended finger, stretching as far as it could. *I want out, let me out!* It pleaded.

You can't! She snapped selfishly. That was the last living reminder of her sister's final moments. Once it was gone, then it was just Catalina Cove again, where dads took their daughters for mermaid lunches, not where fourteen-year-olds met their demise. The walls were supposed to echo giggles, not screams.

No. That tape *had* to remain.

"How have things been with your mom?" Hart had been slowly building the courage to ask—if he went too far, too fast, she shut down. Peeling back her bandages was a delicate game. Where he saw wounds needing care, she saw rot.

"She's been extra...Cashmanian lately." She answered tentatively.

Hart took no time cutting to the chase. "Is she hurting you?"

"Things are fine, Hart. I can take care of myself."

"That's not what I asked." His voice took a firmer tone. "Lennon, I know you're more than capable of handling things on your own. But you need to know that *my* priority is keeping you safe, even if that means protecting you from yourself."

This was always when things got tricky; when she reached the edge of the cliff of vulnerability, and he asked her to jump. He'd been able to catch her so far, but the cliff grew higher each time, and that look down was becoming nothing short of terrifying. At some point, the jump would crush him.

Not to mention that this cliff in particular was her mother. And despite their hardships, she wouldn't blame a rocky base for hurting her. It came with its existence—it couldn't help it.

"She's just going through a lot right now. I mean, imagine how guilty she feels...and it's not just her. We all failed her." Lennon's voice wavered. She wasn't sure if that truth was more painful than one where her sister had been murdered, but the feeling was still crippling. She gripped the railing for support, legs growing weak.

"God, Hart. If we were the ones who pushed her to...ugh, I swear to—"

"Okay, wait, hold on a second." he interjected over her shallowing breath. "Breathe, baby."

The effects of her self-medication had waned off long ago. She reached for the emergency pen, taking a deep inhale into her throbbing chest.

"There you go," he coaxed, only hearing her deep breathing. "That's it."

Lennon poisoned herself until her mind went quiet, bending her knees to avoid fainting. She focused on how her fingers struggled to hold on to the dewy railing, the way Hart's voice breezed calmingly through her ear.

"Keep breathing. You're doing great, honey."

She licked her cracked lips, brushing messy hair out of her eyes and readjusting her cap. "I don't feel like I am."

Her eyes lifted to the cove, begging for answers while his voice soothed her waves of grief. "I think...I need to..." She trailed off, distracted with something in the distance..

The yellow plastic snagged, and her breath with it. She watched it fly into the wind for a fleeting moment before the ocean spray weighed it down, taking it into its belly. It was gone.

She was gone.

14

Lennon had just finished the second load of dishes when her phone erupted into a symphony of wind chimes from the living room. It rang three times before penetrating through the THC coating her senses. She'd gotten a little carried away with the pen; it was almost all air at this point, but there were hints of yellow swimming around the edges. Her soapy hands left her unable to answer, and with two more rings the phone silenced, sending whoever it was to voicemail.

By the time she closed the washer, the call had been entirely forgotten. She moved on to the laundry room, where a pile had grown nearly as tall as the machines. Each Mayfield had their own unique stink; Stacy's held notes of the pond he fished at every other day, Cash's reeked of booze masked with expensive perfume, while Lennon's dipped into a more earthy, natural scent.

She lifted a small, floral print shirt with pause, and immediately buried her nose deep into the scrunched material. Lavender and lemon; Page's signature scent. She set that one to the side and folded the rest into a basket, balancing it on her hip and taking the hall to her parent's room. She kept her eyes down as she passed her mother, who was lying facedown on her bed and shaking with silent sobs. Lennon might have comforted her, but Cash wasn't alone; three empty shooters kept her company on the nightstand. Lennon winced as she set the basket down, thinking back to the electric box in the park. Those bottles were the same as the three scattered on the nightstand.

Something invisible stopped her before she left the room. Maybe it was the lemon and lavender still permeating her nose, but something in her ached to help.

"You okay, Mom?"

Cash wailed again, and Lennon's jaw flitted uncomfortably. The Mayfield's weren't good at condoling, or compassion; that had been Page's specialty. Lennon walked toward the outer wall, where every curtain had been lowered to shut the room in darkness. "You know, you'll probably feel better if you got some light in…"

Cash cried louder when she lifted the curtains, the pitch high enough to reach Stacy from his office. "No, no, shut it! I can't look out there, I don't want to see!"

Lennon stood frozen. She'd seen Cash in all shades of anger, but never this amount of grief. Stacy rushed in, making sure everyone was safe before hurrying to close the curtains. The metal rings grated against the rod as he pulled with a sharp *whoosh*. Lennon flinched.

"Sorry," she whispered, though she wasn't sure to whom.

She remembered the missed call on her way back. The sun had long begun its descent below the horizon, leaving the sky flushed in amber reds and petal pinks. Conrad's name lit up her phone, split in half by the crack scarring the screen. She put the phone on speaker and picked up a drying towel.

"Hello?" His voice sounded like it'd been dragged over a cheese grater.

"Hi, Conrad." She paused for a moment, trying to remember why she'd called him in the first place. *Oh*, she thought as she saw the vase. *Right.* "I saw the flowers you brought by. That was…thank you."

She cringed at her awkwardness. The utter failure in Cashmere's room proved she wasn't good at niceties or talking in general, but this was the icing on the case.

"It's the least I could do." He cleared his throat, trying to think of something else to talk about. "You guys put a dent in that pile of food yet?"

She laughed humorlessly, and placed a clean bowl in the cabinet.

"Right," he muttered. "Well...when's the last time you ate?"

It should have been an easy enough question, but it left her stumped. She'd skipped breakfast to go to the park, and burned through chores the rest of the day. Investigating Emery had preoccupied most of her time yesterday, and the drugs had suppressed her appetite for dinner... *Holy shit.* It had been at least two days, maybe three, since she'd ingested anything.

At her silence, Conrad clicked his tongue. "I was going to grab some food at Rum Social in a bit, if you wanted to join me."

He wanted to hang out even after the way she'd spoken to him? Maybe he didn't find this relationship as difficult she did. It wasn't his fault, but all she could think about was Wyatt or Page when she saw him—both felt like taking a shotgun shell to the gut.

She lifted her pen to her mouth, already thinking of an excuse. A blinking red light interrupted her before she could speak it, spiking anxiety through her like pins and needles.

"*No!*" she hissed.

"We don't have to go there," he said quickly.

She tried again, and was met with the same red blinking. Empty. The comedown was leaving her particularly low, and this was the only thing helping her keep her sanity. It was a little past seven—stores and dispensaries would be closing soon. Cons of a small town.

"No, wait. Sorry. Rum Social's fine, I can meet you there in thirty?"

Her ETA was a little off. Lennon had to run past the gelato shop without saying hi like she'd planned, sliding into the booth of the quiet restaurant forty-five minutes after pressing end.

"Sorry," she breathed, attempting to tame her windblown hair.

"Looks like a good haul." He nodded to the bag sitting beside her.

There was no shame in her crooked smile. "They had a sale. Figured I'd stock up."

She poured over the menu, looking for something cheap to minimize the damage two hundred dollars had already done to her bank account. Stacy would definitely be asking about that later.

"Get whatever you want. My treat," he said, his eyes trained on his own menu.

"I'll be good with water," she said, nodding to the passing waiter.

He looked at her amusedly. "I meant food."

"Oh, you don't have to—"

"Seriously. It's the least I can do."

She waited for him to look up, knowing her intimidating look would get her her way as it had so many times before. But, almost as if he knew, he kept his eyes down to the menu he'd had for over fifteen minutes. She shook her head, fighting off a smile as a waiter dropped off a chilled glass.

"Did you just get out of the shower?" She gestured to his wet head of loose curls, resisting the bubbling wince. She could hide her awkwardness under her features and figure, but as soon as she opened her mouth, the mystery crumbled.

He lifted his hand to his hair, as if he too was just noticing. "Oh, no." He chuckled. "I swim a lot, diving n' stuff."

"Wyatt loved that, too." It came out of her mouth before she realized. She knew how that felt now—to go about your day, feeling normal, and then have someone remind you of the deepest pain in your life. It was happening to her a lot lately. Eyes widening, she raised a hand to cover her mouth. "I'm sorry."

"Don't be. He did. It's nice, actually...nobody talks about him anymore." When his eyes did finally lift from the menu, she sucked her water down the wrong pipe and choked, coughing loudly. They'd distantly reminded her of the ones she'd seen in her dream, towering behind her with a sinister stare.

It wasn't real. That's not him. Her fingers twitched for her pen,

Missing Page

but it was no use. It had already provided all the relief it was capable of.

"You okay?" he snorted.

"Yeah, just swallowed wrong," she croaked. "So...what, people just...stopped talking about him? Moved on?"

He shrugged sadly. "Eventually, yeah. It was almost seventeen years ago now, he was so young...I kind've get it. I know my parents don't talk about it for their own reasons. Still feels wrong."

"I'm the opposite. I feel like people are *always* talking about Page, I can't get away from remembering." She rested, her chin on her hand. "I wish people would stop...*inserting* themselves into our grief, y'know? Every day it's a different bouquet, a new casserole..."

"I know you won't believe me right now, but someday you'll miss it. Most people don't want to listen to stories about someone they'll never meet. Nobody'll say it out loud, of course, but you can feel it." He lifted the amber-colored rocks glass to his lips, letting the dark liquid sift through his lips. "It sucks, people forgetting about someone who was so real to you."

"I'll never forget him," Lennon said. "He was my best friend. I didn't have Page yet, the other kids thought I was weird. He got me through a lot."

"You *were* weird," he smiled, his eyes suddenly far away. "But yeah, I remember you two being attached at the hip. And you were kind've a bad influence on him, right?"

Lennon laughed, the sound shaking her stomach in an unfamiliar way. When was the last time she'd laughed? "Yeah, I guess so. I was the one always wanting to sneak in and try your Xbox out. And I was the one who convinced him to run away with me—"

"Right, right...you made it all the way down the street." A smile tugged at his lips. "God, I remember being so *annoyed* by you two sometimes. And now..."

"You'd do anything to hear his voice again."

Their eyes locked together for a flashing moment before she broke away, busying herself with the table cloth.

The waitress came by, drawing his attention. "You want another? Jack Honey and rum, right?" she asked, sweeping her hair behind her shoulder.

"I'm okay, actually. I'd love to get her some food, though." he said, nodding to Lennon.

The blonde took their food orders, giggling softly and batting her lashes every time Conrad spoke. *What's so funny about Alaskan salmon and scallops?* Lennon wondered. He didn't seem to notice though, or perhaps he wasn't interested.

The waitress brought back steaming plates of their first course, and Lennon's stomach growled ravenously. The two were silent for a moment while they scraped their silverware against the porcelain, placing the first bites onto their tongues.

"*Fuck*, that's good," he groaned.

Lennon blushed at his quiet outburst—it sounded almost titillated. She couldn't quite blame him, though; her own belly cried out once the fish entered, and she had to press her fist against it to stifle the noise.

A group of kids on their bicycles flew past the window then, one after the other, their bells ringing happily through the air. Lennon blinked, her smile fading.

"We found her bike, you know." She murmured. Conrad's eyes lifted from his plate.

"Where was it?"

"Emery's. Under the balcony."

His chewing stopped, his eyebrows raising subtly. "Really."

"They're trying to say she left it there, but my dad and I went there that night. I would've seen it."

He ran his fingers through his honey waves, revealing two lines between his brows. "Surely they have to be looking into—"

"They say they are. Doesn't seem like it though."

He crossed his arms on the table, leaning forward with new intensity. "What do you mean?"

It appeared as though Conrad was ready to believe—or at least be

Missing Page

open minded—to whatever Lennon was about to say. It made her want to tell him exactly what she thought Emery Felton's hands were capable of. But she had little more than a theory to back it up, and she couldn't risk losing the one person who might believe her when she finally *did* say something. Her teeth chewed on her lip, hovering over the tender part she'd bitten through the day prior.

"Do you have anybody supporting you, Lennon?" He lowered his voice. "I don't want to get into your business, but...I've been there, during some of your mom's episodes. She has a lot of bad days. I worried about you girls. Still worry about you."

Though humiliation was tearing her apart beneath the surface, Lennon took the words with a blank expression. She silently thanked whatever instinct had kept her mouth shut just before, which would have surely written him off for good—Conrad was worried she was going insane.

"Yeah. Of course." Every syllable was perfectly enunciated, each colder than the last.

"Who?"

"Hart, my boy...friend." She wasn't sure what made her add that last lie, as if having a boyfriend made her more credible. Or maybe she was scared he would start treating her differently if she said she was single; they were not-friends, and she liked it this way.

Conrad wasn't convinced with her answer, but he used it to change the subject. "Hart, huh? How long has that been a thing?"

"Ten months." she mumbled, stuffing another bite into her mouth.

"I can't tell if you like him or not," he half-teased, but soon cowered under the glare she shot him.

Don't be crazy, she reminded herself. She sat back, minimizing her height and softening her gaze. "I do...it's complicated. With me, not him. Relationships aren't my forte." She swallowed her bite. "What about you?"

He shrugged. "I was seeing someone off n' on for a while. Been off for a bit, though."

"What happened?"

"Oh, I dunno," He stretched his long arms, his height becoming even more apparent. "Distance, I guess."

"She lived in Washington?"

He nodded, but said nothing more. It wasn't enough to alleviate Lennon's curiosity. "So you just...grew apart?"

"That's the basic answer, yes."

"What's the complicated answer?"

"For one, she calls California 'Cali.'... I can't stand it. *When can I visit Cali, How's Cali,*" he mimicked. "That kinda stuff."

"You broke up with her over that?" Lennon asked, slightly impressed. She thought *she* was cold...

He grinned, amused at her surprise. "No, that's not why. But it did help." He moved his empty plate to the side with a sigh. "I've been through a lot. I want to make sure that whoever I love, whoever's my *partner*, is strong enough for everything that comes with that. I need somebody who can handle my shit, because it's not easy—probably isn't much fun, either. And it definitely isn't fair...so what kind of love would that be?"

He didn't realize until then Lennon had leaned closer to him. Even she had failed to notice her elbows finding a place on the table, chin nestling into the crook of her interlaced fingers. Lennon had never heard her feelings put into words that simple before; it resonated deep within her chest, rattling her ribcage.

He cast his eyes down to avoid her pointed stare. "Sometimes I think people like me aren't meant for love," he mumbled.

"Like us, you mean."

His eyebrows creased. "Haven't you found love?"

"Well...I'm not sure. I think so."

"Who said it first?"

She brushed a flyaway strand behind her brow, growing warm. "We haven't."

He laughed, dropping his eyes to his glass. "Well, you *are* a little intimidating."

Missing Page

She didn't smile this time. "I can't be soft when I'm trying to figure out if I'm safe."

"Do you? Feel safe with him?" A new expression took over his face, solemn and humorless.

She nodded without hesitation. That, she was sure of.

"So what's the issue?"

Her phone buzzed from under the table, a notification from her senior's groupchat. Lennon flipped her phone face-down, piqued with a new question.

"Would you happen to know anything about Page's pen pal?"

"Pen pal?" He tilted his head.

"Twofor2. Some of her friends mentioned something about an internet friend she'd been talking to."

He snorted. "*Ohhh*. Yeah, think I know who you're talking about. He got in the way of tutoring a time or two....whenever you weren't."

"He?" she pressed, ignoring his playful jab.

"Well, I don't know for sure. I just guessed by how much attention he got. She never talked about him, though."

Lennon rested her chin on her fist. "I feel like I'm missing so much. Why didn't she tell me about any of this? Or how bad it was getting with Emery?"

"Maybe she was worried it would bring you down. You got a new start, she didn't want to drag you back into it."

Her throat tightened. "If she was in hell, I'd still go to her."

The waitress returned then, dropping his card off. Conrad bent his head, signing the receipt and stuffing his card into his wallet.

Lennon frowned. She hadn't even seen her come by. "Hey—"

"Don't mention it." He shook his head, sounding final. "Thanks for eating dinner with me."

"You know, Conrad, I hate what we have in common. But it does make things a little less lonely." She grabbed her bag, standing up. "I'm glad you're back."

Knowing a returned compliment would bring the red flush back to her cheeks, he simply nodded. But he didn't seem ready to say goodbye. "I'll walk you to your car."

"Bike," she gently corrected. At least she didn't fight him this time.

As they walked through the complex, she noticed an older woman locking the door to the gelato shop, murmuring in frustrated Italian.

"Mrs. Cappelli?" Lennon asked, eyes widening.

The plump woman turned, her eyes widening with recognition. "Lennon! *Buonasera, Bella...*" She began to reach out for a hug before remembering her timidness, and instead she took her hand securely in hers, squeezing. "Good to see you, again."

Lennon smiled softly. Her former boss moved to the tall man standing next to her, hugging him as if he wasn't a stranger. Mrs. Cappelli was always so welcoming; she'd been the only one to offer Lennon a job. Everyone else said she came off too unapproachable, but Mrs. Cappelli valued work ethic over all else.

"Buonasera, Conrad."

Lennon's head swiveled, eyes narrowing with confusion. So she *did* know him. He greeted her back, but not before shooting a confused glance in Lennon's direction, not understanding her sudden change.

"How are you, sweetheart?" Mrs. Cappelli asked her with sad eyes.

"We're managing."

Mrs. Cappeli nodded, her wrinkles deepening. "Well, it's good to see you two are sticking together. That's all you can do, right now..."

Lennon was too deep in her head to listen to the rest. Conrad was shrinking into the background now, as if he felt her mental deliberating. After a few minutes of small talk the women bid farewell, and the two were silent until Lennon reached to her bike.

"What was that?"

"Huh?"

She crossed her arms. "How did she know you? Why were you

being weird?"

"I wasn't being weird," Conrad said defensively. "I just knew what that conversation was about to be, and I didn't want to hear it. It's always the same, it's awkward."

"For me, not for you." she retorted. He wouldn't have reacted that way if it had only been about her. "How does she know you?"

He looked at her strangely. "As the guy who dropped Page off for work...? Her bike fits in my truck bed, and it gave us an extra fifteen minutes of tutoring if I took her on my way home. Mrs. Cappelli always came out to say hi..."

Lennon stared. *Why had she attacked him like that?* Maybe she *was* going crazy, but there was something else there, hidden deep beneath—*jealousy*.

Conrad had become so interwoven into their world this past year, tucked into places and moments that Lennon missed out on. He knew of Page's pen pal, he helped her with school; he even knew how scary Cash could be behind closed doors. Lennon wasn't used to sharing these feelings—these secrets—with anyone besides her sister. Before this year, Lennon and Page had their own corner of life to themselves, and though it wasn't perfect, it was *theirs*. Now even that had changed.

However, as upsetting as it was, that didn't make it Conrad's fault.

"I'm sorry," she murmured.

"Don't be," he responded. Even if there were anything to forgive, it had been given instantaneously. She looked up to see a deep understanding settled over his face1. There was no trace of resentment in any part of his hazel eyes.

The way her body leaned and tensed seemed as if she were about to hug him. But she simply nodded, climbing onto the bike instead. There was a bit more muscle in her calves now, strengthened by the hills she went back and forth over. She pedaled away and out of view without a goodbye, leaving Conrad with an invisible, unwelcome friend who went by the harrowing name of Solitude.

15

Lennon had spoken figuratively about following Page to Hell. But when she entered through the large double doors, she was reminded that Hell wasn't too far off from home.

Most of the tin-foiled glass dishes were now shattered in a glass painting across the glossy tile, victims of Cash's wrath. Based off her guttural growls of anguish, Lennon knew the Devil had returned.

Her dad was still trying to calm her when Lennon entered the kitchen. Cash's arms were outstretched, her eyes wide and animalistic, swaying in a struggle to keep herself upright. Lennon could smell her from the dining room.

"You piece of *shit*," Cashmere seethed, spit flying through her teeth. "Anna Tannem, *really*? That's who you chose to mourn your daughter's death with…where did you find the time? Did you squeeze it between planning Page's funeral and abandoning your family, or is that what your 'fishing trips' really were?"

"You're drunk, Cashmere." Stacy coaxed.

"That doesn't change what you did!" she screamed, her voice filling the room with a vibrating intensity. Lennon flinched, her fingers trembling with adrenaline.

"Cash, *stop*—" He tried to approach her, but she screeched in response, backing against the countertop like a cornered animal. Her hand stained the cool marble with red, and she hissed from the pain.

Though frightened, she'd been desensitized long ago. Lennon remained perfectly still, only moving her eyes. They flitted around the room, connecting as many dots as she could see. Bloody shards of a broken wine glass were scattered across the sink like a crime scene. The adrenaline spread to Lennon's feet, keeping her on her toes and ready to escape; her hands twitched, ready to defend the body it belonged to. Cash's fury could be felt like an electric charge through the air.

Stacy's whittling patience with his wife washed over onto Lennon, surprising her. "And where the hell have *you* been? Two hundred dollars?"

"I was eating dinner, with Conrad—"

"I *told* you, Len, I need to know where you're going!"

"It wasn't planned!" Why was he focusing on *her* when Cash was the one acting like a feral animal?

"I'll—you'll be dealt with later. Cashmere," He took on a stern tone. "You're very drunk, and we will be speaking about this tomorrow. But right now, I need you to stop swatting waters out of my hand and *drink them*, or go to sleep."

"Why," she spat. "So I'll forget that my husband is cheating on me? During the worst possible time—"

"Are we really gonna do this right now? Our daughter is standing *right here*, Cash! I did not cheat on you because I spoke to another woman. You know that. You're doing this to distract from the fact that you've been—"

"You're *LYING!*" she yelled, lunging.

It all happened in a few seconds, but Lennon's adrenaline slowed everything to be able to witness in perfect detail. Less than a second after Cash lunged, her foot slid on a chunk of spilled casserole and sent her flying. The fall was long—she'd caught an impressive and wince-inducing amount of air—but eventually her body collided the tile with a hard thud. Even the air froze over, wondering what would happen next. After a few moments, Cash gasped for the breath the wind had stolen from her, and a meek cry leaked out of her.

Maybe not a feral animal, Lennon thought to herself, still shaking. *But a wounded one.*

Stacy stepped carefully, holding out his arms with a tired sigh. "Will you let me help you get cleaned up?"

She wailed louder and held up her arm to keep him away, soaked in her own humiliation.

"What were you saying, Dad?" Lennon asked, looking to her father. "What was she distracting you from?"

This was exactly what he'd been trying to avoid. His disappointment would be a speck compared to Lennon's, and the last thing he wanted was to deliver more bad news, but Cash had brought it on herself, and Lennon was an adult. She deserved to know.

"*Stacy,*" Cashmere warned. "Do not—"

"Your mother's been lying about going to therapy."

Cashmere seethed, avoiding both of their eyes.

"What?"

"I was checking our accounts after I got the ding from your little splurge," Stacy shot a pointed look her way. "There's been no charges from insurance or the therapist...."

His voice drowned into a low buzz in her ears. She was inexplicably disappointed, but not surprised. *No wonder it seemed like nothing had changed.*

Lennon walked forward, lifting her mother's arms to help her up. Cash was too weak to refuse, and thus was forced to let her daughter muscle her down the hallway, fading their figures into black.

"I knew you would help me," she slurred, muffled behind the running water Lennon had started. Stacy started to enter, but Lennon stuck her arm out sharply to keep him out.

I can handle it, she mouthed. His eyes pleaded with hers, but she kept her arm outstretched until he left. Once he was gone, she turned, helping her mother out of her clothes.

Missing Page

    She had a rare freedom of speech when her mother got to this point. Lennon could ask questions without any repercussions or grudge-holding; Cash wasn't coherent to enough twist Lennon's curiosity into something sinister, as she often did, and she would remember nothing of it in the morning. Lennon lowered her into the tub, watching over her like a mother would her toddler.

    "Why do you think Dad cheated on you?" she asked, collapsing onto the toilet with exhaustion.

    "*That fucking bitch,*" Cash grumbled. She reached for the buttons to start the jets, but her hands were gently moved back to the water by her overseer's hands. This would not be prolonged any longer than it needed to be.

    Already forgetting about the button, Cash returned to Lennon's question. "I went through his phone. They've been talking for *months*...she's been Perfect-Friend-Anna. She's been checking on him every day since Page." Her lip trembled for just a moment before her emotions hardened over again. "I'm sure she seems like this shiny new toy—no kids, only married once..."

    "And that's cheating? Her checking in, them talking?"

    She glowered at Lennon. "He doesn't *need* another woman to grieve his dead daughter with!"

    "You're hard to talk to sometimes, Mama." Lennon didn't know why she was truth-bombing her right now; maybe it was the fact that she felt safe. Her mother couldn't fight her or her questions. She couldn't even hold her bladder. Lennon had noticed the slight tint of yellow minutes before, but didn't see the point in saying anything. *Just keep the water running.*

    "That's bullshit." she sneered. "I'll talk to anyone, s'long as they talk to me with *respect.*"

    "Your definition of respect changes every day," Lennon argued, exasperated. "You can't expect us to read your mind."

    "Look, I'm not *perfect*, okay? I know you guys love to make me the villain, but *I'm* the one putting food on the table. *I'm* the one who put this roof over your heads!"

Lennon sighed. That argument was fraying from the amount of times Cash used it; for some reason, money excused every bad thing she had ever done. And it wasn't even the truth—Lennon couldn't count the number of times Cash had yanked her funds as punishment. The girl would have starved in college if her dad hadn't secretly sent her cash, or if Hart hadn't noticed she wasn't eating. It was even harder in high school. If Stacy was away for work and Cashmere had gotten angry, she'd lock herself in her room and order takeout, leaving the girls to fend for themselves. In those times, Lennon took on many titles: chef, chauffeur—parent. She'd gotten three detentions for tardiness her junior year because she had to take Page first. Groceries were paid with the money earned from her summer job, because the consequences of using her mother's card were painful and long-lasting.

"*Thief!*" she screamed once. "*My own daughter, stealing from me...next time I'm calling the police and sending your ass to jail!*"

These punishments could go on for days—sometimes weeks—until the girls' father returned home. Worse, Cash couldn't be held accountable for her ways, because she so adamantly refused responsibility. Stacy was left to do the apologizing, filling the pantry up with their favorite snacks and promising the next work trip would be far in the future. Those promises were almost never kept, but she thought the gesture was sweet enough.

Now she was twenty-one, and things were still the same. In fact, they were worse—much worse. Lennon blinked away the glassy film that had covered her eyes, checking on her mother once more. All of Cash had sunk below the water except her eyes, peeking above like an alligator waiting to strike. She was glowering at her daughter, festering a resentment burning for so long that she herself was not sure where the flames had originated from.

Nether of them knew it had built up since Lennon was a child. Cashmere had grown to hate the very thing she'd worked so hard to provide. Lennon had her own brains, natural beauty—she'd grown up with money that would someday become her own. Lennon wouldn't need to pay for or marry into those luxuries like Cash had.

That's why Lennon's angst could never match her mother's. Cashmere was what Lennon could become; bitter, anguished, trapped in a family and town who held no respect for her. But Lennon was a reminder of what Cashmere once was—full of potential and possibility, with a long life and the whole world ahead of her. But what infuriated her the most was that, for whatever reason, Lennon didn't want it.

Cash caught the jet button in her peripheral, pressing it before Lennon could stop her. Feeling a bit more in control, she sank fully into the bubbles, her bleached hair floating back and forth around her; Lennon thought it made her look a little like Medusa.

"He doesn't need to be speaking to other women when he has me," she grumbled again once she came back up.

"He doesn't have you!" Lennon snapped, her patience breaking. "None of us do. Do you honestly think anybody could trust you, after everything you've done? We're taking turns picking your drunk body off the floor or from the bar every night, or protecting each other, from *you!*"

"You can't tell me how to cope, Lennon. You have no idea what I'm—"

"Stop," Lennon breathed, bristling. Her body was quivering with fury. "If you're about to say I have no idea what you're going through, *stop.*"

Cashmere opened her eyes, now slits. Her tongue held itself for no one. "She was *my* daughter..."

"She was *my* sister." Lennon hissed, standing abruptly. "And *I* didn't need five years to realize I loved her."

The room was silent. Not even the water dared to drip and interrupt it.

Cash was rarely speechless, but Lennon's words held her by the throat. Instead of retorting, she closed her eyes, leaned her neck against the lip of the tub and rolled her head back and forth. Lennon couldn't expect rationality out of her in this state, but for some reason, the apathetic response hurt even more.

"I was so sure that Emery was responsible for this." Lennon's chest tightened, frozen over with grief. "Whether it was on purpose or not, I didn't know, I was trying to figure that out. But maybe the truth is that she got tired of you, of *all* of us. Maybe she was exhausted with being let down."

Lennon stumbled back, shaking her head. "That cove was the only place we didn't have to think about you, or worry about being *hit*, or *screamed* at. We could pretend like we were happy."

Looking at her mess of a mother in that giant tub, it seemed so clear. From her never-ending bender, Stacy's lack of leadership, and Lennon's abandonment, perhaps that destination had been Page's plan all along. Something Lennon had never been able to do, because of that very girl's existence. While turning to leave, Lennon's reflection startled her.

What had her past done to her? What had she done to herself? And why couldn't she stop?

"I wanted it to be Emery so bad, because I didn't want it to be us." she choked, staring at the hands she was wringing. "But I—I think it is, Mom. I think it is, and you—*we*—are gonna have to live with that, for the rest of our lives. We'll have to live with that forever."

Lennon waited for the blow-up, or the denial. She wanted to be screamed at, she longed for the pain of being hit, to be punished for being truthful. But nothing came. Cash was lying unconscious, her mouth slack and drooling. Lennon lifted the back of her hand to her mouth, silencing her sobs.

She could've left her there, let fate decide whether she lived or drowned in a tub of piss, blood, and tears. It scared her how strong that small part wanted her to–but she couldn't. Her shell was hard, but it was there to protect her, not harm others. She could not punish a viper for being venomous just as she couldn't condemn herself for being poisoned, or her sister for being fragile.

Missing Page

She shakily pressed the button to cut the jets off, opened the drain, and draped a few towels over her mother's naked body.

Her father was gone when she returned to the kitchen. She couldn't find her breath—it was hiding in that discreet black bag, rolled into small pieces of paper. Despite her desperation, she left it alone, too helpless to even try. The hopelessness had become a part of her.

Cashmere's drinking was getting worse. She wasn't going to therapy or getting help. How long were Lennon or her father expected to endure this? How long before it bled into Cash's work, the only escape from them, and them from her?

The last Mayfield daughter grabbed a broom and swept the spilled food into a pile, illuminated only by the dim light above the oven. The aging meats splattered across the floor had filled the entire house with a sour combination of rot and death. These gifts had been in Page's memory, but Cash couldn't even leave that untouched.

"Here, let me do that," Stacy said, startling her. He took the broom from her hand, stepping between her and the mess.

Lennon turned to the pantry and scrounged for a dustpan. The silence became heavier over the room each time a pile of food hit the bottom of the trash can, waste after waste.

"I'm gonna need your phone," he said once they finished, the lateness of the night wearing on his voice.

"What?" Lennon asked.

"Give me your phone, Lennon." he repeated. She handed it over awkwardly. "I'm over this disappearing-without-telling-me act."

"Are you grounding me?" She couldn't hide her amused smile. "You haven't grounded me since I was thirteen."

"No. That never worked, anyway." He squinted, trying to navigate the technology. The LED from the screen lit his eyes, giving them an artificial life that had previously been missing. "I'm making sure I don't lose you again."

"I really didn't mean to scare you, Dad. Conrad asked me to get food, it wasn't—"

"Conrad? Like, Conrad Bates?"

She nodded. His expression shifted for a moment, eventually returning his attention to the screen. "I'm glad you're spending time with him. I think it'd be good for the both of you."

"Yeah," She tucked her thumbnail between her teeth. "Maybe."

"It's nice to have someone who understands. Maybe it'll help with the night terrors."

She stilled. "You can hear those?"

He didn't answer, but his look was telling. "I was worried about those coming back...I could tell by your screams. They're no joke."

"Night terrors," Lennon repeated confusedly. She leaned against the counter, crossing her arms. "Did you mean nightmares?"

He peered at her, surprised she didn't already know. "Terrors are different. You can't wake someone up from those, and you're not supposed to try. I'd hear you screaming bloody murder in the middle of the night, like someone was hurting you...first few times had me sprinting out of a dead sleep." His eyes lost focus. "Your eyes would be wide open, and you'd be *screaming* for help, for *me*, even when I was right in front of you. All I could do was hold you...."

She frowned guiltily. "I'm sorry, Dad."

"There's nothing to be sorry for, baby. Good news is, they turn into nightmares with enough time. And I promise, as long as I'm around, I'll always wake you up."

She smiled softly, nodding appreciatively.

"And if you ever want to talk to me, you know—"

"Dad," she interjected. It lacked sharpness, but was final nonetheless.

He cast his eyes down, stuffing his frustration. "Agh, I know."

If Lennon were a coiled spring, the ball was the Bates and that summer they shared. Every question her dad asked pulled back the lever further and further, but releasing was not an option. Instead she was left with this taut, uncomfortable pressure, with nowhere to exert it.

"Feels like I'm watching you through a movie screen sometimes, is all. I'm your dad, I should know you better than anyone, but a lot of times I feel like we're strangers." His expression made it clear he wouldn't push any further, but there was a dissatisfaction buried between his brows.

The oven light was weak, saving him from the look on his daughter's face. Despite her youth, there was so much regret in those pale eyes. She took a few steps to plant a kiss on his stubbly cheek. "Mom's in the tub, by the way."

His sigh was quiet, taking her goodbye with as much grace as he could muster. "Great."

The shadows began to curl around her as she walked upstairs, but his voice stopped her just before the dark completely swallowed her. "You're not gonna ask about what your mom said?"

Her brow furrowed in confusion. "What's there to ask?"

"She accused me of cheating. I figured you'd want to—I don't know, *discuss*..."

"Honestly, Dad, I don't know if it'd make a difference if you were."

It had come out dismissively, but it hit Stacy like a bullet—yet another blow to their family's stability. "What do you mean?"

"Just that I...I would understand if you did." She was being more blunt than necessary, but she had her mother's tongue after all.

"Well..." He scratched the back of his head, searching for a response. It still hadn't found him when she turned back to the stairs, leaving home alone in the entry.

There were nothing he could say that would confidently reassure her in the strength of her parent's marriage, or even their future. Lennon wasn't sure he—or anyone else for that matter—would ever have the vocabulary to make the world look beautiful to her. Since she was little, she'd seen it for what it was; there were no words, no melodies that could ease someone's mind on a sinking ship.

She lie awake for what felt like hours, thinking of possible passwords to Page's next journal entry. Her last thoughts kept rolling back to Twofor2, wondering how much Page confided in them.

All of a sudden, sleep snatched her beneath the waters of consciousness, trapping her in cold, uncomfortable porcelain.

She was freezing in lukewarm water sloshing against her goosebump-covered body. There was light outside her lids, but this time, it provided little solace. The shock only last a moment before she was being moved, her plastic hair cover crinkling against the giant's chest. Before she get could her bearings, darkness surrounded her, and her stomach plummeted.

Now having a moment to collect herself, she put all of her focus opening her eyes. They only opened enough for her to see the large dresser directly in front of her, but everything on it was draped in shadows, fuzzy between her lashes. She finally made out a jewelry stand, some glassware, a lotion bottle, and a bigger container of dark, stagnant liquid that smelled sweet and peaty.

It was too late. The curtain swished closed, and her throat tightened.

She wouldn't make it out this time.

16

A LOUD GASP BROKE THROUGH THE ROOM, FOLLOWED BY THE crinkling of the duvet under her clenched fingers. Her raspy scream immediately cut off with her newfound consciousness as Kaiser jumped into the bed, coming to the rescue with wet kisses.

When had she fallen asleep? Lennon last remembered trying to think of passwords when the answer hit her like a meteor. She'd meant to go downstairs right then and enter it; sleep must have beaten her to the punch, and now she couldn't remember.

She checked the ink on her arm to prove she was back in real life and her twenty-one-year-old body. Her heart came back cautiously, unsure if her mind was done putting it through the torture of vivid memory.

Oddly, the first thing she did was text Hart a heart in her best attempt at reassurance. Her phone dinged a few minutes later with the same heart, stirring a warmth in her stomach—he was staying. *For now*, the small voice in her head warned her.

Shower. She needed a shower.

Though she went through every step, it still went by quicker than she'd wanted. The scalding water made Page's laptop feel extra cold to the touch as she clicked her way into the documents, getting to work on attempts. Each was rejected time after time, and every third try added five minutes to the lockout time.

Lennon paused, concentrating. Page must have chosen passwords that were relevant to her in the moment she was writing them. She waited anxiously while the lock time drained down, tapping her fingers in a nervous beat against the thin metal. What was she trying to hide?

She never told you about the pen pal? Theo's voice echoed.

Twofor2.

Once the text box opened again, she hesitantly typed in her guess. Seven characters, one number, *enter*. The circle loaded, rolling around itself in an agonizing slowness, like a game host waiting to announce who won. It felt so silly, it'd couldn't possibly...

After a beat and a slight glitch, pages of text loaded before her, straightening her spine. There were still so many questions, still—maybe this would be her answer.

3/13

So...you're me. You know who I'm talking about.

I don't really know how it happened. I just really needed someone to talk to, I didn't think we would message again after that night. But we've talked every day for a month or so now. Honestly, it's embarrassing how much I look forward to that notification. And if I had options besides Emery who bullies me almost every day, or kids who want to do drugs and talk about sex all the time, maybe it'd be different.

But it's getting harder. We were messaging in math. Emery got annoyed because she kept trying to get my attention and I wasn't listening. He sent me a message saying something super sweet, and she ripped the phone out of my hands! I literally had to lunge at her to get it, and Emery was being obnoxiously—thank god for autocorrect—loud about how I was 'in love.' It was humiliating. Zach S asked me why it was such a big deal anyway, and Emery goes, "it's not, she's just being an attention whore." She called me a *whore*.

I think she's getting obsessed. I've never had someone care so much

Missing Page

about my personal life. Is that a friend thing? Zach told me she tried to check my phone when I went to the bathroom the other day. If I hadn't changed my passcode that morning I would have been screwed... Anyway, now I have to be extra careful.

Why can't I have one piece of my life that's just for me? Why can't she respect that? I can tell him anything...he's up late anyway, which is usually when I need to talk. It's my little corner of safety. I don't want everyone messing with that. So because of that, I had to delete EVERYTHING, it was too risky. Which sux because there were some really cute messages. Nobody's ever talked to me like that before, and maybe the circumstances are a little odd, but it feels nice. And when he found out that Emery hurt me, I thought he was going to actually fly here, he was so upset. My head still hurts, by the way. But it's his dad's birthday in a few days, and it's super important to them.

I was able to convince Mom and Dad I tripped, but I don't know if I can see her the same anymore. You never know what someone's capable of until they show you. She cried to me on the phone, apologizing...I felt terrible. But I'm doing the right thing, right? I know what Lennon would say.

I miss her so much. I miss hearing her sneak back in after whatever trouble she got into, her little footsteps on the stairs. It was always wild listening to her stories, but I'm still mad at her for going to Vegas with a STRANGER.

She's always turned out okay, though...the stories are actually kinda fun to hear, once enough time has passed. Lennon's too smart to get herself hurt. I just wish she'd use her brains for something better.

Mom left her beer out on the deck last night. I don't know what happened, it was like an intrusive thought, but I really almost took it. Everyone at school drinks, and they're not crazy. Moderation's key, right? But if Lennon ever found out, she'd actually kill me.

I'm just tired of the extremes this family goes to. Nobody ever thinks to live in the middle.

Lennon tossed the computer to the side. Page *did* end up drinking, and it killed her. How could she be so naive?

Because she's fourteen, Lennon thought, soothing her anger. And if she hadn't been so strict about alcohol, maybe Page would have felt comfortable enough to talk to her about it. At the very least, Lennon could have told her that rocky coves, high tides, and booze do *not* go together.

And what about this secret internet crush? She still didn't know their identity, and she'd learned nothing more about Emery, but there was one final journal to unlock. After ten failed attempts to get into the last one and another berating from her intestines, she slumped upstairs, fishing a box of Cheerios from the pantry.

Each bite felt like a rock. The cereal filled the hole in her stomach, which only brought attention to the void everywhere else. She plucked a strawberry from the fridge hoping for more flavor, though deep down she knew it wasn't the food. Everything tasted like failure.

Lennon's cracked phone lit with an onslaught of text tones. Now that everyone was back home, they wanted to drive up to Los Angeles and finally use their real ID's. Lennon hated the city—it smelled, the people sucked, and the traffic was hell. But the idea of getting out of this fishbowl for a night sounded exactly like the kind of distraction she needed. A crowded, stinky distraction.

> MICHAELA
> I'll take care of the goodies!!

Lennon scrolled through the string of texts, typing out a quick request to carpool. Trick confirmed, and she slipped her phone into her pocket.

He parked his car at the bottom of her driveway at nine o'clock sharp, beeping his horn in quick succession. Lennon swiped a clear gloss over her lips and stuck the tube in her pocket, along with a small wallet containing all of her necessities for the night; packing light was essential.

"Just to Los Angeles, right?" her father asked, leaning against the stair railing.

"Promise, Dad. I'll be back tomorrow morning...maybe afternoon."

He pursed his lips. "What if we watched a movie tonight? We can make popcorn...I'll even make the jalapeño cheese dip. You can pick—"

"I just need to get out of the house for a little," she said in one breath, already halfway through the door.

He sighed defeatedly. "You still owe me a fishing trip, by the way."

She faltered, fidgeting guiltily. That feeling had started to make a permanent home in her lately. "I haven't forgotten. We'll go soon, okay?"

"All right, kid. Love you."

"Love you, too. I'll be back tomorrow. "

"Be safe, Len!" His words felt like fingers reaching out, racing down the driveway to meet her before the car door shut.

"You ready?" Michaela reached from behind, squeezing her shoulders.

"I guess we'll find out." Lennon mumbled, letting her eyes drift shut.

She'd just started to dream when a bump shook her awake.

"You look like you're in a music video." Trick said, bringing Lennon's mind and body back into the present. She peeled her chin from her fist, checking in with the group. The twins were smoking in the back, waving at the car driving next to them filled with the rest of their friends.

"How long was I out?" Lennon stretched, her best attempt at a joke.

"Are we close yet?" Michaela whined. "I wanna take this tab already."

"We're ten minutes from my buddy's place. I don't trust the valet here," Trick said. "He'll have an Uber ready for us."

Lennon shook out her ponytail and shed her hoodie. Her

underlying top was deep onyx, with a snaking rip sown loosely over cleavage only God or a surgeon could provide.

She rolled the tinted window down, unveiling the scene like a movie screen. Lights and buildings passed in colorful blurs, turned to watercolor by the glistening tears wind was whipping in her eyes. The car speakers thumped deep in her ears and chest like a heartbeat, and for a moment, she was alive.

Eventually it came time to change cars, and the heartbeat stopped inside her chest. She crossed her arms and looked to the girls huddled on the curb, spotting a flash of a plastic baggie.

In times when she wanted to run full-force at these things, she considered it balance to walk and feign nonchalance, despite the saliva filling her mouth.

"Bottoms up, bitches!" Michaela cheered. Lennon stared longingly at the crystals glittering from the girls' pinkies before disappearing into their mouths.

"C'mon, Len," Macy urged, nodding. Lennon swallowed the excess of spit, blinking away the desire. She'd said one more time, she'd promised...

But she'd known what she came for. Lennon dipped her finger and swiped it over her tongue in a single second, pushing the guilt deep into her mind. She'd had enough of that feeling to last a lifetime.

The girls talked, and Lennon listened, waiting for her nerves to unwind. She didn't first feel it until halfway through their ride. Faces and sounds began to melt inside the car, interesting enough to anchor her in the present. Things were good.

Until she was spit out of a car she'd forgotten she was in.

"Sorry sir, you're getting five stars, don't worry!" Macy called to the driver, sticking her hand up. "Jesus, Lennon..."

"What I'd do?" Lennon giggled. Michaela shook her head, guiding her to the entrance guarded by an intimidating pair of security.

"ID's," the brute grunted.

Lennon smiled innocently, fishing in her purse for her wallet.

Credit card, credit card, debit card...her brows furrowed. She started over while the others flashed theirs, forehead creasing as she flipped each one. *Where was it?* She must have forgotten to switch it over from her sling bag...

"Would you accept a picture?" she asked, showing her teeth this time in her smile.

"Physical only," he said, his Australian accent thick.

Time to go to work.

"C'mon, all of my friends are of age." Her lashes fluttered, melting her pale eyes into ocean water, inviting and treacherous.

"We graduated the same year," Michaela added earnestly, brushing his arm with her nails.

He was locked onto Lennon, pulled in by her gaze. He unthinkingly licked his lips before speaking again. "You want me to let you in without showing ID?"

"Of course not," She sunk her top teeth into the flesh of her bottom lip, feeling her dimple crater into her cheek. "But maybe you could look down the road while I slip in?"

"Wouldn't really be doing my job then, though, eh?" He smiled, enjoying this game. "Could probably get fired over it, in fact...so why should I?"

"Because you'd be making my night. I'd remember you forever." Her voice was dripping with praise and false promises.

The bouncer glanced at his partner, and back to her. "And what do *I* get?"

The opportunity practically threw itself at Lennon, as it always had. She knew *exactly* what he wanted. Her fingers plucked a fifty from her wallet, extending it to him.

"Here."

He frowned, disappointed. "I don't want your money—"

"I just wanted to give you this so you can use it when you take me on a date. Call it a...*security* deposit."

He looked over her hungrily, lost in the idea of having her all to himself for a night. "Yeah?"

"Let me in, and then find me upstairs." she said quietly, her pupils beginning to swell. He glanced at his partner once more, and after an unspoken conversation, stepped to the side. She smiled sweetly as her friends swept her away, the fifty still tucked between her fingers.

Once they were in the elevator, Trick shook his head. "You're fucking insane."

"She's fucking *incredible*, you mean," Rowan said, beaming. "You just sweet-talked a bouncer, dude. You're badass!"

"That's why we keep her around!" Michaela cheered, slinging an arm around her shoulder. Lennon laughed, trying to stay upright as the elevator jerked to a halt. Bass boomed from behind the doors, which slid open like curtains to reveal a sea of dancing, sweaty bodies.

"Whoa..." The twins marveled, pupils dilating with excitement and a flood of endorphins. Lennon could feel the music pulse through every part of her, involuntarily swaying to the beat.

"There she is, she's back!" Rowan whistled. The twins squealed, taking her hands in theirs as they danced toward the middle of the floor.

Time didn't mean much when she felt like this. The chemicals dissolved her nerves with each new song; by the sixth, she found herself swallowing another half a tab with the twins, wanting to see how far she could push the euphoria.

"You wanna dance?" A hand touched her waist, squeezing gently. She turned, expecting to see the bouncer based off the accent, but Trick's eyes met hers instead.

"Gotcha," He winked. Maybe it was the drugs, but the daunting way he looked at her, as if she were a meal instead of a person, made her take a step back.

"I need some air." The last thing she saw was his confused expression before turning away and pushing through the crowd. She reached the edge of the bar, leaning her sweaty forehead against the cool, protective glass. The world below buzzed with so much life that

Missing Page

it sounded like electricity through wires. It was overwhelmingly beautiful—almost too much so, she thought, as tears crystallized in her eyes.

"*Oh my God....*" She lifted her fingertips to the transparent glass, her voice sounding much deeper and slower. Lines of cars twinkled through the city, spreading out like veins.

"Lennon!" She didn't know which friend was grabbing her arm, dragging her back into the crowd. "C'mon, we're dancing."

It was Rowan, gathering the group like a bunch of ducklings. Soon she was surrounded by sweaty, bouncing humans, indistinguishable and invisible in the human sea. She felt free here; Lennon didn't have to be anybody other than a girl dancing at a club. There were no obligations or responsibilities, no recognition to worry over.

A small pair of fingers slipped across her sweaty palms and through the spaces between her fingers, tightening with concern. "Hey..."

Lennon expected the hand to belong to one of the twins. But the girl was one she'd never seen before, with lemon-colored hair that glowed pink from the overhead lights.

"Are you okay?" The girl yelled over the music.

Lennon realized she had stopped dancing, and was simply basking in the light show happening behind her lids. "I feel *so* good."

"Wanna come to the bathroom with me?"

She didn't get the chance to answer before being pulled along with her. Lennon glanced around for a familiar face, but they had driven deeper into the crowd, closer to the stage. Her bladder complained then, urging her to say yes.

"Sure." She shrugged, following the pink lemon head.

The two went downstairs, groaning at the line that snaked outside the door.

"You've gotta be kidding me!" the girl groaned.

Lennon glanced at the nearly empty bathroom next door and tugged her new friend's hand.

The girl grimaced. "That's the men's."

"They've all got the same thing!" Lennon freed her hand to push the door open, rushing past the urinals and keeping her eyes down.

"Hey! Wrong bathroom!" one called in protest.

"Sorry, emergency!" She slid the lock into place, hovering over the dirty porcelain as she relaxed her muscles.

Once finished, she hurried out again, finding an open sink in the ladies'. The girl that had saved her was now inside, staring at her in awe.

"You actually did it?"

"I'm not pissing my pants over a sign," Lennon scoffed playfully, scrubbing her hands.

"I like you." She grinned. "I'm Marissa. Everybody calls me Issa."

"Lennon," she replied with a friendly nod.

"Lemon?"

"*Lennon,*" she corrected.

"Oh. That's cool!" Issa pushed her lashes up with her index fingers before taking Lennon's sweaty hand again. "Are you feeling better? Please tell me you're not alone."

"Yes. And no, I'm not." She shook her head. "My friends are upstairs. We came from Laguna."

"Laguna Beach! My dad loves going down there!" Issa shouted over the music. She gestured to the view outside the bathroom. "Do you like the city?"

Lennon looked around, shrugging. "It's all right. I was hoping for something a little less clubby."

Issa bit her lip, thinking. "This place is kinda lame, huh? My boyfriend was telling me to come to this house party up in the hills..."

Issa's brows suddenly furrowed. "This is gonna sound weird, but you seem *so* familiar. I feel like I've seen you before, your eyes..."

Lennon tilted her head. "Really?"

Issa's eyes widened with recognition. "Oh! I know what I'm thinking of, now...there's a picture my family's had for years of a little

Missing Page

girl's eyes, they look like ice. They look *exactly* like yours, you wouldn't believe it!"

Lennon's lips parted in disbelief. *It couldn't be...could it?* "Do you know who the photographer is?"

"I don't know, we've had it forever! But my mom got it on a little roadtrip down south, it was..." She trailed off, shaking her head as the pieces clicked. "*No!*"

Lennon laughed, amazed with the universe's sense of humor. "Yes."

"Is that actually you?"

"My dad took it when I was seven. That picture got really popular, he sold a few thousand copies—"

"Well, your eyes are fucking incredible, that's why. Holy *shit!*" She beamed, dancing in place. "This is crazy, I gotta get your autograph or something!"

Lennon laughed, shaking her head at Issa's contagious excitement. The blonde tucked a stray wave behind her ear, blinking her doe eyes. "I think I'm gonna go to that house. If you wanna skip this and come to a *real* party, I'd love to send you the details." She reached to steady Lennon as she wavered, giggling. "Your friends can come too."

Lennon knitted her brows. She couldn't believe this girl was so trusting, but it was LA, after all—stranger things had happened. "Seriously?"

"Yeah! You can join my Uber if you want, I hate riding by myself anyway. Everyone deserves the *LA experience* once in their life."

Lennon tossed her paper towels in the trash, worried more for the girl's safety than her own. She'd never invite a stranger into a car with her, girl or not.

"Er...yeah, I'll think on it."

Issa extended her hand out for Lennon's phone. "I'll give you my number. You can text me if you decide you wanna come...you sure you're okay?"

Lennon nodded. Issa hugged her, pulling back after she stiffened.

"I'm leaving in twenty, but I'll order an XL just in case. Text me when you decide."

She disappeared into the crowd, leaving Lennon alone to find her friends. It felt like she was being stuffed through a tube as she traveled, eventually spat out near her friends at the bar.

"You got invited to *what?*" Michaela asked, lifting her ear to Lennon's mouth.

"*Where?*" Rowan asked.

"House party! In the hills!" Lennon shouted.

"How the fuck did you manage that?" Macy asked incredulously, eyes wide.

She shrugged. "Got lucky, I guess."

Michaela looked to the others. "I mean, of course we...don't we...?"

"Fuck yeah! Let's go!" Rowan yelled, ushering the group to follow. Lennon shot a text to Issa, and soon they all loaded into the elevator, racing to the curb to meet her. A black Escalade pulled in front two minutes later, driving them through the winding roads of West Hollywood.

"Oi, where are you going?" An Australian voice called behind her. She whipped around to face the bouncer, but couldn't fight the current of bodies rushing her inside the car. "I never got your number!"

"Sorry!" Lennon grinned unapologetically, waving until the door closed. Trick flipped the bouncer the bird before the Escalade sped off, sending the group into a fit of laughter.

Lennon had gone on autopilot during the drive again, but was brought back by Trick's large hands gently pushing her off his lap to exit the overcrowded SUV.

"C'mon, pretty girl, wake up," he grunted, helping her out of the car.

"What the fuck are we doing?" Lennon whispered breathlessly to herself.

The house was buried into the hill, hidden behind a privacy gate

Missing Page

and thick bushes. Deep house music pulsed through her as she entered, trying not to stare at the beautiful humans inside. She recognized a handful of people from movies and shows, and was once again reminded of how strange this city could be.

Issa locked lips with a tall, broad-shouldered man, and then waved to Lennon. "I'll find you later!"

Lights sparkled like kaleidoscopes behind Lennon's closed lids; her concept of time had all but disappeared. She couldn't think about anything other than how she felt in that exact moment—it was bliss.

Michaela called her over near the pool with the rest of the group. Something about the water looked ethereal, inviting Lennon into its turquoise embrace. It was an undeniable force, hypnotizing her like she had the bouncer. She kneeled next to it, her nose close enough to brush against the surface.

"Lennon, what are you *doing*?" Michaela laughed.

Her pupils had sucked up most of the ice around it by then. She turned, reaching out to take her hand. "C'mon. Let's get in."

"Bitch, you're *cra-zy*," Michaela smiled, but her laugh was less humored. "We're not getting in the pool."

"C'mon, Mic!" Lennon whined. "It'll feel so good."

"I'm in a mini skirt and a full face of makeup—"

"Get in the pool," Lennon whispered, wiggling her eyebrows.

"Who are you, Angelina Jolie? I'm not getting in, and neither are you!"

Lennon jerked her hand, angling them toward the twinkling water. Michaela tightened her grip, planting her feet. "Hey! I said no!"

"If you don't let go, you're coming with me!" Lennon warned melodically.

"Lennon...Lennon, stop—!" Michaela squealed, slipping her hand out at the last moment. Lennon threw her body back, and crashed through the liquid glass.

Everything went quiet once she broke through, and she let herself sink to the bottom, away from the world. The bass vibrated through the water molecules, surrounding her in a trembling bubble. Cheers of a crowd could be heard from above, but she was content being submerged. This was the true quiet she'd been wishing for all this time; that brief nothingness that silenced her mind and every thought that crossed through it. That's what she loved about drugs.

And then a hand yanked her upwards, breaking her head through the surface. Lennon gasped, wiping salt water out of her eyes. The hand belonged to Trick, who matched the twins' fearful stare and panicked expression.

"Are you okay?" Michaela demanded, kneeling to check Lennon's hair for blood in a rare moment of concern. "Did you hit your head?"

"Why'd you pull me up?" she breathed.

Their expressions morphed into confusion, and in the next moment, a laugh escaped from Trick. More roars of encouragement erupted, and Lennon shielded her face with her hands from the explosions of water as others cannon-balled in.

Trick's interruption combined with the sudden addition of bodies had cracked her bubble of bliss. The deafening loudness that had once brought so much beauty now overstimulated her, and her pulse pounded painfully through her chest. Lennon clamored for the wall, suddenly feeling imprisoned.

This was what she hated about drugs.

"I think I wanna go home," Lennon shouted over the noise. The twins glanced at each other, and Michaela stepped forward.

"What do you mean?" she asked. "You just got this party started, we're having fun!"

"I'm not anymore." Lennon's teeth chattered through her words. "Can you...can we go home?"

Rowan's lip jutted. "Yhu whalla lief?"

Lennon stared at him. "What?"

Michaela stared at her as if she'd grown a second head. "Lebbeh, arg yhub ubay?"

She was too far. The edges of black that had been swimming around her eyes took over her vision.

You promised.

"Sorry," she whispered to the dark, before it completely took her. "I'm sorry."

17

SHALLOW BREATH FOUND HER WHEN SHE REAWOKE. Her fingers squeezed the material underneath, feeling a slight sense of relief when she recognized cotton. *She woke up*—that was a good start. Waking up in a bed was even better, though an uneasiness returned upon realizing it wasn't hers.

She was baking underneath the heavy blanket, preheated by the rising sun. Her eyelids, sticky with sweat, peeled open and surveilled the unfamiliar room.

Where am I?

A body next to her jostled, and she closed her eyes again, pretending to sleep as her hands trembled.

Please don't be a guy. Please don't be a guy...

Once the body stilled, she turned her head, careful and quiet. Tangled platinum strands tickled her cheek right before she saw Michaela's slack mouth; Lennon almost laughed with relief, thanking a God she didn't believe in.

She'd never been in the True's house before. Michaela's room was huge; she could only imagine what waited outside the door. There were two others sleeping on the floor, all in pitiful makeshift pallets. Lennon reached to pull the duvet off her, stopping when her knuckles came into view. Four were bruised, and the middle had dried blood caked over a scab. *What the fuck?*

She slipped from the room and padded down the hall, opening every door in search of a bathroom. Eventually she found a walk-in supply closet, in which she found a spare toothbrush and toothpaste tube. When she exited, a golden knob glinted at the end of the hallway, shining like a holy grail.

She startled when she saw a bed instead of a toilet, with one lanky arm hanging from the side. *Oops. Sorry, Ricky,* she thought, pulling it closed. This house was disgustingly big, and somehow she still had yet to find a bathroom. *Do these people not pee?*

She tiptoed across the kitchen, taking in the scene with dry, itchy eyes. Pizza boxes and snack bowls littered the bar and counter…was that there before or after they'd arrived? She could only remember bits and pieces after they got out of that first Uber, and nothing at all after they went to the house party. Lennon swiveled her head to the living room, where another three were passed out on couches and the floor.

Her head was still fuzzy, trying to remember the details of the previous night. She recalled weaving through infinite crowds under kaleidoscope lights, glinting crystals in dark alleyways, feeling suspended in vibrating water…*lots* of driving in overcrowded cars. There was no telling reality from delusion in this state.

After opening another few doors, she finally found what she'd been looking for. She rushed the sink, splashing cold water over her perspiring skin to wash away the mess on her face and the sweat from her underarms. *Why did Michaela need such a heavy blanket?* This was a beach town, for Christ's sake. She flushed the urine away and soaked her hands in foamy soap and hot water; mint toothpaste filled her rancid mouth, washing away a pinky's tip worth of crystals, a tab, and two—no, three—joints that had found a home between her lips throughout the night. Her refusal of alcohol kept her safe from any headaches or hangovers, but the impending comedown would be another beast.

Mascara bled under her eyes, her lips were cracked from lack of moisture. There were matted curls scattered through her hair, worse than after jumping in the ocean. And her knuckles...they were growing sorer by the minute, darkening into deep blues and violets.

"Oh my God, I thought someone was breaking in!" Macy gasped, holding her hand to her chest. Lennon whipped around, biting down on her tongue hard enough to taste iron. She winced, and spit out the rest of what was in her mouth before responding.

"You thought an intruder came in to *brush their teeth?* You have like ten people in your house, Mace."

"Don't be mean," she chastised, pressing her fingers to the bridge of her nose. "I don't know up from down right now. I didn't recognize your clothes, and you were being so quiet...you don't have to sneak around."

Lennon swished the inside of her cheeks with water, trying to make sense of her words. "I got crazy last night, didn't I?"

Macy watched her carefully, as if waiting for something. "Yeah... it was something." Her gaze trickled down to Lennon's knuckles.

"Do you, er–d'you know how this happened?"

"No idea. Looks bad, though. What do you remember?"

Lennon wasn't convinced; it seemed more like Macy was scared of being the news-breaker. "Not much, honestly. Just the club...it gets blurry after we got to the house."

"We got split up for a while. It was Michaela and me, the guys, and you. You disappeared after you jumped in the pool—"

Her eyes bulged. "That was real?"

"You ended up fine, obviously. We found you in those clothes around three." She gestured. "You were sitting on the curb. It took forever to get Michaela to leave, she was making out with that guy from Finding Paradise all night."

Missing Page

Lennon looked down, finally registering her sweats and T-shirt. She'd assumed the twins had given her pajamas...were these stolen? Flashes of the night flickered behind her eyes in indiscernible blips. The random blonde she'd met—what was her name? Rowan spinning her in circles, Trick's scrunched face tipping back a shot, his face washed in purple. Were those memories from the club, or the house? Were they even real?

Macy left for a moment, returning with ice wrapped in cloth. "Here."

"Thanks," Lennon mumbled, pressing it to her tender flesh.

"I think I heard Michaela getting up. I'm gonna try and wake the others."

Lennon nodded, retreating to the room she came from. The person closest to the door was still asleep, tufts of auburn hair poking out from under the throw pillow. Michaela was sitting up next to another girl, groaning with reluctant consciousness.

"So you *are* alive," Lennon rasped, sitting on the edge of the bed.

"Hey, Len," she croaked.

Something was off. Growing up with Cashmere as a mother required the ability to detect a mood shift in something as little as breath changing, or how heavy car keys were set down.

"What'd I do?" Lennon asked, wanting to cut straight to the chase.

Michaela glanced dramatically at her knuckles, and then back to her. She treated these moments like reality television. "Look, I wasn't with you guys, so I don't know exactly what happened, but you...punched...Trick."

"I *what?*"

She'd meant to take whatever Michaela said without emotion so she could avoid the smug, satisfied smile present on her face. Not much surprised Lennon; she had done a lot of crazy things on drugs. Stolen for the thrill of it, out-crazing men who catcalled her on the streets—she even climbed a water tower her first year of college.

There was a polaroid somewhere out there to prove it. But she had never gotten in a fight before. She'd never hurt someone.

"I wasn't *there*," she said with a sense of remorse. "So it's all hearsay. You found us on the balcony with new clothes and a bloody fist, said 'I decked him,' and left again. We didn't know who you were talking about at first...honestly, I just thought you were tripping. But you were in shock, or something." Michaela glanced at the girl listening from the floor. "Trick went home by himself."

"Did he say what happened?" Lennon pushed.

Michaela couldn't hide the impatience in her voice. "I *just* woke up. I think we're all pretty much on the same page...I was kind of hoping *you* knew what happened—MACY, TURN THAT FUCKING MUSIC OFF!"

Lennon found her phone hidden under a pillow. There were two missed calls from Rowan and one from Trick, asking to talk. She scrolled through her notifications, hoping for context; all she found was an incomprehensible string of misspelled words she'd sent to Hart, followed with an audio message apologizing and letting him know she was okay. Lennon dragged her hand down her face, groaning. How big of a mess had she made?

Macy came in, matching her sister's curious eyes. The way they watched her made Lennon feel like a zoo animal; her destruction was their entertainment. Michaela wasn't annoyed because of Lennon's actions, she realized, but because she hadn't been there to witness them. Even the half-familiar face on the floor had peeked her head out, perking like she'd smelled a hot cup of coffee.

"I think I need to go home." Lennon said quietly, her face growing hot.

"Maybe if we get some breakfast, you'll feel better," Michaela suggested, sitting up. "You might remember—"

"Save the fucking niceties, Mic."

Lennon hated how humiliation felt on her skin; she felt like she was soaked in it. But even more than that, she felt shame for falling back to her old habits. These people weren't good for her, and she'd known that from the beginning. Maybe that's why she went—it wasn't the drugs or recklessness she was addicted to, but the suffering.

"I want to go home," she repeated harshly.

"Lennon..." Michaela said, trying to deter her. Lennon ignored her, using her phone to get a quick route home. It was only a ten-minute walk. She stood up, and Michaela followed. "At least let me get you an Uber."

"I'll walk, thanks."

She gathered her things, hearing a quiet murmur as she stormed down the hall.

"Didn't her sister just die?" An auburn haired girl asked, just as she entered the living room. She followed the heads and paled when she noticed Lennon.

"You're awake," she squeaked, petrified with fear.

"Don't let me stop you." Lennon growled, slamming the door behind her.

Once down the street, Lennon's angry tears had been dried by the morning sun, and seagulls cried for her instead. Walking gave her time to think and put the pieces of the night she could remember into place. She strolled slowly, making sure she was calm before climbing the driveway.

Her dad was busy in the kitchen when she entered. "You're back early," he said with a mouth full of scrambled eggs. "Whose clothes are those?"

She looked down, finally noticing the crass design on the T-shirt. "Got them in LA."

"How was it?"

She scooped the remaining eggs from the pan onto a new plate with the intense kind of focus that only comes from avoiding something else. "Should've stayed and watched movies with you."

He could hear the deep sadness in her tone and reached to pat her shoulder. She drifted to the pile of bills spread next to the stove. *Water, gas, license renewal, West Coast Funeral Services...*

She looked to him, silently asking for confirmation.

He nodded. "We set a date. June tenth."

Lennon blinked. "That's just over a week."

"Gotta do it at some point, Len." he murmured. "We got the results back, too."

"What?" she squeaked. "How'd you get them so fast?"

"Tom Wells, we went to Stanford together. He works over in...."

Of course he knows someone, she thought to herself. He *always* knew someone. A sharp ringing drowned out his voice in her ears as she processed what this meant.

"So...what was it?" she asked. "The cause of death?"

Discomfort twisted his lips, deepening the lines around his mouth. "There was a pretty big lesion in her head that matched up with a part of the cove wall. They think she tripped. Detective said it would have been a miracle if she didn't bleed out from it, but she—she drowned before anything else."

Lennon drew a staggered breath, struggling to fight against her emotions. A part of her wished he would take her hand, but the other part wasn't sure she'd accept it if he did.

"Her blood alcohol level was point two-eight." he added more quietly.

"That's a lot," Lennon guessed rigidly.

He nodded tightly. "That's probably why she fell. Hit her head just right, and the water took care of the rest. But they're gonna do a thorough investigation of it, just to make sure. I, uh...I mentioned your concerns about Emery to them. She's not completely off the hook yet."

Lennon's eyes welled. Her father's were swimming in the same ocean of grief when he placed his hand over hers, and though she was reluctant, she allowed it.

Her question could barely reach above a whisper. "Was it...was it quick?"

Missing Page

He gave one, tight nod. Her chest depleted.

"Okay." She nodded, swallowing. "That's good, that's...I'm glad."

There was silence for a few minutes while she processed. The backtrack noise of birds and ocean seemed too pleasant for their subject matter, but there was nothing she could do about it.

"What happened to your knuckles?" he asked, his brows knitting.

She retracted her hand, lifting it to inspect again. Hearing this about Page made her want to yell at herself. How could she risk her life for a few hours of artificial happiness? How dare she so carelessly offer her fate to the same hands, and make her dad go through this all over again? And she'd had the nerve to jump into a pool, of all things...

"Honestly, I'm not sure."

"Lennon," he started.

"Doesn't hurt that bad. I'm okay." She didn't know if the sick feeling in her stomach was from her digestive track or her conscience.

"Did someone hurt you?"

She thought of Trick's lingering hands at Seadog's, the way he'd shadowed her throughout the night. Even so, she couldn't fully justify her actions when her perception had been so distorted. Trick was ambitious, but he'd never overstepped before. There was no way to know for sure, and she hated that the most.

"No, Dad. *I* hurt someone."

She went upstairs to submerge herself under the heavy streams of her shower head, boiling under the scalding water. Lennon avoided her reflection in the mirror this time, too ashamed to be with herself. *No. More. Pills.*

Just as she washed the last of the suds away, her phone rang from outside the door. She wanted to chuck it off the balcony, but she begrudgingly stuck out her good hand to answer, twisting the knob with the other.

"Hello?"

"Bitch, what's *up* with you? The twins just told me you blew up at them." Rowan's voice echoed off the tile. Lennon rolled her eyes, not caring enough to defend herself. People would think whatever they wanted to about her; it's not like the Mayfields had much of a reputation to live up to, anyway. "Trick just left my place. There was a pretty good bruise on his jaw, you happen to know anything about that?"

"My hand does," Lennon grumbled. "I do not. Did you ask him?"

"I tried, he wouldn't say anything. He was super stressed this morning, though."

She closed her eyes, racking her brain with all her might, but nothing came. "Everyone thinks I'm going crazy."

"Girl, you've *been* crazy. Now they just think you're a bitch. So unless you can give some justification, I don't have much to defend you with."

"I remember him taking a few shots..." She retraced her steps as far as they'd take her. "After the pool, I went to the bathroom..."

"Then what?"

Hart. "I was texting Hart on the curb," she breathed, as if worried she'd forget if she didn't say it right then. She recalled furrowed brows, spit coming out Trick's mouth while he spoke. "We argued about Hart. I think Trick was trying to confess his feelings, or something..."

"So you punched him?"

"No." Lennon sighed, exasperated. "You know me, I don't just punch people."

"You are literally chaos incarnate's daughter, so I don't know anything."

She chewed her thumbnail, wanting to get off the phone. "I'll keep thinking."

"You could also try, I dunno, *talking* to the guy you punched." Their sarcasm took no time springing into action.

She groaned. "I will, I will. I'm still getting my bearings."

"I'll leave you to it. But you better get to thinking, because I'm currently still mad at you for hurting my friend."

"Okay. Bye, Rowan."

Missing Page

They looked at their phone in confusion. "Did you just say *okay—?*"

Click.

Lennon barely saw her parents that day, too busy with funeral preparations to stay longer than breakfast. She spent those hours re-reading Page's journal entries and attempting new passwords; because of last night's guilt, there was extra obligation to put in the work, erase the regret with retribution. She deep-cleaned the house, took Kaiser for a few circles around the neighborhood, and made sure to avoid the cove entrance. Even when he pulled, she couldn't be persuaded.

Trick had called her twice during that jog, silenced both times. On the third call, she stopped, lifting the phone to her ear. "Stop calling me!"

"Lennon?" Hart's voice jarred her. She choked, looking down at her phone.

"Oh my God, Hart, I—I thought you were someone else, I'm sorry..." She burned with humiliation and the ache of missing him. "How are you?"

"I heard your message but I couldn't get signal out there. I drove back first thing this morning...are you okay?"

"Out there?" she asked, confused.

He paused, equally perplexed. "Yeah, my family's on a camping trip, remember? With Cooper, Peyton and her boy—fiancé?"

The guilt she felt was indescribable, immeasurable. Lennon only vaguely remembered Hart mentioning a proposal, and now she was ruining his time with his siblings. It was bad enough fucking up her own life, but did she have to include his too?

It seemed so clear then. The worry in his voice, the difference in the air between them. Everything felt too guarded, too careful; that wasn't Hart's way. Lennon was ruining him. He couldn't be the man she fell in love with when she was in his life.

She gripped the phone tightly in her hands. "Everything's fine. I'm really sorry about the messages."

"I wish I was there—"

"No you don't." she assured him. "I promise. Hart, I'm—I'm really sorry, but I..." She trailed off, unable to find the strength to finish.

"What?"

She clenched her teeth, trying to find the strength to say the necessary words. It was one of the most difficult things she would ever have to do, but she could do it for him. She would.

"I don't know if we should keep...seeing each other...anymore."

The phone was silent for a painfully long beat. The part of her heart reserved for the boy on the phone—which had unknowingly grown in size since the last time she checked—shriveled, breaking off with an excruciating, nearly audible crack. *Is that what love can do?* she wondered, marveling at its power.

Despite an impressive pain swelling in her lungs, this wasn't world-encompassing agony. The past few days almost served as a cushion for the pain she was experiencing now. She'd still be able to see him at school, or be able to check on him through pictures throughout his life. It gave her enough space to process each string of love in its concentrated form of pain, instead of a protective numbness.

"I don't understand," he finally said.

Technically, there were nothing to fight for. Without a label for their relationship, Hart had no feet to stand on, except for the underlying love they both knew lied under the surface. It was the kind of love that ascended words and relationship titles; their hearts had known each other too long for those silly things.

His voice was brazenly hurt, but calm. "You want to break up?"

"We're not dating, Hart." she uttered, wincing at her own cruelty. She hated how hurt he sounded, but a clean break would be best. She had to believe that.

"So you don't want to be friends anymore," he corrected, unrelenting.

Lennon prided herself on not owing anyone anything. This

emotional parachute of casualness usually felt relieving, but with Hart it felt heavier, more like an anchor hurdling her toward concrete. She felt his pain on top of hers. Lennon wasn't his girlfriend, just as she wasn't his friend; she was just *his*—the same way the rest of her heart had been Page's. And in some twisted way, because she loved him, there was no way she could be with him.

"I'm sorry." she whispered.

"Lennon, please, *hold on a s–*"

She hung up, her scabbed knuckles whitening around her cracked phone. As much as she'd tried to avoid the cycle, here she was again, sitting in the ashes of her own self-destruction. And she would do it again, and again, and again.

Kaiser tugged on his leash, and she looked up, realizing they were at the trail's entrance leading to the cove once again. Winds whispered through the branches swooping overhead, giving a stark eeriness to a place she once considered an oasis. The song nature was singing felt like a siren's, pulling her in almost against her will. Lennon reached down, slipping a finger in her shoes one at a time and stuffing her socks in after them. Kaiser trotted next to her, sniffing every crack in the stone stairs leading down.

Whathefuckamidoingwhatthefuckamidoing was the only sentence rolling in her mind, growing louder with every step she took. By the time she reached the entrance, her brain was screaming.

The winds coming from within whipped cold ocean spray against the walls, speckling her jeans. The tide was low and weak; it could barely make its way into the cove before sand swallowed it. If it wasn't so dangerous, it'd be fascinating how quickly everything changed. There were a few times during those mermaid picnics where it seemed fine one moment, and in the next they were wading through waters with their baggies of half-finished lunch. It was nature's way of letting them know they'd overstayed their welcome, but for now, she had a few hours of safety left.

You treat the ocean with respect, her dad had warned them during one of their first visits. *Do not underestimate her. She will not hesitate to kill you.*

It had always sounded harsh to her; their dad loved dramatics when telling stories. It was the artist in him. Now her lip trembled as she stared at the sand banks, the walls. Where had her sister been when they found her? How long was Page stuck in here before it took her—was she scared? Did she cry out for her mom, her dad, her sister?

Her fingertips brushed jagged rocks, toes burrowing into the sand for stability.

"P..." She couldn't finish. The voice that came out sounded foreign, weak. She swallowed, gripping the leash.

"Page?"

The ocean roared as it splashed against the rocks, hissing in retreat.

A guttural, animalistic scream rumbled from her belly. One of grief, guilt, and the most unimaginable pain. Kaiser stood close to her as it echoed off the walls, shocking them both into a brief silence when it screamed back.

"You took my sister!" she bellowed, tears staining her cheeks. "You took her from me!"

Again it yelled her words back to her, refusing to take responsibility.

Even Kaiser hung his head a little lower when they left, less interested in his surroundings than before. When she returned to the stairs to rinse her feet and slip on her shoes, the sun peeked out from the clouds, its warmth sticky on her skin.

She wanted to be high. That's how fast and deceptively addiction worked; it erased all the bad parts to make you miss the good. She wouldn't have to think about how fucked up she was, or how lost; she wouldn't have to think at all.

Page would be so disappointed. As terrible as Lennon felt, she would take a thousand comedowns, a million withdrawals, to have her back. She would give everything up, even for one more day. She even missed her sister's scoldings. *What's the fun in getting so messed up you can't protect yourself?* Page had once pleaded with her.

Lennon dropped the leash in shock, her gasp of clarity piercing the air as everything rushed back to her.

Last night.

Trick.

18

Lennon would remain a prisoner to her own mind for days and nights to come, ridden with heartbreak and grief. She kept her phone close on her nightstand, selfishly hoping Hart would call so that she could take everything back. He never did. She couldn't go in public either, without risking an encounter with Trick; she wanted to at least wait until her knuckles had healed more. Her parents had enough to take care of without tending to her self-induced illness. All of this, along with the fact that it was the night before her sister's funeral, had concocted into a terrible bout of depression.

Burying herself beneath her blankets had started off comfy. Besides the tightening of her bladder and the stench of sweat permeating in the bubble she'd created, she didn't have to think about anything else. Staying still helped, but it weakened her; it had been eight hours since she mustered enough energy to sit on the toilet. The slightest movement angered her insides all over again, but she'd been doing well the past ninety-six minutes.

The nightstand suddenly rattled outside her bubble, interrupting her mindless stare. She hadn't even realized her eyes were open.

Missing Page

Lennon reached out instinctively, already smiling at the idea of Hart's voice crackling through the speakers.

A white-hot pain seared her gut, throwing a tantrum over the sudden move. There was no escaping her body—as much as she wanted him, she couldn't evade herself any longer. Lennon scrambled for the door, wincing as she sat down on the toilet. Her muscles felt hard, calcified after days of idleness. Every part of living had become painful for her; even breaths came labored, exhausted under the load of its maker.

It took thirty-six seconds for the stream to slow into a trickle. She'd had time to blink herself awake and notice the dark sky outside her window; there was just enough light from the waning moon to illuminate droplets on the tile leading to the toilet, evidence of Lennon's failing body. Before, it would have been second nature to hop in the shower, take five quick minutes to rinse off. But now the thought alone made her muscles quiver with exhaustion.

Lennon sighed, dropping her head into her hands. Her numbness took too much space to make room for shame or embarrassment. Surviving was ugly.

The nightstand buzzed with a second call, reminding her of what had started all of this. She hobbled towards the sound, peering down in confusion. The first missed call was from an unknown number—not Hart. To her surprise, Conrad's was the one currently displayed in big white letters. Her finger tapped the speaker button and then stretched above her head, encouraging the stagnant blood to move faster through her protesting limbs.

"Lennon, can you hear me?" Conrad yelled over thumping music. She furrowed her brows, dropping her arms at his tone.

"Yeah," she rasped, clutching her throat. When was the last time she'd drank water?

"I think you and your dad should come here, like...now. Cash is here...she's not doing well–"

Lennon lifted the phone to her ear, sure she'd heard wrong. "My mom? Are you at Seadog's?"

"Yes!"

Shame filled her more than surprise did. There'd been countless times Lennon and Page had called different bars or taverns in search of the woman who was supposed to be taking care of them. Although, this was the first time the bar had called her. She checked the time, cursing—less than twelve hours until the service. At least Lennon had the courtesy to indulge her bad habits in private. "How bad is she?"

Conrad didn't know how to tell her. When the lady told him there was an inconsolable, hysterical woman in the restroom, Page's and Lennon's mom was the last person he expected to see.

"Well, she's... You know, you guys should just come get her. As soon as possible."

The discomfort in his voice made her skin crawl. "We're coming."

Her father's grumblings served as the background music to their ride, grinding Lennon's ears like static from a radio.

"How long has she been gone?" Lennon asked, exasperated.

"Two, three hours?" Stress was twitching Stacy's lip. "She was supposed to be—are you okay? You look terrible."

Lennon avoided his gaze. Rotting away in bed must have taken its toll; she hadn't eaten, and she only drank water when she remembered to brush her teeth and could sip straight from the faucet. Each moment awake was spent waiting for sleep—or death—to take her; anything to avoid facing the behemoth of a day that waited for her. She was even wearing the same hoodie and sweats she had on when she'd walked Kaiser nearly a week ago, and she smelled like it too.

Stacy lingered on her bloodshot eyes, frustration bubbling under tanned skin. "We do *not* have time for this!" He slammed his hands on the wheel, punctuating his sentence.

The wheels of his Bronco rolled over rocks onto pavement, slowing to a stop just outside the wooden saloon. His door slammed a few moments before Lennon's, following him with her arms crossed over her chest.

There were twice as many people as she'd expected. The kids

Missing Page

were home for summer and could afford to party on a Tuesday. Stacy was too focused to worry about keeping Lennon close, leaving her to wedge between sweaty bodies on her own, searching for a familiar pair of eyes.

A couple of clammy, grasping fingers closed on her shoulder from behind. She was only tall enough to reach the man's chin, but she recognized his dirty blond hair, and his yellowing jaw.

"I've been calling you!" Trick shouted over the music.

"I can't do this right now," she yelled back. He craned his neck to listen and she leaned away, her eyes of ice freezing over his chestnut pools. "I'm looking for my mom. Have you seen her?"

She tried to shake his hand off, but he tightened his grip instead. It was firm, but not painful. "Why haven't you answered?" he demanded.

Her teeth sank into her cheek, working her anger down. "I didn't want to!"

Unsatisfied, his hand moved down to her bicep, cuffing her arm to keep her from escaping. "I think there was a big misunderstanding, I just wanna talk!"

She looked around for Conrad, begging him to appear in every face she saw. Realizing there was no escape within arms reach, she turned to him.

"You locked us in that bathroom after the pool." Lennon seethed. "I was fucked up, and you cornered me and tried to kiss me!"

He stood agape, eyes as wide as his mouth. "Whoa, *whoa!* That's *not* what happened! I mean, I wanted you kiss you...but I told you to say no if you didn't want me to. You said nothing, so I leaned in!"

"You had no business even trying when I was like that, Patrick. You know how I feel about you!"

His brows lifted in disbelief. "You're calling me *Patrick* now?"

She stood there fuming, wishing the heat from her skin could melt her out of his grasp. Of course *that's* what he would focus on.

"Lennon, you can't be serious."

There wasn't a lot of material to defend herself with. She

remembered his lips taking up most of her vision, but there wasn't much else. The locked door, the alcohol...she remembered the discomfort she'd felt most of all, and the steps she'd tried to take to keep him from being exactly who she was afraid every man was. And yet, despite that initial alertness, Lennon hadn't been quick enough. Their relationship—their trust—was ruined all the same.

Her eyes lingered on the large bruise wrapped around his jawline. Even when she'd forgotten, their skin remembered.

"Do you really expect me to believe that wasn't the plan the whole time?"

"I'm not some evil mastermind, I was fucked up too! Why are *you* the only one allowed to make mistakes? You've got this way wrong, Lennon, Jesus. I'm not a fuckin' predator." He wrinkled his nose. "You've known me for five years. You think I'd change that much in one night?"

Had he always been this naive? People changed all the time, and it took less than a night to do it. Her glare traveled down his tensed arm, landing on the hand holding her in place. "You gonna let me go now?"

Trick released her quickly, and Lennon took her opportunity to duck into the crowd, doing her best to avoid contact with anyone else. But after just a few minutes of searching, a dancing patron pushed her into the bar. Her already bruised hip cracked against the wood and her vision went fuzzy. It was almost too much, all of it. Her brain wanted to give up like her bladder had earlier, but she dug her nails into her palms, forcing herself to stay awake.

She finally found her target shaking tins in all six arms—*ugh*, she couldn't see straight. Her heart was pounding from her previous interaction, pumping adrenaline around an empty stomach. It took all of her will to stay conscious while the three heads of blond curls merged into one.

"Conrad," she uttered breathlessly. Whatever he saw when he looked at her made him abandon his cocktail and dash around the counter. His coworker hadn't noticed Lennon as quickly, and knit her brows in confusion as he bustled around the side.

"Hey, where are you...?"

Lennon lost focus once his arms caught her mid-fall. His concern softened into worry, emotion tugging at the fine lines near his hazel eyes. Conrad hooked an arm around her waist, craning his neck to find her parents. The female bartender followed after, crossing her arms and scowling in disapproval at Lennon's state.

"I gotta get her out of here," he huffed, grimacing with the effort of keeping her upright.

"Just make sure you come back this time." she sneered, narrowing her eyes.

Conrad rolled his. "Jesus Christ, Syd, *let it go!*"

"Enough with the chitchat, we're waiting on our drinks!" A bearded man complained from his stool.

"I'll be back in five minutes." Conrad growled.

"They'll be watered down by then!" the man shouted.

"Then make 'em yourself, asshole!"

Lennon was the first to find her parents through a brief gap in the crowd and pointed, guiding Conrad forward. Stacy was urging Cash along with little progress, waiting to carry her unless completely necessary; Cash's rage was worst when sprouted from humiliation, and right now he had to hold onto any dignity the Mayfields had left.

Both were breathing hard by the time they reached the other side, but Lennon was in significantly worse shape. At first glance, there didn't seem to be too much wrong with Cash. Her eyes were half-open, and she was swaying heavily, but that was pretty typical for Cash after dark.

"*Finally.* I was looking for you!" Her mother called.

Lennon looked up, bewildered. "*Me?*"

"Cash, it's time to go home. We have a big day tomorrow." Stacy reminded tiredly.

"I can't do it, Stacy." Her head shook frantically, eyes widening into glassy, reflective orbs. "I'm not ready!"

A few people turned their heads to watch with wary amusement. Lennon glared until they looked away, wishing her dad would scoop her mom up already. It didn't look like Cash would leave here on her own; why was he insisting on dragging it out?

"You can, and you will. A hangover's only going to make it worse—"

"You're not *listening!*" she wailed, pushing his arms away.

"C'mon, Mom. We can't do this tonight," Lennon said, placing her hands on Cash's shoulders. "Not tonight."

"I'm an adult, Lennon. I'm perfectly capable of—"

In a brief, rare moment, Lennon took her into her arms, settling her chin into the crook of Cash's neck. "I know. Nobody's mad. But we wanna go home." She lowered her voice to a whisper only her mother could hear. "You're not gonna find her here. Let's go home, Mom."

Cash slowly came to, looking around at the few who had gathered while holding in her bubbling cries. Something in her daughter's voice had reached the right corner of her mind, and her resistance went lax. It was then Lennon realized—though her emotions were magnified with liquor, grief was mainly responsible for this breakdown.

Stacy glanced at Lennon before they exited, hoping she could see the gratitude in his worn face. For a moment, it had really seemed as though Page had come back to Earth and spoke her mother back to sanity. But, as long as their family had been broken for, that moment of togetherness would be twice as fleeting—the Mayfields had never been one for balance.

At some indeterminate point, Lennon had started watching herself from outside her body. Stacy was right, she *did* look terrible. Conrad's mouth was moving, but his voice went in and out. *Like a radio,* she thought with a dazed expression.

"C'mon Lennon, we shouldn't fall too—hey, *hey!* You okay?" Conrad stuck his arms under hers before she fully collapsed. It was

Missing Page

too late for her mind, however. A deafening silence swallowed her, just before darkness came in for the kill.

∼

Consciousness boomeranged back and forth, blurring the lines between dream and reality. Her body felt small, swaying in someone's arms. *I'm dreaming,* she decided, even though it felt frighteningly vivid. Even more terrifying was her paralysis, and the realization of where she must be going.

No. No, no, no!

She had to wake up, but everything was slow and immovable, including her eyes. No, her body had to wake up, otherwise bad things would happen. She didn't want to see the face of the giant that carried her.

Like all the times she'd practiced before, she stopped trying to calm her pounding heart and instead focused all her energy into moving her toes. It felt like an eternity had passed before she felt a flicker in her pinky toe. But it wasn't too late; she was still being carried, could still see flashes of light behind her eyelids. She worked the feeling throughout the rest of her toes, and then her feet. That feeling moved into her fingers, her lips, her nose. Finally Lennon's eyes broke free, allowing dim light to enter through weak lids. Blurry blond hair came into view, and she took a staggered breath. When he looked down at her, she screamed.

She shoved against his chest to jump out of his hold, fighting tooth and nail to get away. Her knees scraped against pavement with an unforgiving sting, but it was the concrete, not the pain, that stopped her. *Concrete?* That wasn't right.

"Stop, Lennon! Lennon!" She felt her dad's hands grasp her, shaking her out of her panic. That was also wrong—her dad didn't belong in this dream-memory hybrid. She choked, relieved beyond belief that it hadn't been a dream after all. The past still lived in the past; it hadn't come back to take her. Gasps forced air back into her lungs, and her eyes fully opened, taking in her surroundings.

They were next to the Bronco; Cash was slumped against the window in the passenger seat, but the back door was still open, waiting for her.

"Did I hurt you?" Conrad asked, looking stricken. She shook her head back and forth quickly, shivering from the adrenaline.

"Conrad, you...I thought..." she whimpered, breaking at the pain in his face.

"I'm so sorry about that, son. For everything. Please forgive us." Stacy shook his hand. "Thank you for all of your help."

"Y...Yeah." Conrad was still unrecovered, watching Lennon. "I'll uh...I'll see you guys tomorrow, then."

"Yes. We'll see you tomorrow." Stacy shut the door, closing Lennon in the bulky car with her mother. Lennon stared down at her bloodied knees, trying to decipher their muffled voices on the other side of the door.

Stacy circled the car, taking his place behind the wheel. Conrad stood for a moment, hands stuffed in his pocket and eyes locked onto the tinted window Lennon was concealed behind. Stacy pulled out of the parking lot, pulling to the side of the road once they made it down the street. He turned to her, eyes wide and slightly accusatory.

"What the hell was that?" he asked.

Shit. Lennon didn't have enough strength or energy for the pinball lever of questions. She bit down on her lip to hold it closed.

"I haven't seen you like that since... that was bad, Len."

She struggled for an answer that would end the conversation. "I passed out. I'm dehydrated—"

"Did he do something to you?"

"No!" she cried out before collecting herself. "No, he never hurt me...I was just...disoriented."

He blew out of a puff of air, frustrated beyond words. The Bronco eased back onto the pavement, engine roaring as they cruised home. *He thinks I'm crazy,* Lennon thought. *And maybe he's right.* He didn't deserve this, any of it.

"Dad?" she asked quietly.

"Yes, dear." He sighed, fighting a yawn.

"I love you. Thanks for...I don't know, sticking around, I guess."

His eyes found hers in the rearview mirror, and he cleared his throat. "You'll never rid of me, Lennon. No matter how hard you try."

She used to think of her dad as the anchor of their family. But right now, as their family's ship was sinking below the surface, she realized he was a life preserver, doing everything in his power to keep them afloat.

A small silver gift bag waited by the entrance of her house. First to the door, Lennon picked it up, squinting at the note; it had her name on it. She stuck two fingers in the small bag, separating the tissue, and felt her blood run cold at the orange that peeked through. She swallowed, clamping the bag shut and tucking it into the coat closet in the cover of night. For one final time, her and her dad banded together to change Cashmere into pajamas and carry her to bed.

"I just needed a break, I'm sorry," her mother sobbed. It was one of the few times she'd ever heard her apologize.

She ran back to the entrance after closing the door, snatching the silver bag and darting to the isolation of her room. Her fingers slipped into the tissue paper again, plucking them to showcase the entire orange case.

A pill bottle that waited at the bottom, complete with a small collection of different colored tabs. A color-coded paper was taped to the bottle, detailed with drug descriptions.

There was a note with it providing only two sentences of context.

Thought you could use some happy pills. Don't forget to share!

Xoxo, Mic

There was no use in trying to stay clean with these girls around. If Lennon wasn't sure this girl didn't give a fuck about her before, she was positive now. Of course these trust-fund babies didn't understand grief or hardship, but were they *trying* to kill her?

Despite her hesitation, a single pill had found its way into her palm. It was a muscle relaxer, according to the code. The weight of her father's and sister's eyes rested on each shoulder as Lennon stared, two angels on the shoulders of a devil.

Justification came so easily in times like these. She hadn't been sleeping nor eating, and ached for relief from her lingering comedown. She *needed* rest for tomorrow, the kind that was deep enough to erase any disruptive dreams.

Functional, she reasoned. *Not for entertainment.*

Lennon placed it on her tongue, swigging from her water bottle to wash it down with a hopeless grimace.

19

Though the coffin stood at the end of the aisle, Lennon felt like the box that carried her sister was right in front of her. Was somebody breathing, or was that her own?

She was a little girl all over again, but the only person she could hide behind was her father, since her eyesight rested just over her mother's hairline. She passed deep blue lilies down the aisle, watching them grow in volume the closer they got. Despite the small capsules of relief still coursing through her, it wasn't enough to prepare her to look inside the casket. This hollow body wouldn't be Page; Lennon guessed her cheeks would be colorless, the smile permanently wiped off her lips. She already had a perfectly beautiful picture of her sister in her mind; hair whipping in the early summer breeze as she pedaled into Laguna's sunset, her cheeks lifted in a smile.

The desire to look was stronger than any magnet, but Lennon was strong—or perhaps scared—enough to keep her eyes down as they walked the aisle filled with whispers from the funeral planner to her mother. Lennon watched her feet like her life depended on it; how was she supposed to get through today? It felt as though any moment she could pass out from the prickly anticipation, and the service hadn't even started. Once she saw her face...

"It's okay, baby," Stacy soothed, rubbing her back. "It's closed."

Her head whipped up, needing to confirm his words. Instead of feeling at ease, another cloud of grief formed in her internal storm, bringing tears like rain down her cheeks. She hadn't expected her choice to be taken from her, and it hurt even more. Lennon counted her inhales while the planner spoke, watching her mother nod every few sentences. Her inner anguish pelted her insides like hail, denting her organs and freezing her blood flow.

"So, we probably won't start *exactly* at eleven," The planner said quietly. "We'll want to give everyone enough time to park, find their seats..."

Noticing her stillness, Stacy reached out for her hand. "Lennon—"

It was too late; Lennon turned and flew down the aisle, disappearing through the wooden doors.

The bathroom was the closest escape. She took a fleeting seconds to scan to the room before doubling over the sink. She heaved like someone had gut punched her, gasping for breath in between.

Lifting her chin, she stared into red-rimmed eyes and watercolored cheeks. Though everything felt monstrous internally, her makeup and genetics kept her fairly put-together; most of her hair was kept secure by a navy, pearl-adorned clip, save for a few strands curling around her face. If she cared, she would think she looked beautiful. Her mother had insisted on this dress from her own closet, and though it would have been too tight a few weeks ago, stress and grief had stripped her curves. The bishop sleeves were long and opaque, the neckline was square and fitted. Most importantly, it covered nearly all of her tattoos—all except the tiny book etched into her collarbone.

Was the damage really so horrid that Page had to be hidden? What did she look like under the cherry mahogany casket? Lennon pulled out her phone, fingers waltzing in stressed debate over the

Missing Page

search tab. She wanted to retake control over her choice, despite knowing she'd see her sister's face in place of every morbid picture. It wasn't likely to make things better, but her moral compass had never worked right. It was compulsivity and weakness that controlled her, influenced by a tortured masochism. Whatever it was, was strong enough to compel her to press enter.

Lennon scrolled through the photos of drowned victims, covering her mouth in horror. Page's eyes reflected in each of them, milky and lifeless. Is this what the ocean had done to her sister? Had it no mercy, even for a little girl? Lennon stifled the pained whimper at the picture of a younger girl with mousy brown hair as a few pairs of heels came in, their bodies concealed behind the stall door.

"I can't believe how many people came. This is crazy," one said in a hushed whisper, her high-pitched voice revealing her youth.

Another laughed humorlessly, speaking in a nasally voice. "Speaking of crazy...did you see her mom? My brother saw her at the bar last night, said she was hysterical."

"A *bar?*" the third asked incredulously. "Last night?"

"It's the *Mayfields*, Nance," the nasally one snorted. "They're all crazy, in their own special ways."

"Page wasn't," the first said. "She was shy, but she was always nice," The soft spoken girl said.

There was a beat. "I mean, something was *bound* to happen eventually, but I think everyone thought it was gonna be Lennon... You thought the mom was crazy? Her sister's borderline psychotic. My brother knew her in high school. She doesn't talk to anyone, doesn't go out except to party...she's always been weird—"

Lennon walked out then, feigning obliviousness as she bent to wash her hands. The girls went white in unison, fear rolling off of them in hot waves while she dried her hands. Finally, Lennon turned to them, keeping her face blank. She took a step forward as the girls all jumped back, lowering her voice.

"I'm not going to do anything, don't worry." She smiled, but there was something sinister behind it. "I just wanted to say that if I see *any* of you in that room when the service starts..."

The girls' eyes widened, glistening with terror.

"I will show you *exactly* how crazy I am."

They nodded fervently, turning and rushing out the door. She followed, only to make sure they turned for the exit instead of the doors. After half a minute, the planner stuck her head out and waved.

"Lennon, honey. Service is about to start."

There were more people than she'd expected; almost every row was filled. The room had seemed much larger that morning, echoing people's voices off its walls like a whispering choir. Now there were dozens—maybe even a hundred—collected in here, all mourning one singular life. There were teens, parents, teachers, family members. Not all of these people knew Page, of course, but they wouldn't miss this for the world. Nothing bad ever happened in Laguna; something of this magnitude was a spectacle, a warning for their own children.

She felt the lingering eyes of her mother as she took her seat. Instead of chastising her, Cashmere lifted her fingers to the clip in Lennon's hair, her nails brushing against the pearls with a foreign gentleness.

Lennon tilted her chin to meet her mother's gaze, glittering with moisture. "You wore her clip."

"Thank you to all those who came to celebrate Page's life today," The priest started, interrupting the brief moment. Cashmere pulled her hand away, moving her focus to the front of the room. "Loved ones, friends..."

Using a priest was an odd choice, in Lennon's opinion. The Mayfields were never religious, and it seemed a little late to start now; none of his words brought the comfort one could hope to receive in a time like this. It wasn't like he'd ever answered her prayers before. She couldn't bring herself to believe in God, not even when she was desperate. If he was real, he was cruel, and the last person she'd want to bring up at the funeral of someone as pure hearted as her sister. Her sister and God had nothing in common.

Missing Page

In her peripheral, she saw her mom squeeze her dad's hand. A new feeling rocked through her, one she thought she'd sealed off forever; loneliness. She ached for Hart's thumb to brush over her healing knuckles and erase her worries as it always did, even if for a moment. She knew her hand would feel safe in his, that his shoulder and her head would fit together like a puzzle piece. Hart always said the right things. And she'd ruined it. Hurt people...well, you know the rest.

Feeling terribly alone in the pew now, she interlocked her own fingers, pretending they were Hart's. Just as a sob began to break through her lips, she felt the weight of her dad's hand cover hers. There was no room for vulnerability—she was sure those girls in the bathroom weren't the only ones hoping for a scene.

Lennon remained in her seat while her parents spoke, nodding in encouragement whenever they looked to her. For some reason, she kept wanting to extend her hand, thinking Page was there needing comforting. That's when it finally sank in—Lennon was no longer an older sister. She'd become an only child again; there was no one to protect, no one to share her experiences with. Though she'd thought it was impossible, grief found another piece of her cratered heart to devastate.

She felt the stares of her peers spreading over her like an itch when she gasped from the pain. Lennon had never ached for that orange bottle more, but tried to think about the small amount of pride she'd felt after resisting. The heat from her finger pads had started to melt the powder of the tab before she dropped it back into the container, but she'd done it.

After the speeches finished, everyone rose from the pews to gather into a line. Lennon went first, placing her body directly behind her father and keeping her eyes to the ground. She didn't want to look at the others' heartbroken eyes that reflected her own, and she definitely didn't need a stranger's pity.

Each person would shake hands or hug her parents before walking forward, letting their fingers brush against the wood. Lennon stiffened when Emery passed, watching her sniffle at the head of the coffin with disgust. Mr. and Mrs. Felton wrapped their daughter in comfort when she began to tremble. Stacy and Cash frowned sympathetically, but Lennon's face was stuck in a scowl, trying to see through a cloudy red haze. *Who invited them?*

Lennon froze when Emery reached out, wincing when she pressed her palm against the mahogany. The girl let out an echoing sob that caused everyone to turn and look, their mouths morphing into pitiful lours. Only the teenagers seemed to know better, watching with grimaces and eye-rolls.

With her blood boiling underneath her skin, Lennon decided right then; if and when she found the final piece to Page's puzzle, she'd remember this exact moment. In case Emery asked for mercy, or forgiveness, Lennon wanted to remember how heartless and calculated one must be to put on a show at her victim's funeral.

Trying to calm herself, Lennon turned to count how many were left. She recognized a few faces—Ricky, Theo, a few girls on Page's soccer team. Even Mrs. Kylie had come to say goodbye, and ended up being the only one to reach out to Lennon, her magnified eyes glossing over when their hands met. Lennon allowed herself to be taken into a hug, feeling the woman's frail hands shaking against her back. She clamped down on her cheeks, needing to feel a pain other than the one stabbing every centimeter of her heart.

"Oh, sweetheart," Mrs. Kylie whispered, after pulling away. "I'm so sorry."

With that, she hobbled a few steps forward, stilling when she reached the end. Her mouth moved in silent prayer over Page's coffin. Lennon pointed her attention to the different pairs of black shoes shuffling past; family members she hadn't seen in years were next in line, an awkward sense of formality weighing over their greetings and apologies. Even combined, their family tree was small. Stacy's parents had died long ago and Cashmere had burned bridges with both of hers, along with her siblings.

Conrad was a welcome face behind his mother's, despite

Missing Page

Lennon's lingering humiliation over their last interaction. He didn't reach for their hands or offer a hug like his mother did. He was quiet, and let Ms. Bates do the talking. Lennon wasn't at all upset with his reclusiveness; this must have felt painfully familiar, an old wound that never healed. At least she'd been too young to attend Wyatt's wake—Conrad was reliving the worst day of his life.

The reception was less dreary. There was more blue than black now, like a slow-healing bruise. Everyone was attempting to celebrate her life now that they had mourned it; Page's friends shared their favorite memories, smiles sprouting out of heartbreak's seedlings. Her teachers spoke of how much they had looked forward to seeing her every day and how hard she worked. Interestingly, in everyone's story, she was referred to as some kind of light in their life, shining especially during hard times. *How radiant you must be to sun-soak people's darkest moments,* Lennon thought. She had learned how powerful love could be through pain, but it was nice to see it in its true form.

People's quiet murmurs became a loud buzz as the speeches droned on, which begun feeling more about the speakers than her sister anyway. Rowan and the twins came to give their condolences during a young girl's stuttering, tear-stricken speech. They wrapped Lennon in a big, unsolicited group hug, as if all past transgressions had been forgotten.

"The service was beautiful," Macy gushed.

Lennon nodded with clenched teeth through their compliments, wishing they'd get it over with. This was charity to them, not support.

"I should probably check on my parents—" Lennon started with a clearing of her throat, shifting her weight to her outward foot.

"Wait, we need to decide what we're doing for Fourth of July! It's a month away, Len, and we gotta make this the best vacation ever. We should go...*away*. Far, far away," Michaela suggested dreamily. "Cuba sound good to anyone?"

"*No*," Macy vetoed instantly. "It doesn't. You don't celebrate

Independence Day in another country. But you know what *does* sound good? Ha-wai-ee!"

Rowan rubbed his hands together, preparing their pitch. "Okay, hear me out...I thought it'd be cute to give the ol' country club another shot."

The idea was immediately met with groans of protest from the twins. Lennon was too emotionally exhausted to hide the disinterest in her dull gaze, instead scouting the room.

"Literally—" Rowan moved their finger in a zipper motion. "I *don't* want to hear it. Your rec was *Cuba*...are you *trying* to get kidnapped and sold into sex trafficking?"

"I'm *trying* to think ahead," Michaela snapped back. "There's easy—and *cheap*—access to things that make vacations fun!"

She glanced at Lennon for backup, but the girl had disengaged from the conversation long ago, now watching people add to the already overflowing gift table.

"*Cheap!* Who cares about cheap, you're a fucking True!" Rowan cried.

Envelopes, picture boards, and black tissue-stuffed bags covered almost every inch of the cobalt-clothed table. She didn't know people were supposed to bring gifts to a funeral—they *were* dead, after all. What could they need?

A girl excused herself past the group then, catching Lennon's attention. Her hair was the color of oil, her red-rimmed eyes a deep oak; she stuck out like a sore thumb against the sea of blondes. Lennon's lip curled once her eyes fully focused, the hackles on her neck raising.

"...well, if we brought enough guys, it wouldn't be a problem. Have you talked to him, Lennon?"

"Hmm?" Her head swiveled back, unsure of which girl asked.

"Trick," Michaela repeated impatiently. "Have you talked to him since we went out?"

"Yeah. It's fine," Lennon said, purposefully short. They'd

overstayed their welcome, but refused to leave her alone. She needed to keep an eye on Emery...

"Well, he's not here...." Michaela pointed out.

Lennon looked at her head-on so that Michaela could receive the full extent of her glare. "Obviously it's not fine, Mic. Look around, does anything look *fine* to you? We're not here to gossip and plan vacations, so take a fucking hint and show some respect." There was enough venom in her voice to make the girls shrink back, and Rowan's brows lifted.

She hated when she could hear her mother's voice woven in with her own. Her breath caught, eyes lowering. "Sorry."

Macy spoke in her twin's place. "No, you're, uh...you're going through a lot right now, we shouldn't—"

"No, it's no excuse. Really, Michaela. I'm sorry."

Arms still crossed, Michaela nodded tightly, although a little smug. She'd gotten her story.

Utterly humiliated, Lennon looked to each of them in a final, silent apology. "I should, uh...I'm gonna check on my parents."

She walked toward her father while scouring for the girl she'd lost sight of. It didn't take long; Lennon's fingers twitched around her water when Emery came back into view, stopped at the gift table. Conrad's tall frame was leaned over just next to her, completely oblivious as he scribbled into the memorial book.

"I thought that was you. Good to see you, brother," her father said from behind. Her ears tuned in briefly to a heavy, labored breathing behind her, mentally flipping through the list of Stacy's close friends. Most of them were all gym rats, like him...

From across the room, partly skewed, Emery held something small in her hands while she closed her eyes. She mouthed something silently, took a deep breath, and then plunged her hand out of sight behind the black bags. As if the girl could feel the piercing stares of her peers burning into her back, she pivoted quickly, searching for the source.

Just as Lennon stepped forward to pounce, a heavy hand gripped her shoulder. The force of it sloshed the water out of her bottle and onto the floor with a splash loud enough to draw eyes. She whipped her murderous glare to the assailant, only to realize it was her father.

"Look who it is, Len," he said.

She followed his gaze to the heavy-set man with a pair of cold, beady brown eyes in front of them. Her mouth had parted to say hello, but now was stuck open in shock. The quiet that followed was as if the world too had stopped, and sucked out all the air with it.

WHOOSH

Their voices fizzled to a high-pitched ringing in her ears. She hadn't seen Mr. Bates since the accident, but adrenaline and fear swirled inside her as if he'd never left. Lennon truly thought she would never see him again after he moved up north, much less at her sister's wake. Conrad had been difficult enough—now her entire world was crashing around her. Flashes of images and sounds started to flood her mind, threatening a breakdown, but she fought to stay in the present with every blink, every shallow breath.

"What are you doing here?" She choked on her words. Her dad looked at her strangely, confused by her reaction, but Mr. Bates seemed to pay no mind.

"You guys are family. I wanted to pay my respects." A goatee wrapped around his thin lips, hiding a dimpled chin. There were more lines around his eyes and lips than she remembered, and he'd gained considerable weight; the sweat beading at his thinning hairline seemed ever-present. His eyes were a few shades darker than Conrad's—identical to his late son's—and impaling, as if trying to see inside her head.

Finally, Mr. Bates bowed his head. "I'm so sorry for your loss."

"I can't tell you how much this means to us, Devin." Stacy nodded, struggling to keep his composure. "And I'm sorry this is how we meet again."

"Me, too."

Stacy's eyes widened, realizing something. "I can't imagine what this must be—"

Missing Page

Mr. Bates finally broke away from Lennon, nodding to her father. "I appreciate the concern. That's exactly why I wanted to be here... you guys were there for us, through everything."

"Thank you, brother. We appreciate you being here."

Lennon winced at her dad's words, cutting through like a thousand knives.

"The most important thing you can do is keep her memory alive. Forgetting has been the worst part."

"We've never forgotten," Lennon said with a subtle sneer. A quiet moment followed. It seemed like only Devin and Lennon were aware of the weight of her words, while Stacy nodded in naive agreement.

"Devin? What a surprise!" Her mother echoed her father's words as she took him into a tight hug. Lennon couldn't stop the building anxiety; the contents of her breakfast would tumble out of her any minute. Having reached her limit, Lennon ducked away, forcing her attention back to the table.

She rummaged through as quietly as she could, trying not to draw attention. So far, she'd only found cards, trinkets, an out of place calculator, probably from Conrad...

A reflective blue piece came into view, sticking out from the other black gift bags. She reached out and took it into her palms, processing with the speed of an overloaded computer. *A shot glass.* The base was deep and moss green; most of the glass was a slightly transparent blue, except for a few clear air pockets at the top giving it a bubble-like appearance. It could have been beautiful, she supposed—if her sister hadn't died from drowning and intoxication.

There was no note, no tag revealing who had brought it. She whipped around, but the girl was already missing from the crowd. *Of course she was.* She checked to make sure Mr. Bates had left before marching to her parents.

"Did you see this?" she fumed, lifting up the glass.

They looked equally confused. "What is that?"

"A *shot glass.*" She trembled with fury. "Guess who brought it?"

Stacy's knowing expression wasn't what she expected; he looked tired rather than angry. "Lennon—"

"*Dad*," she retorted.

He pursed his lips. "Did you *see* her put it down?"

Her throat tightened, making it difficult to get the word out. "No."

"Look, I couldn't even tell what it was at first," Cashmere murmured. "It could be decoration. It lacks thought, sure. But Lennon, honey, you have a nasty habit of seeing the worst in everything—"

"How else am I supposed to see this? She was drinking and *drowned* to death! This isn't 'lacking taste,' Mom, it's...she's mocking us!"

Cashmere caught the glances from passerby, smiling reassuringly before whispering in her daughter's ear. "You're going to lower your voice," Cashmere warned. "And if you need to take a break, we can go outside. But you will not make a scene here—you will *not* ruin this."

Lennon narrowed her eyes, laughing darkly. "You won't let *me* ruin this?"

Cashmere's stare hardened, glowing embers burning in the blacks of her eyes. Instinct prickled over her daughter's skin, an embedded defense shooting up her spine. In a last effort, Lennon looked to her dad. Stacy cleared his throat and begrudgingly placed his hand on her shoulder, shaking his head. Lennon's nostrils flared as betrayal rammed through her. They wanted peace over the truth, and Page wasn't even in the ground yet.

"*Fine.*" Lennon slung her crossbody over her shoulder, already mapping out the quickest path home in her head. "I'm going. Call me if you need to be picked up from the bar again."

She put up a good fight against the tsunami building behind her eyes. But a half-mile into her walk home, a tear broke the dam, and an endless stream followed. The birds and elements orchestrated a song around her quiet sobs, giving her safety in her solitude. The sun was

Missing Page

warm today, caressing her skin like a soothing mother. People normally wished for rain and gloomy weather under circumstances like these, but Lennon thought this felt fitting. It was the light Page's peers all talked about.

She heard the engine first. Lennon wondered who could be the only other person in town not at her sister's funeral, but wasn't curious enough to look. Even stranger, rather than passing her, the engine eased into a following pace behind her. Lennon's heart picked up a half-beat, preparing for the worst as she turned. But she recognized the soft yellow truck, and the driver too.

"Your dad said you left," Conrad called over the loud engine, rolling down the window. "They're heading to the cemetery. I figured you were going home, but they asked me to— "

"I'm not going," she snarled, staring ahead.

"I didn't think you were. I was gonna offer you a ride, actually. Figured those shoes would be killing you."

Her heels scraped against the pavement, and an anguished scream coiled beneath her tongue. It leaked from her eyes instead, and she reached to wipe them with shaky fingers. "God, it was so…I couldn't stay there another second."

"I get it," He nodded.

"It's bullshit!" she exclaimed. "And your dad…I can't believe he came."

"I didn't know, either. I guess my mom told him about everything. I didn't find out he was coming until after he'd already gotten on a plane."

Lennon swallowed. She was crumpling like paper inside a fist, weak against the pressure of grief. "I couldn't—it was too much. This entire day has been blow, after blow, after… I keep thinking it's gonna be over, then something else just…"

"If I had known he was coming, I would have told you. I know how hard that was for you. It was hard for me, too."

Lennon looked at him cautiously, holding her breath. *Was it? Did he understand her fear of those beady eyes?*

"It's like looking at a ghost," he mumbled.

She exhaled as her brows pulled together, opting for silence. He pressed on the brake, and she instinctively stopped with it.

"Come on. I can drive you home."

She shook her head. "I need to think."

"It wasn't actually a question." Conrad cleared his throat apologetically. "Cash's orders."

"You don't work for her anymore!"

"I'm not stupid enough to tell that woman no. She's terrifying," Conrad shuddered.

She glowered at him. "You're almost double her size."

"I don't think she cares about that."

She huffed. It's not like he could force her in, but if he went back alone, it was likely he'd receive the brunt of Cash's anger. While Lennon was used to repercussions, she couldn't inflict them onto someone else in good conscience, especially if it was preventable. And, if she were being truthful, the loneliness was gnawing at her.

She sighed, lifting her foot to step into the ancient Toyota.

"Are you feeling better from yesterday?" he asked, once the noisy truck settled.

Her cheeks flushed with shame. "Oh—yeah. I'm really sorry about that, by the way...think I was just disoriented when I woke up."

"Don't apologize. I was just worried about you."

She peered around, eager to shift the subject from his uncomfortable pity. "This is quite a relic you got here."

He patted the wheel absentmindedly. "It's all right. She's an old girl, on her last legs." His hand moved expertly with the gearshift, flowing like it was an extension of him.

"I drive stick, too."

"Yeah? What kind?"

Her brows furrowed. "The Jeep. At the gas station, remember?"

Conrad faltered for a moment, glancing at her. "That's yours?"

Her smile was confused. "Who else's?"

He shrugged. "Your mom made it seem like it was kind of a...

throwaway car, like for off-roading and stuff. She let me borrow it while my truck was in the shop. I figured you'd brought yours to school."

So *that's* what Cash's master negotiating skills had consisted of. Lennon resisted rolling her eyes. His thought process wasn't hard to follow. As preposterous as it sounded, 'college cars' were a common thing, and Lennon hadn't done herself any favors by hanging out with the kids who had them. It was only natural he'd extended that perception to her, as well.

"No. I took the bus, or walked. Until Hart..." She trailed off, feeling a stab of pain at the mention of his name. Before that loss could interweave with the others she was currently juggling, she changed the subject. "So she gave you my car? How long?"

"Few weeks," he admitted, avoiding her gaze now. "I'm sorry. I really didn't—"

"It's fine." She sighed. "I usually bike, anyway."

Her thighs, calves, and ass were evidence of that, although it was a little less full since depression had stolen her appetite. Her bony figure settled into the seat, fingernails trailing absentmindedly over the scratchy material.

"Did you see Emery leave anything at the gift table?"

He thought for a moment. "I don't remember seeing her at all, actually."

Their conversation ended on that note. She opened the door before he even parked, narrowly missing her head as she ducked out. "Thanks for the ride."

20

Lennon only made it halfway up the stairs before her legs gave out. She had to crawl on her hands and knees to her bedroom, reaching one wobbly hand in front of the other. *They didn't even let me see her...*

Everything was finally processing, all through the lens of excruciating pain. Her arms stretched out in front of her on the floor, nails digging into the carpet as she gasped for air that wouldn't come. It had to come out—she was in agony holding it inside. A wail filled her mouth, powerful enough to shake every part of her body. It touched each corner of her little tower over and over, in constant waves that made the ocean look lazy in comparison. With each gasp, her nails dug deeper into the carpet, aching for some sort of relief.

With time, her sobs weakened into whimpers, she turned her head to press a wet cheek against the floor. A flash of orange peeked at her from under the bed; without thinking, two fingers and a thumb crept tiredly across the ground, closing around plastic and pulling it back to her chest. The lid opened with a crisp *pop*.

Lennon had never felt so desperate, so miserable. She wanted to be done, but how was she supposed to bear this pain on her own? For the first time, she finally felt as though the poison she'd bottled up throughout her life might finally be potent enough to kill her. If she didn't take this, she was sure she would die.

She stared lifelessly at the ceiling after swallowing, watching the colors of her room bloom in front of her, but unable to enjoy it. Outside, the wind began to whisper, gossiping with the birds.

"Lennon!"

She sat up and checked over her shoulder. Her room was empty, but the voice had come from behind her; was someone playing a trick?

She didn't remember deciding to move, but somehow she'd left her floor, walking through the mini-kitchen as if puppeteered. She opened the door that led downstairs, faced with a landing void of life —no one would have been able to disappear that quickly. Paranoid fear prickled the hairs on her arm, and the air felt thick with the kind of tension you get just before a jump scare in a horror movie.

Now that it wasn't a hurdle to breathe, she went through the motions of a shower, rinsing off all the hands that had touched her today. The water was extra hot, turning her skin a deep red; her nerves cried out when she drug an exfoliator over them, begging to ease up.

"Lennnnnon," the voice called again, singing now. She gasped this time, clutching at her throat where it caught.

The sun had said goodnight by the time she exited, wrapping herself in a terrycloth robe. She turned every light on before pulling a hairbrush through her tangles, trying to ignore the intermittent voice calling out for her. Her reflection caught her attention after a moment, eliciting a snort—she'd been using the backside of her brush.

To most, that might be the telltale sign to sign off for the day, but she wasn't quite ready. She never was, but this time there was something real keeping her from it, anchoring her in consciousness.

Something drew her to her sister's closet. The scent of Page's perfume hit her as soon as the doors opened, causing Lennon's lower lip to tremble. The chemicals went to work right on cue, dulling her back into a numb state, and she was able to stuff her limbs through the sleeves of Page's favorite hoodie and into drawstring sweatpants. Lennon sat there for a long moment hugging her knees to her chest, breathing in the memory of her sister. Soon this would go missing, too.

Again the whispers came. Her brows furrowed—it *was* the pills, right? The line between reality and her mind was melding together, becoming impossible to distinguish. She decided to follow it this time, letting the calls lead her to the living room. It only took a minute of silence to feel silly and want to give up. *So stupid...*

It hissed from all around, startling her. "Lennon!"

That was real, right? It had to be. She rushed to the balcony, her bare feet cold against the wooden deck.

It became embarrassingly clear, then, that there were no ghosts. The whispers she'd heard were from the wind whipping against the lime-wash walls combined with the crickets singing in the greenery below. The fear dissipated, replaced with awe at her view. Her vision was dizzying, but the things she could see were beautiful; above, the moon cast a black glow over the ocean, calm and collected. The energy of the cove could be felt coursing through the air, drawing her almost involuntarily. It was so alluring she didn't notice the lounge chair in front of her, tripping and hurdling to the ground at wince-inducing speeds.

She sacrificed the flesh of her palms to save her nose, hissing with the sting that came when they slammed against the wood. She moaned, before slowly lifting herself to her feet.

Is this what her life would be now? She'd already felt lost out in the world, but home no longer brought comfort. Not even the balcony could fill that void, for now it served as a perfect view of the cove that harbored the final moments of Page's life.

Something darker than night glinted under the soft moon, drawing her eyes to the anomaly. She blinked, sure she was hallucinating again. But alas, the shadow glinted again at the mouth, exposed under the moon's dim light. Lennon rushed to the railing—

making sure to move around the chair this time—and leaned forward to get a better look.

It didn't leave when she blinked. A dark, human-like figure stood at the mouth, barely moving. She didn't believe in the paranormal, but something felt off to her, as if it were aware of her presence. Lennon tried to chalk it up to drugged visions again, and she got close; except that it dove into the water, shooting up a spray of water and ripples in its wake.

She barreled through the sliding glass door, sprinting out and down the street. Bare feet traversed over smooth pavement, and then cold sand. The impact was painful and felt like bricks against her ankles, but the muscle relievers made it bearable. She might be able to catch the shadow, if she was fast enough.

Without the bike, it took six minutes to reach the entrance. She steadied herself against the wall while she caught her breath, clutching her wheezing chest. Every droplet sounded like an explosion; combined with the darkness, this cove became more terrifying than whimsical. The tide pooled around her, claiming her calves; there was little time before things turned dangerous. The flashlight of her phone was weak, but she held it above her head, squinting for any evidence that the figure had been real.

"I won't hurt you," Lennon called. "Just show yourself."

Condensation dripped from the ceiling, counting the seconds. *Was it her, or was the cave breathing?* She thought of a whale's mouth as gusts of wind traveled back and forth; it wanted to swallow her, take her just like it had Page. This had all been a trap, a collaboration of mind and nature.

Lennon's head was low as she stumbled out. It was the same cursed cycle—following whatever trouble her warped mind led her to, and somehow escaping without a scratch. Not even her sister had made it through. Why was the universe so insistent on preserving a life that didn't care to be saved? She had nothing to give, nothing to cherish—just a house she didn't feel at home in, operating a body that didn't feel like hers.

Maybe there is a God, she thought, *but he must not be all-powerful.*

It would be the only possible way for him to exist in her mind. Because if he was all-powerful, then there was no way he was all-good; the two could not coexist.

Her luck only ran so far. She'd gotten out alive, but it'd never promised to get her home. The last thing she remembered was feeling the cool sand between her fingers, and then under her cheek. After that she could only see the stars, even after she'd closed her eyes.

∽

When Lennon awoke, she thought she was dying. It wasn't pain that brought this conclusion, but a deep crimson staining her duvet and white T-shirt.

The blanket cracked when she peeled it away, raining sand over her bare skin. How had she gotten back home? Her stomach came into view first, appearing unharmed. The blood stains were too high to be from her period, which she wasn't expecting for another week. It was when she lifted her bloodied hands that she realized the culprit.

The skin around her nails was caked with dried blood, layers ripped off in different degrees on almost every finger. She must have picked them in her sleep.

Panic wasn't the right word. Death didn't scare Lennon—if anything, it was long overdue. It was more disgust—not only at her current state, but that she *wasn't* dying. What a waste of hope. Confusion came next, unable to recall anything after she stumbled out of the cove.

Her fingers were sore to the touch, raw enough to elicit a sharp hiss when she tried to sterilize them with alcohol. She stripped off her shirt and entered the bathroom, twisting the faucet handles. Cries erupted involuntarily as the water traveled over her wounds—she had peeled clear around the pads of her fingers. The rest of the sand trailed down her legs, swirling around the drain in a useless fight against fate.

The family med-kit was buried in the bottom drawer of their entry table, and only had eight bandages left. Lennon let her left ring and right pinky be the odd fingers out, since they were the least damaged. The plan had been to dart unseen into the laundry room, but her mother was sitting at the dining table, flipping through mail.

"What's all over your shirt?" Cashmere asked, narrowing her eyes at the clump in her daughter's hand.

Lennon froze, caught red handed. "Uh...blood. We're out of Band-Aids, by the way."

Cashmere shook her head, curling her lips. "I can't believe you're doing that shit again."

She must not know Lennon went to the cove, otherwise she would have already started berating her. *Better not to bring it up,* she thought.

"I didn't mean to. It happened in..." She gave up, knowing her words were useless. Cash's heels clicked forward, stopping in front of her daughter. She grabbed Lennon's hands, lifting them for closer inspection.

"Jesus, Lennon. They'll ruin if you keep this up. You'll have old lady hands by twenty-five, all scarred and wrinkly."

Lennon's eyes widened, her mouth opening in faux worry. "But what about my hand-modeling career?" With that, she pulled her hand out of Cashmere's grasp, rubbing her wrist.

"Just don't complain to me when it happens." Cash said snippily. "They don't have surgery or Botox for that."

Someone's extra feisty this morning. Must be left over from yesterday. "How was the rest of the service?" Lennon adjusted the shirt in her arms, hoping to change course,

"It was fine. We were all very disappointed you that you didn't come...we could've used your support. Can't say I'm surprised, though. It's not like you've ever stayed for the hard parts before." She'd managed to pick a fight out of that, too. Lennon knew what this was, now; Cashmere wanted her own distraction, and the quickest route was chaos.

"You asked me to leave. I was trying to respect your wishes."

"You were trying to punish us," Cashmere snapped. "Making sure everyone was as miserable as you were, as always."

"You have no idea what I was thinking, or feeling." Lennon kept her eyes to the marble bar, staring at a bowl of cereal growing soggier by the minute.

"I'm your mother, Lennon. I think I have a better idea than most."

"Then you know how hard it was for me to see Devin? Or Emery, who shouldn't have even *been* there. I can't believe you invited her!"

"So that gives you an excuse to make a scene? For Christ's sake, the girl's fifteen, you're being ridiculous!"

"I wasn't trying to make a scene. I'm allowed to have a reaction, I have feelings."

"Your 'reaction' was selfish and *embarrassing*," Cash interrupted. "Lennon, I can and will not try to justify your behavior any longer. You've been babied long enough. You think I was hard on you before?"

Lennon laughed humorlessly. "You're right. I better be careful, or else I'll wind up dead, too—"

The slap rang like a shot through the air. Lennon pressed her palm to her stinging cheek, realizing the magnitude of her words. She hadn't meant it that way, though she now saw her error.

"How *dare* you," Cash whispered, breathless.

If Page were still here, this is when Lennon would tip-toe downstairs, and seek asylum in her room. Page would try to make her laugh and forget about whatever was hurting, but even that would have to be a quiet exchange; if Cash heard laughter after a fight, it sent her even deeper into rage. Nobody could have fun while she was upset.

She went down anyway. The closest she could get to Page would be guessing that final password.

Missing Page

Emery—071103—project—beautifulboy—
After the fifth lockout, giving her an hour-long cooldown, her hope had frayed down to the last thread. Lennon might never read this last entry. It felt strange, knowing there could be pieces of Page she'd never get to see—or in this case, read.

I should've written those down, she thought, extending a few bandaged fingers to Page's nightstand. She fished around for a piece of paper and pen, jotting down all the passwords she remembered entering.

"Lennon..." Cash's voice said her name softly from the door. The girl lifted her head, meeting a pair of glistening eyes.

"What's wrong?" Lennon asked, immediately stiffening.

Cash took a few steps toward her. To Lennon's utter shock, she kneeled in front of her, taking her daughter's injured hand in hers. Just as she was about to ask what was going on, Cashmere lifted her manicured fingers to her daughter's recovering cheek, holding an unprecedented sensitivity.

"I'm sorry," she whispered, her thumb brushing over Lennon's freckled skin.

Lennon was frozen. She couldn't remember those words leaving her mother's mouth before and had no idea how to react. Would Cash take offense if she said that she forgave her? Would it be worse to say nothing? Was this a trap?

"What?" Lennon finally responded.

"I...I don't like how I've been handling things. I don't like the way our relationship has been going—is going...I just..." She sucked in a deep breath. "God forbid anything happened to you or me, and that was our last interaction? Lennon, I haven't been a very good mother these past few weeks, and I'm so sorry."

Then, she uttered a sob—a real, genuine cry. Tears rolled down her cheeks, her voice changing as her nose filled with mucus. "You don't have to forgive me. I know I've handled things wrong, I would understand if you don't forgive me." Her body quivered with vulnerability, and she squeezed her daughter's hand even tighter.

"But I would like to make these past few weeks up to you. Would you let me do that?"

Cashmere never admitted she was wrong. Not for anything, even the little things; it had become a bit of a running joke for her, like it was quirky to refuse to be accountable. She had *definitely* never given someone the choice to forgive her. Lennon couldn't remember a time where she had ever seen her mother in this state—it was jarring, almost frightening.

Nothing Cashmere suggested could make up for years of neglect and abuse. But something in this seemed true, and heartfelt; Lennon didn't want to discourage her from trying. "Thank you for apologizing," she started slowly. "I appreciate that, Mom. Really."

Cashmere sniffled, wiping her eyes.

"I...er...I don't really need anything from you, though."

"We haven't spent much time together since you got back. I know things have changed since Christmas..." She broke off, clearly struggling. "Let me take you out to dinner. You and I could use some one-on-one time."

Dinner left lots of room for one of them to say the wrong thing and mess up everything that was happening right now. Why was she rushing this? Cash had to know real forgiveness came only with time.

"Mom—"

"C'mon, Len. Anywhere you want," she pleaded. Lennon cleared her throat, trying to give herself time to think. This act was obviously more for Cashmere's peace of mind than hers; she must have had a rare moment of guilt, a feeling she couldn't bear. She needed this dinner to live with herself.

"Okay. Okay, yeah. You wanna go to The Deck?"

Cash's elation contrasted strangely against her tear-stained cheeks and swollen eyes. "Perfect. I have some meetings, and a showing, so I wanna say..." She counted on her fingers. "Seven thirty?"

Lennon nodded. "Seven thirty, sounds great."

"Perfect. And we'll bring some back for Dad so he's not grumpy."

Missing Page

She didn't recognize this woman at all. Was she having a psychotic break? Cash patted her leg, kissed her hair, and left as quickly as she had entered.

Lennon tried to scribble more entry attempts onto the piece of paper, summoning the last few drops of ink with vigorous shaking. But it was done for; no amount of resuscitation would bring it back to life. She went for the nightstand again, glancing up at the clock which read two o'clock; if the wait time kept increasing like it did, she only had a few more attempts before she'd have to start getting ready.

A crumpled piece of paper cut through her skin during the rummaging. She lifted the knuckle to her mouth, trying to alleviate the pain of her new paper cut. Hadn't her hands been through enough? She smoothed the culprit on the nightstand and faltered at the smeared ink. Page never kept clutter.

There was a short string of words displayed across the paper. They were messy and cut off a few sentences in, but words nonetheless.

Sorry about my clumsiness—I was kinda nervous ;) I got them online, but I hope its cl

Always the perfectionist, Page had given up after a small mistake. Lennon rolled her eyes in amusement. She *would* toss a paper over one imperfect letter. This finding did bring a slight ping of happiness; uncovering anything new about her sister made it feel like she was still alive, if only for a moment.

Lennon continued pondered the note as she put away dishes and swept the floor. Whom had it been intended for? It took hours to clean the house and was nearly dark by the time she threw away the last antibacterial wipe, but she still hadn't come up with any answers when the time came to get ready.

A black off-shoulder sweater stood out in her closet when she first opened the doors, one of the few clothing items her mother gifted that she actually liked. Kaiser huffed with boredom from the bed as she sponged concealer and blush into her skin, tapping her tired skin into perfection. It was during her last coat of mascara that a light bulb finally came.

The note said it was from online, idiot. Just check her orders.

She had to leave soon, but it would only cost a few minutes and clicks to get to the site. Lennon sprinted downstairs, her hair bouncing in pins. Page had Etsy bookmarked, placed at the top. *Profile, Orders...*

She stared at the results, dumbfounded. Page's most recent purchase was a little less than a month ago, and oddly enough, Lennon recognized the item. A pair of shot glasses with a deep, moss green to blue gradient. Flecks of gold and bubbles sprinkled at the top, identical to the one she had seen at the funeral. That was one... but where was its pair?

Was this a draft of the note Page was finalizing the night she died? Lennon remembered how fast she'd clutched it to her chest when she entered. Of course she'd want to hide this; it'd raise too many questions. Lennon wished she knew the questions Page was worried about being asked, though. *That* was the key.

Her parents might know, but she couldn't risk it, especially now. Her father was out of the question, at least until she gained back his trust. It seemed she might've made a breakthrough with her mom, but if this didn't go over well, it could ruin everything.

This letter was a clue—a great clue—but not the entire puzzle piece. She was self-aware enough to see that it could seem trivial to anyone else, or maybe entirely unimportant.

Her watch beeped at her, letting her know it was time to go. Arriving late would definitely start things off on the wrong foot. She hurried upstairs, removed her pins and swiped gelled palms over her flyways, smoothing her waves into a sleek ponytail. *No hat tonight.* She hoped her mom noticed the effort she was putting into this.

At 7:20, her white Jeep slid into The Deck's parking lot, letting the valet open her door.

Missing Page

"Ms. Mayfield, it's been a while." the short man said with a smile, pouring unabashedly over her. She nodded awkwardly, turning to take in the view. The outside lights were dim, giving the moon all its glory to reflect off the ocean's waves and into the restaurant's windows. The call of the seagulls overhead disappeared once she stepped inside, approaching the host stand in a timid manner. A large mirror stood in a half-moon behind her, and Lennon accidentally caught her reflection. She needed to touch up her roots; her natural dark brown was starting to grow in, and brunette was Page's thing, not hers. Otherwise, it was the closest she'd looked to normal in a while. She looked...pretty.

Blegh.

"Hello," The hostess barely shot her a glance before returning her attention to her computer. "Do you have a reservation?"

"Er...maybe–"

"Last name?" She held her fingers above the screen readily.

"Mayfield," Lennon said, matching her impatience. The hostess finally looked up then, swallowing nervously. Was that look because because of her sister, her mother, or her? She didn't look older than seventeen, so Lennon was willing to bet it was Page or herself. Her stories were notorious here, passed around to this day as legend amongst the youth, and as warning for the adults.

"Oh, Len—Ms. Mayfield. Hello. Let me just..." She typed for a few moments, and then frowned. "Hmm...I'm not seeing anything. Could it be under—"

Lennon interrupted her this time. "No, she probably got busy. Just a table for two, please."

"Would you like to sit at the bar?"

"A booth. As far away from the bar as possible, please."

Despite getting a booth tucked into a corner on the opposite side, the restaurant was tiny enough that the bar was still visible. *So much for out of sight, out of mind.* She clasped her hands together, trying to take deep breaths. She'd only have a few minutes before hearing those heels click toward her.

At 7:28, she texted her mom, asking for an ETA. At 7:40, she got a response.

Had to pick some stuff up from the market. Should be there by 8.

She was *grocery shopping?* Lennon switched apps, tracking her mother down in their family app. She took a deep breath through her nose, trying to calm herself down.

Cashmere was lying.

Her location was near the store, but Lennon knew that a tavern resided next door. Lennon breathed again, trying to exercise patience and place herself inside her mother's mind. Being vulnerable and apologetic probably constituted as a long day to her; with work, as well as that moment between the two of them this morning, maybe her nerves had piled too high.

Eight came and went. Then it was 8:30, and her waiter was asking if she wanted to place an order again, sounding as annoyed as Lennon felt.

"You don't want an appetizer or anything?" he asked.

"Sure, I'll take one." She kept her tone light, trying not to take her anger out on him. "Surprise me."

"I, well, what do you—okay," He sighed, giving up and walking away.

She wouldn't normally feel this let down; after all, this was perfectly Cash of her. But it stung extra to realize her mother hadn't meant anything she'd said in Page's room. The tears, the apologies... all of that had simply served to ease the guilt eating her in that moment. Lennon could send another text, but why give her more ammunition to disappoint? Either she'd reply with another excuse, or be too drunk to respond at all. Both would hurt.

"Sorry, miss, you can't smoke in here." An approaching waitress stage-whispered.

Lennon slowly pulled the pen out of her mouth, finishing her inhale before she spoke. "Gotcha." Her words came with a plume of smoke, wafting toward the ceiling and casting a haze of light over the already dim room.

Missing Page

The waitress pursed her lips as she set a steaming bowl of Brussel sprouts down. Professionalism kept her from yelling, but the sound of her feet stomping away made her feelings clear, murmuring in a hushed tone to a coworker.

Lennon stabbed a fork into the vegetable, jaw tight as she chewed. How could a mother do this? How could Cashmere break down, beg for forgiveness, and fuck up the first time she tries to make it better? It hadn't even been twelve hours. The weed wasn't working; it was just sending her into an endless loop. *This was so shitty of Mom. Page is gonna—*

Page couldn't do anything. Page was dead.

Lennon felt the betrayal deep in her bones, but more than that, she just felt stupid. It was stupid thinking tears meant change, that it meant anything other than Cash's inability to look at herself in the mirror. And when it finally came down to it, she'd chosen a bottle, a vice, over her own daughter. It felt like Cash had slapped her again, but this one stung much, much worse.

21

She'd only been able to stomach two more Brussel sprouts before tucking her head into her crossed arms on the table. It was because of that view that Lennon was able to see shadows of black shoes approaching before she heard them, and prepared herself for another barrage of questions or complaints.

"Would you like—"

"I told you, I'm *fine!*" she snarled. Lennon lifted her glare to find Conrad, with that same surprised expression she always seemed to draw out of him.

The pen fell through her fingers, bouncing against the table with a soft thud. She could tell he'd meant to be teasing, but had quickly rethought at her tone.

"I was just gonna ask if you'd like some company."

Her eyes squeezed shut in shame. He always happened to be there right when she lost her temper—or sanity. "I'm sorry. Shit, I'm sorry...yeah, have a seat."

Conrad trying to fit all six foot three of himself into the booth was a gentle reset. He grunted as he got comfortable and smiled after, which she returned, although hers was much weaker. If only she could forget her outbursts as easily as he did.

"How—what are you doing here?" she asked, feeling slow.

"Well, *I* came for a drink, but then I saw you sitting here all by yourself. I thought if I sat with you, you'd feel better...now I'm kind of regretting it."

Despite his wink, she grimaced. "I'm sorry."

He waved it dismissively, but Lennon's chin remained shamefully buried in her fists. He watched her, frowning. "What happened?"

She chuckled darkly. "I got stood up."

"Oh." He furrowed his brow.

"By my mother," she finished.

"*Oh*," he repeated, frowning. "Damn. That's...uh, that's unfortunate."

"She has a ten percent show-up rate, anyway." She shrugged.

"That shouldn't be the way things are." Conrad said genuinely, not letting her make light of it. "I'm sorry."

Lennon eyes followed his gaze down to her pen and held it forward in offering. He shook his head, and she placed it between her lips with a shrug, taking a small drag. "You can stay if you want, but don't feel obligated. I know I'm shitty company."

"You're not shitty. Even if you were, so what? You've earned a shitty moment or two."

"That's..." She had prepared something sarcastic, expecting a less understanding response from him. His words were disarming. "...nice of you, actually."

He didn't look away from the window, which she was grateful for, but she had a feeling it wasn't the view that had brought a smile to his lips.

She pursed her lips, intertwining her fingers in her lap. "I've been curious about that, actually."

"Hm?" he said, finally looking to her.

"Why *do* you want to hang out with me?"

He chuckled. "What d'you mean?"

"I'm not...pleasant to be around. I told you we couldn't be friends. I'm not nice—"

Conrad was amused now. "How would you describe yourself, Lennon?"

"Difficult. Hard to get along with. Maybe even a bitch, depending on the day—"

"Bitch or not, at least you're real. That's about as much as anyone can ask for these days." His tone grew more serious. "There're bitchy people out there. There're bitches as much as there are assholes, geniuses, or jocks. It doesn't matter what you are, as long as you can be honest about it."

Lennon's forehead creased with doubt. "I don't know about that."

"It's hard to be mad at someone for being themselves. For being real—"

"People don't want real," She rolled her eyes. "They want convenience, they want somebody who will make them feel like a god."

"I was starting to think you were making this person up!" The waiter returned, shooting a look at Conrad. "Sir, you had this lady waiting for over—"

"He's a surprise guest, actually." She couldn't look at Conrad as she said it; it was too embarrassing. She apologized to his hands instead, noticing a fresh collection of small scratches the ocean and its inhabitants had given him. "But he is going to be joining me."

"Ah, my apologies. Welcome, sir." The waiter nodded, and turned to Lennon. "So, are we ready for drinks?"

"She doesn't drink," Conrad answered. "But I'll have a Manhattan please, well's fine. And I'd love a fresh plate of those Brussel sprouts."

Lennon's eyes darted to him, narrowing slightly. "Make it WhistlePig, Boss Hog if you have it. Thank you," Lennon adjusted, offering a smile to the waiter. He walked away before Conrad could stop him.

"On me," she nodded. "For suffering through my insufferableness."

"See? You are kind of nice."

Lennon rolled her eyes. "How did you know I don't drink?"

His shrug came after a short hesitation. "You ordered water at the bar, and when we ate together. I just assumed...."

"That's very observant of you." She cut her interrogation short, letting her eyes fall.

"How do you know about Boss Hog?" he countered.

"My mom's a rich alcoholic," she answered with his same cadence. The two of them traded glances, and then smiles, as if sharing a dark inside joke.

The waiter dropped off his Manhattan then, along with a steaming plate of fresh Brussel sprouts covered in a melting balsamic glaze and warm goat cheese. Conrad sipped, nodding in approval. "Damn. That's good. Thank you."

Lennon still felt weird seeing people she cared about drink alcohol—it had only brought ruin to her life so far. It'd been hard to watch Hart, too, despite him being more responsible than her other friends. It suddenly occurred that this had been the longest they'd gone without talking since the day he offered his bag of chips to her, and she was hit with a new wave of pain. *Distraction, distraction...* she recalled Page's entry, about being scared to tell Lennon she wanted to try drinking. *Nope, that's worse.* She tried putting it out of her mind altogether and return to the present, only to remember she'd been forsaken by her own mother. *Perfect,* she thought glumly.

Lennon laughed humorlessly, stabbing a Brussel sprout and placing it on her tongue. "This was supposed to be a make-up dinner for us. My mom and me."

"What was she making up for?"

"The last few weeks. Being worse than usual."

"Grief makes people do terrible things," he said softly. Old, grainy memories flashed behind Lennon's eyes, but she disguised it with another bite.

"Sometimes people just do terrible things," she muttered.

"This is a step though, right?" he asked, not hearing her. "She's admitting fault, I know that doesn't happen very—"

"It would have been, if she showed up. Now all of it feels like bullshit. It was for her, all of this." Lennon gestured around her. "I'm embarrassed I even humored her."

"It's not embarrassing to be hopeful." He took a full swig this time, draining his glass to the quarter line. "I'm still waiting on a make-up dinner from my dad."

"For what, making you guys leave?"

He nodded. "A lot of people want to get away from their past, I get that. But his past is his family…and nobody ever asked what *I* wanted to do." Sympathy drained from his voice. "Ever since then, he's seemed weak to me. I love him, but I don't know why he thought the right answer was to…I wouldn't've…"

"Run away?" Lennon finished.

He tapped his thumb against the side of his glass. Watching his jaw work under his skin, clearly still in pain over it, sent a pang of guilt through her. The words escaped before she could stop them. "Maybe that wasn't the only thing he was trying to get away from. It could have been the cherry on top."

"What else would it have been?"

She stirred the straw in her nearly empty glass, immediately regretful. "I don't know. People are dealing with demons on their own all the time."

He lingered on her for a moment, brewing thoughts behind calculating eyes. Whatever they concocted into, he swallowed them down with the last of his Manhattan, and slid the empty glass to the edge of the table.

"You always talk about dark shit." he said.

"I told you, I'm shi—"

"It's not a bad thing," he assured. "It's refreshing, actually. You talk about hard things the way most people do small talk. But I like that. Because if you don't talk about those things, then eventually

Missing Page

conversations start feeling like a Jack-in-the-Box, y'know? Something's gonna spring out after it's too late."

Their waiter came by to take dinner orders, but Lennon slipped him her card after ordering another Manhattan, making sure the card was the one attached to her mother's account. As she signed the bill—complete with a tip that doubled the total—and Conrad took his first sip, she felt a presence stumbling toward her. She feigned obliviousness when it stopped next to her, but couldn't pretend any longer when it spoke,

"Don't tell me you ate without me," Cash uttered, trying to mask her slurring.

Lennon shot a warning glance to Conrad before taking on her mother. "It's twenty past nine. You're almost two hours late. I was starving."

"Y'could've texted me. I lost track of time in the store... I came as soon as I realized."

"Let's stop with the bullshit, okay? You got drunk, you messed up, and now you're feeling guilty."

Conrad looked between them, frozen with uncertainty. His stillness kept him invisible to Cash, still glaring at her daughter.

"See, *this* is what I'm talking about! I make one *tiny* mistake... You could've texted me, called me, but you didn't. You *want* to be angry, you like making me look bad!"

"That's not true," Lennon said simply.

"So why can't we eat right now?"

"I just ate with Conrad," she answered. "We're finished, I already paid."

Cash finally looked across to the man in the other booth, and straightened her posture. "Oh, Conrad, honey. I didn't realize...."

"Because you're drunk," Lennon said. "You're drunk, aren't you?"

"No!" she exclaimed.

"You're swaying." Lennon's voice was flat.

"I had two drinks." Cash was growing annoyed now. "That's not illegal."

"You're not in trouble with me, I'm not the police. I'm just not eating with you."

"Lennon, I just *stopped by*," she spluttered, not listening. "I didn't even sit down! I can't believe you're acting like this over—"

"Where are the groceries?" Lennon asked. Her question had Cash's mouth opening and closing like a broken gate, struggling for answers. "You just came from the store. Where are the bags?"

At her silence, Lennon felt tears crystallizing in her sapphire eyes. "You didn't even go, did you?"

"I said that because I was scared you'd judge me, exactly like you are right now! You're treating me like I'm the worst mother in the world, when all I've ever done is—"

"Mrs. Mayfield," Conrad gently interrupted. He took Lennon's elbow in a guiding manner, trying to lead her away. "I think we should have this conversation somewhere else."

"I'm not leaving," she spat, taking a seat at the booth. "I'm here now. You barely touched the Brussel sprouts, let's order a meal."

"No, Mom. You're gonna have to deal with this one on your own."

Cashmere gritted her teeth. "Lennon, if you don't sit down *right now*—"

Conrad tugged Lennon's arm. "I'm sorry, Mrs. Mayfield..."

He pulled her out of the restaurant and led her to the Jeep, opening the passenger door and gesturing for her. She climbed in, stretching to open the driver side just before he reached the other side. Once he settled, the locks slid into place.

She felt a tremble threatening her lip. "I don't know what to do. I can't go home, not until she goes to bed."

Conrad cleared his throat. "She *was* right about one thing."

Lennon craned her neck at him, betrayed fury bubbling inside her stomach.

He met her gaze bravely. "You barely touched your Brussel sprouts."

A strange sound erupted from her throat. *A laugh*, she realized,

Missing Page

and it was snowballing. Had it changed, or had it been so long since that she'd forgotten the sound? Conrad joined in, and together they laughed—slightly hysterical—in her car, heads thrown back like hyenas. It pushed out tears that were already brimming, but she was okay with that. People could see laughing tears.

"That was fucking crazy," Conrad breathed, wiping his eyes with his sleeves. "Your mom's crazy."

Lennon nodded in small, quick movements, unable to speak. The laughter had died, but she held gratitude tight between her lips. His words could come to some as a stab, a gut-twisting knife of truth. To Lennon, who had always considered herself a realist, it was closer to a gasp of air—the freedom of getting a rotten branch sawed off her tree. Cashmere had instilled for years that Lennon was delusional, and so skillfully manipulative that she'd convinced herself she was the victim. Her mother promised if anyone else thought she was did so only because they knew *her* side of the story, otherwise they'd run.

Well, Conrad saw both sides, and he *did* run—and he took Lennon with him.

"You wanna go somewhere else? Get you a real meal?" he asked, his voice softening.

"What about your car?"

"We'll come back for it later."

"I'm not really—"

"I know. But..." He tugged at the baggy sleeve of her sweater. "You should eat."

She pulled her arm away, trying to ignore the warmth that his fingers had left. At her yielding nod, Conrad drove them to a cheap sushi restaurant he used to frequent, ordering a few plates of rolls to split. They talked about her school for a little before he finally noticed her Band-Aids.

"Jeez...." he murmured, squinting as he turned her hands from side to side.

"I've never done it in my sleep before."

He nodded slowly, preoccupied with roaming thoughts as he

stared at her fingers. Her sudden concern of oversharing made her realize her high was waning, but she was doing oddly okay—the emotion wasn't overwhelming. His head turned a few moments before hers, blinking as a petite girl with a blonde pixie cut had approached the table.

"Sorry for bothering," she said shyly, with a too-big smile. "I just wanted to say, you guys are *so* cute! I was out for a smoke outside and saw you, and just *had* to—"

Lennon opened her mouth to correct her, but Conrad was quicker.

"We're not dating," he said, dropping his hand. Lennon side-eyed him, before returning to the girl who was now blushing.

"Oh! Oh my God, that's embarrassing. So sorry!" She scurried away, leaving them in a heavy silence. Conrad glanced to the window next to their seat, reaching to jerk the thin curtain over it.

WHOOSH.

The sound stiffened the hair on Lennon's arms, but she forced her head to stay in the restaurant; the nightmares hadn't come in a few days. She chalked it up to the new horrors unfolding in her life combined with heavy relaxers, although that didn't bring much comfort.

Conrad busied himself with his sushi, but Lennon was staring at him inquisitively, having abandoned her appetite. He'd corrected the girl faster than Lennon had, even though *she* was the one in a relationship—or, at least, she had been. Obviously they weren't dating, but why did he denounce it like that? Conrad had seemed almost...offended, or perhaps even grossed out by the notion. Lennon had never gotten that kind of response from men before—usually they were ecstatic if someone thought they were fucking. She was used to being treated like a trophy, not an embarrassment. She hated both, but this new reaction made her wonder *why*.

She watched his eye contact dwindle with every passing second, his words grow shorter with every sentence. *He's acting different.*

Missing Page

Once so open before, her walls had now reinforced even stronger, solidified into concrete.

Lennon could only think of one thing; Conrad was ashamed to be associated with her. The troubled girl, the slut—that was her reputation here, even though only half of it was true.

A question raised its hand from the back of her mind. Was that why he was so careful around her? She had noticed he never flirted with her, not even in a joking manner. In fact, him grabbing her hand was one of the only times he had initiated any kind of contact between them. She'd been downplaying how nice that moment felt— not because it was romantic, but because it *wasn't*. She didn't remember the last time a man touched her without her gut squirming, knowing that he was yearning for more.

So that was it, then. He didn't *actually* like her, didn't want to be friends. He pitied her, or worse; she was merely a mirror for his grief, a different face to look at after years of boring through his own. She winced, cursing as fresh blood seeped from a piece of new skin her fingers had found. She reached for a napkin and wrapped it around the wound, scooting to the edge of the booth.

"Ah, shit, you okay?" he asked. She looked up to him, and only then did he notice her expression, knitting his eyebrows in response. "Lennon, what's wrong?"

"I'm gonna go," she said shortly, slipping her sling bag over her head.

"Whoa, wait a second. Did I do something?" His eyes were wide with confusion.

"No, you haven't done anything." There was no anger in her voice. How could she be? His intentions were pure, she was sure of that. But it didn't stave off the humiliation drowning her in that tiny booth. Lennon wasn't a stray dog; she didn't need food and comfort from whoever was willing to offer.

"Goodbye, Conrad."

Her feet couldn't carry her fast enough to the door; every step felt like it was taking her farther from the entrance, trapping her in an endless tunnel. He rustled in a struggle to get out of the small, constricting space, which quickened her pace in response. She didn't turn even when he called her name, cut off by the ding of a door chime. Lennon only paused once in her Jeep, realizing she was leaving him stranded. In a rapid fire of taps and clicks into their message board, she sent him forty bucks, more than enough to get an Uber back.

She wiped her tears with her sleeve as she drove away, choking back the tsunami wave clawing at her chest. Conrad was right—she was good at the dark stuff. No matter how much she tried to stretch the light, night would always come.

22

Lennon was nine years old when she broke into her first home. She was in fourth grade, and shared a class with a girl who lived down the street from Lennon's humble home. *Lindsay Kellowitz*—she had a two-story house, which seemed like a mansion when you're nine. Lennon had been one, too, but she'd seen how much work her parents had put into it. It was Cash's first flip; there were still holes in the wall, stained carpet. Apparently the cabinets were expired—she'd heard her dad say they were out-of-date. Little did they know the project would end up being so successful that it would give them the means to purchase an even bigger house, twice as big as Lindsay's, just two years later.

The Kellowitz's home had stone around the entryway that complimented the brick, connecting the entrance to the garage. There were large windows and a hammock in the backyard. It was practically a castle.

Lindsay was not as nice as her house. She liked to play tag, but Lennon always had to chase her, even after she caught her. Similarly to Conrad, Lindsay's pranks were more cruel than funny, like telling Lennon to meet her at a spot outside the neighborhood—usually outside of how far she was allowed to bike—and then never show up. She'd tell boys Lennon had crushes on them when she didn't, which would be where a lot of those rumors that followed Lennon throughout school first originated. Most recently, Lindsay challenged a barefoot Lennon to a footrace, knowing spiky stickers hid underneath the blades of grass.

But sometimes Lindsay would let Lennon choose the game at recess, or be there waiting when she parked her kid-sized, sparkly ribboned bike. There were days where Lindsay would tell Lennon that she was her best friend. So she wasn't *all* bad.

On one particular Thursday, Lindsay invited Lennon to sit next to her at their lunch table. Usually her other best friend Karly would hold that seat, but she was at home, sick. Lennon's heart pounded underneath her small ribcage, and she blushed, sure Lindsay could hear it. Lennon breathed as the plastic ripped from her pizza Lunchable, in disbelief of what Lindsay had just asked her.

"Like, to your house?" Lennon asked, trying to seem nonchalant.

Lindsay reached over, taking a pepperoni slice from Lennon's box. "Duh. That's what *coming over* means."

Lennon watched her chew the meat, pushing down her indignation. Mommy said she needed to be better about sharing. *It's just one pepperoni,* she'd say. Instead, Lennon focused on the excitement building in her gut, almost nauseating. She'd never been to Lindsay's house before, she'd only seen the outside of it. She knew that Lindsay had an aquarium inside stocked with sea fish (and a *real* electric eel!) *and* a Yorkie, who just had a small litter of puppies. Lennon didn't have any animals—they had a cat for a few months in first grade. But her dad traveled a lot for work, and Mommy was too busy with her budding business and two young children to make sure the cat was back inside during a storm, or that it hadn't jumped in the fridge before she closed the door. Daddy said the cat was on its last life when they gave it away.

Lennon smacked her lips, realizing she forgot to answer. "Okay. I just have to do my homework first—"

Missing Page

"If you do mine, you can be my best friend for another day."

Lennon scoffed mid-bite. "No way, do it yourself!"

"What about just the odd numbers?" Lindsay tilted her head, jutting out her lip. "Pweaseee?"

Lennon chuckled when she did that voice, and the kids surrounding her joined in, giggling at Lindsay's dramatic expression. She *did* like being Lindsay's best friend—especially if it meant sitting next to her at lunch, getting to see her house. The homework was easy, anyway. "Fine."

She sped through her and Lindsay's math homework before she could even change out of her school clothes. She changed into the cutest of her thrifted T-shirts, checked Page's room to make sure she was sleeping—she did that a lot—and ran out the door, screaming bye to her mommy. Her legs burned as they pedaled feverishly down the street, rainbow ribbons streaking from her handlebars as wildly as her long, brunette locks. Turning the corner, she sailed to the two-story house in the cul-de-sac, gawking at the behemoth with the black SUV in the driveway. Once at the mahogany door, she held her hand above her eyes, trying to see through the frosted window. Shadows of furniture loomed behind, the only sign of life being a chorus of barking that erupted once her knuckles hit the wood.

The wait felt like forever. After a few minutes, she knocked again, riling the dogs into another fit. *She said come after school, right? Maybe she's upstairs, can't hear the knocks.*

She wasn't sure what compelled her to test the door handle. This *could* be another one of Lindsay's pranks. The door swung open easily, it was as if the house itself were inviting her in. A small breath escaped her as she peered around the dark home. Bubbles could be heard from the entrance, and her heart jumped as the door swung shut behind her. *The aquarium!*

"Lindsay?" she called. Her footsteps echoed against the tall ceilings, closing the distance between her and the bubbles. Small fingers brushed against the cool glass, her nose leaving a smudge. It wasn't what *she* would call an aquarium, but the fish tank was huge.

Her eyes focused on the piece of coral just in front of her, and she jumped back when she noticed the eye of an eel staring back, retracting into the shadows.

"Lindsay!" she yelled again, swallowing. Nothing.

Had she come too early? If nobody was home, she had just walked in without permission—she was breaking in. *But she was in.* She wasn't going to steal anything, and how much of a crime was it to look around? The adrenaline pulsing through her felt good, she couldn't deny it. She let curiosity lead her, through the kitchen first, ogling at the shiny appliances she watched her mother circle in catalogs. She peeked into the guest bathroom, nodding in admiration. It had a ba-day, the thing that shot water against your privates to clean it. She'd heard her dad talk about using one in Tokyo.

A chorus of sniffing greeted her from behind a closed door with a few whimpers thrown in between. Her hand barely touched the handle, but she pulled away like it was hot. *I just want to play with them.* She hadn't played with a puppy in a long time, and they sounded like they wanted out...

Her hand twisted and pulled the knob, and out spilled a litter of three-month old puppies, pawing at her legs in earnest. Lennon immediately bent, giggling as their wet tongues licked her nose, her cheeks. She ran chipped nails through their fur, lifting her chin to avoid drowning under their kisses... She'd never felt so loved. Lindsay had been entirely forgotten up until the door knob twisted, and she remembered whose home it was.

The blood drained from her so fast it made her lightheaded. *They were home.* She dashed for the back door, forgetting to put the puppies back into their room. Using all her might, she was only barely able to push the sliding door shut before the litter came out with her. Once it was closed she whipped around, spitting out strands of her hair as she looked for an exit. The fence was too tall, but there was a gate that led to the front.

My bike! She gasped. It was all over. She couldn't believe what she'd done—her mom would be so mad. Lennon opened the door and

Missing Page

stepped through the gate, nearly combusting with guilt. But her parents were gone, as was Lindsay; it was only Ashley, Lindsay's older sister, and their seventeen-year-old brother.

Ashley was in seventh grade, and even meaner than her sister, with a frown permanently etched into her freckled face to prove it. "Were you in our house?"

"Lindsay told me to come over," Lennon stuttered, straddling the bike. She started to push her foot onto the pedal, but Ashley gripped the handlebar in her fist, holding her in place.

"You can't go in if nobody's home, dipshit. I should call the police!"

"I just went inside and played with the dogs!" Lennon cried out in one breath, yanking on her bike handle.

The brother groaned, throwing his head back. "You let the fuckin' dogs out?"

She opened her mouth helplessly, still trying to grasp the situation. Ashley pinched her lips together in concentration, pulling on the handle of Lennon's bike, a cherished Christmas present. Lennon heard the rip before she saw it—rainbow strings detaching from the bar with its rubber cover, exposing the ugly metal inside. Ashley's hand cocked back, and she threw it towards the roof with as much force as she could muster, watching it roll until it fell into the gutter.

Lennon wailed, seeing red. "You ruined my bike!"

~

She killed the engine of her Jeep, headlights fading fast as the darkness feasted. The only sound left was the hum of her cooling engine, and the occasional tapping of her nail against a glass screen. In the distance on the second floor of a deteriorating home, a bedroom light was on, tucked behind a pair of half-open blinds. Her eyes drifted to the driveway, void of any cars.

According to Facebook, Emery's parents had just checked into a hotel in New York. Her husband was attending a work conference, and Paola decided to go as emotional support. She'd also decided to boast about it online, letting the world know they wouldn't be home tonight.

Emery must have forgotten to turn off the lights before she left.

Lennon popped her door handle, stepping out and moving with the shadows along the street. She'd noticed a new camera near the stairs, but it was no matter. Near the back, she lifted herself onto her tiptoes and for the deck. Her fingers gripped the wood with surprising strength, hoisting her up and over the rickety fence. Landing in a surreptitious crouch, she was able to sidle to the window leading into Emery's bedroom. Before anything else, she listened first, making sure it was empty.

Now, maybe it was a coincidence the first time...

Whoosh

It hadn't been—Emery left her window unlocked again. Lennon bit down on her bottom lip, heart jumping the same way it had twelve years ago. It felt like overkill to check the park, but she couldn't risk skipping any precautions. There was a complex at the far end, but the apartments were tucked between layers of trees, blocking any kind of clear view. She could almost hear her younger self whispering in her ear.

Park down the street.

Wear gloves.

Check for witnesses.

Quick, but thorough.

She pulled herself through the opening, hit with the heavy scent of dirty cleats covered in perfume as she reached the other side. The walls were sage green, decorated in academic and athletic certificates as well as self-made art pieces. Not bad, actually, though they looked childish compared to Page's skill. A white cross hung above her bed, detailed in frills that didn't seem to match the rest of her tomboyish room.

Lennon opened nightstands with the same delicacy as she would

Missing Page

moving an injured limb, searching her desk drawers like the papers would crumble at her touch.

There was a sudden creak from outside on the patio. Lennon darted for the desk, ducking her head underneath. The sound passed without any following footsteps. Expelling the air burning her lungs, she cautiously lifted her head above cover.

Quick, but thorough.

Her tired blue eyes settled on a rectangular piece of metal, glinting under the moonlight like a chipped diamond. She lifted the screen of the laptop, wondering if it really could be this easy. If this was connected to her phone, Lennon could have most—if not all—the answers at her fingertips. The screen stared back at her, unresponsive, but after a few moments, whirred to life with a groan of protest.

Lennon's was even more audible when a password box appeared. She slapped a hand over her mouth, remembering her circumstances. Once she made sure she was in the clear, Lennon closed it, glancing at the stickers covering the logo. A soccer ball, a small rainbow, palm trees, and a trio of numbers in big, bubble lettering with *Bahamas* in curly writing beneath it. This made her pause, gazing down.

242.

Twofor2.

Was *Emery* Page's pen pal? Why would she go to the trouble of posing as someone else to get close to her? Humiliation? She'd been nose-deep with this internet friend for months, and the way Page wrote about him was the way every young girl wrote about their first crush. It wasn't hard to imagine Emery doing something like this; Lennon already thought she was guilty of worse crimes.

She pulled out Page's cellphone, searching quickly as her head cowered below the desk. To her surprise and frustration, there was nothing. Twofor2 no longer existed. Lennon snapped pictures of the numbers on Emery's computer, not wanting anything else to go missing. She was so close, she could feel it on the tip of her tongue, but another creak rose from outside, farther away.

This time, whispers followed after.

Panicked, Lennon scanned the room, looking for somewhere to run or hide. Closet? *No, too risky.* Also, she worried the door would creak as loudly as the rest of the house if she tried to exit. This house was old; every part of it complained. Maybe she should just jump out the window, try to run away before they could get a good look. She was fast, but she remembered Emery sprinting down the path in the park. It would be hard for anybody to outrun that. The whispers turned into giggles as stumbling pairs of feet bounded up the old staircase to the elevated deck.

"I can't see straight!"a girl giggled. "Oh, shit."

Oh, shit was right. Lennon dove for Emery's bed, bowing her head and scooting underneath. In a quick, small movement, she reached to tug the comforter until it brushed the floor, and forced her breath to slow. At that moment the window complained from the girls muscling it up, their grunts and *ouches* filling the room. They were inside.

"Wait here. My parents just installed a camera in the living room, I'm dead if they see you."

Lennon's eyes bulged with this knew knowledge, and her lips sealed shut.

"More dead than if you snuck out?"

"They don't know I sneak out—this window's supposed to be sealed shut. I used to work at it in the night with this old knife I'd hide under my pillow. Dad only put a few layers on... It was more tedious than anything."

The other girl giggled again, interrupted with a hiccup. "Oooh, you're *bad*."

Three feet below, Lennon lay petrified with a heart pounding out of her chest. She was sure they could hear it; any moment, their conversation would taper off, and one of them would rip the duvet up, exposing her. She was trying to think about what the next step would be—if she left right now, all she'd get charged with was trespassing, breaking and entering. It crossed her mind to push them hard enough to disorient them so they don't see her face. But then, if caught, she was also facing battery. Not to mention the fact they were minors. *Fuck, Lennon! How could you be so stupid?*

Her blood ran cold as Emery's feet passed, padding into the living room. The girl was even sloppier than the night Page went missing; she was taking this hard. It left just Lennon and the girl behind the curtain, or duvet, rather. The shadows of her feet were softer as they moved from one side of the bed to the other, eliciting an eerie creak with each step. If Lennon moved a muscle or breathed a little too deeply, this house would betray her. She tried to distract her rising claustrophobia with the shadow, guessing its next move.

She assumed the girl was taking in the room, just as she had ten minutes ago; perhaps she was trying to gauge who Emery really was. Was she not frightened, being in the same room, under the same circumstances, that Page had been her final night?

Emery's clumsy outline returned, her silhouette bleeding into the girl's. "Here you go."

A few liquid droplets rained onto the wood, inches from Lennon's cheek. But she remained stoic, unblinking. Removing herself from stressful situations was a talent of hers; it was easy to take her mind out of her body, to abandon ship. Terror helped things less than crying did... Adrenaline could be messy. She'd learned long ago how to hold tension inside her like a quivering arrow in a bow. The energy was searing inside her heart, its white flames licking everything it could touch, and yet she stilled herself into nothingness, into something bigger than the pain.

"Why can't you just get the bottle?" The girl laughed at whatever Emery had brought in.

"My mom can tell when it's moved, it's like a superpower. I literally had to siphon these out with a straw, that's why it took so long."

"You did all that for me?" the girl asked with a rough southern accent, her voice stretched by a cheesy grin.

"Shut up," Emery mumbled. For a split second, their shadows

disappeared, like they'd vanished. But before the confusion could fully hit Lennon, the mattress sank down against the floor, stopping centimeters above the tip of her sloped nose.

A separate, new tension hung damp in the air as the bed creaked. "Can you say something to me in Spanish?"

Emery chuckled, pausing for a moment. "*Estoy muy borracha.*"

The bed creaked again. "What does that mean?"

"I'm very drunk." Emery sighed.

"No, c'mon...Spanish can be so pretty. Say something pretty."

There was a pause before her next words, which came slower, softer. "Um... *Valentina, eres muy bonita, y divertida. Me recuerdas tiempos mas felices.*"

Valentina's laugh was elated. Shy, even. "*That* sounded pretty. What did it mean?"

"It means, well...it means you have a kind of beauty that's... nostalgic. You feel familiar."

Creaaaak.

There was a strange, brief noise then. A sound so recognizable, but it wasn't computing in Lennon's overloaded brain—

"Was that okay?"

"Yeah." Emery whispered.

"...Are you sure? You look...not sure."

"No, Val, it's—ugh. Sorry."

Lennon wanted to crawl out of her skin. She couldn't believe that breaking into a stranger's home was the second most surprising thing to happen today. Teens were so painfully awkward; she was cringing out of her skin to escape. She had to get out, but how? And, after that, there would be a lot of new information to process. Some pieces clicked into place, while others tore to shreds.

"I know you've been through a lot, Emery. I like you, obviously—I have for a long time, and I think you know that. Don't think it's lost on me that we didn't start hanging out until Page died."

"I'm sorry. I didn't mean to make you feel like...."

"What, like a second choice?"

Missing Page

Lennon winced for her.

"Don't be sorry, Em. I know you're hurting. I'm happy to be here for you, really." There was a quiet moment, then the air broke as Emery's emotion cracked, body convulsing. She was crying.

"I *am* sorry, Val, I feel awful! The least you deserve is an apology, I've dragged you along through everything, and you never left, not once. I've just—I've never lost someone like this. I didn't—" She hiccupped, genuine grief spilling out of her in quick confessions. "I didn't know I cared about her like this until she was gone, y'know? And—and now there's this...I have this huge, gigantic hole in me that will *never* be filled. Because I never got to tell her how I felt. I never got to tell her...I loved her, Val. I really did."

If any part of Emery had ever hated Page, it was only because she loved her even more.

23

Emery was Twofor2. She had to be, it made the pieces fit together perfectly. A girl too ashamed of her truth to try in real life, so she created this online persona to get close without subjecting herself to vulnerability. It was a hollow shell of love, young love at that, but for the first time, Lennon understood. Although their loves were different, the power in them was transmutable. It didn't seem possible to have such massive love for a tiny girl, to despair for her time and attention enough to settle for the ghost of her.

Despite these revelations, a building cough had begun to dry Lennon's tongue, begging for release. Dust bunnies littered the floor underneath the bed, water bottles waited to be kicked like plastic spring traps, and a cobweb that was most certainly home to something nonhuman rested inches from her hand. But she wouldn't move, keeping her breaths slow and shallow so that they didn't tickle her throat as much. Lennon would sooner pass out than expose her presence.

The bed raised an inch, losing the weight of a body. Their feet left and came back in under a minute, eliciting a disapproving click of the tongue from whoever had stayed.

Missing Page

"Oh, Emery..." Valentina murmured as liquid guzzled from where Emery stood. "Aren't you supposed to not move the bottles?"

Emery swallowed loudly. "I wasted so much time trying to make sure no one knew I liked her. My parents, my friends, *her*. I made her cry so many times to protect myself, I was so selfish!" She took a breath, trying to calm her sobs. "Do you know how shitty this feels? I thought the worst thing that s'meone could call me was a dyke, and now everyone's calling me a *murderer*! The police keep coming back to question me, even her family thinks—"

"Stop. They don't think that."

"You saw the notes! Dozens, on dozens, all saying I'm—"

Val interrupted her again. "People love having a witch to burn. Especially rich, racist dickheads like Ricky. I mean, look at his sisters... They're all bullies."

"B-But her sister..." Emery blubbered. "Oh my God—gosh—Val, talk about *murderer*. She would k-k-kill me if she c-could!"

"Their whole family is fucked up, Emery, you can't take it seriously. Lennon would rather hate you than admit that her sister committed suicide."

Lennon clenched her fists and teeth with a denying fury. She couldn't help but notice her own reaction, and wondered if maybe there was a harsh truth to Val's words.

"I can'neven defend myself. I was so *mean*, no wonder they think that." Emery sniffled. "I just feel s-so *guilty*. And I couldn't even give them anything good, all I brought was her calculator."

"Listen to me. You have no idea what Page was thinking about or going through." Their shadows melted together again. "But she clearly cared about you, too. You were the last person she wanted to be with before she left."

"We don't *know* she killed herself, Val. We'd been drinking, maybe it was an accident. I should have gone with her..." Her voice hardened into anger. "But she had no business being there! What was she thinking? We were almost as drunk as you n' me are. She seemed perfectly fine, and then, out of nowhere, she got so —" Emery's breath slowed, her voice muffling against Val's shirt.

"You have to stop this, Emery. You're *fifteen*, and a freshman, for God's sake! We're teenagers, not psychologists. This was not your fault, do you hear me? I need you to say it with me. This—is not—my fault."

"This...is not..."

"My. Fault." Val repeated.

"My—"

A phone erupted caused everyone to jump, including Lennon. The wood creaked from underneath and her life flashed before her eyes, jaw clenching in fear. She tightened her elbow against her jean pocket where her phone resided, heart exploding out of her chest.

"Hello?"

It was Val's. Her noise had been covered by the girl's scrambling, loud enough to conceal the small gasp that followed. "Okay, okay, sorry, we're coming!"

The two pairs of feet fled toward the window, grunting as they climbed through the opening. The window squeaked as it slid back into place, confirming their absence.

Lennon counted to thirty after she heard the last step. Finally, she allowed her chest to expel the dust it had been force-fed. It punished her mercilessly, wreaking havoc from her stomach to her throat. She didn't even cough this hard when she hit a bong for the first time. She maneuvered a hand through the narrow space to wipe them away, and wiggled herself out, emerging like a miner from a cave after a twelve-hour shift with suffocated tears and beading sweat.

As she stood alone in Emery's room, it hit her that this was in fact the last place Page had come to. Lennon removed her glove, letting her hand hover just above the duvet. Page had been here—laughing and drinking just like these girls had been. 'Perfectly fine,' in Emery's words.

Her fingers brushed against the fabric, lips folding into a tight line. Finally she turned and lifted herself through the window, sneaking around the worn patio to take a final look at the park. The trees swayed back and forth, waving goodbye. Her brows furrowed in confusion. The cove was a mile or two in the opposite direction, though Emery had said she saw her go through the park...

The shooters in the park. Had she drank more after leaving here? Is that why she came in the first place, to drop off her bike and pre-game? Pre-game for *what*, then? Nothing was making sense...

The confusion plagued her the entire ride home. She thought clarity would come in the shower, but she was just as perplexed as she'd been before.

Lennon pressed her forehead into the cool tile, letting the water travel like molten lava down her back. There was no justice that could be given, no closure to take. Valentina was right—all this time, Lennon was looking for someone to crucify. Her wound was gory, and fresh; the knife might as well still be in her chest, but there was nobody to push away. She'd have to pull this one out herself.

She took extra time to scrub off her mother's apology, Conrad's pitying touch, and Emery's dust bunnies. There were no phone calls to interrupt her this time, but she found herself missing the blaring tone. Tired, scabbed fingers massaged her scalp, sending suds rolling along the delicate lines of ink traveling down her spine.

A knock at the bathroom door spooked her. "Len? It's Dad."

"Yeah?"

"When you're done, I'd like to talk to you."

Whatever it was, it couldn't be good; he never stayed up this late. With her pessimistic inner voice, she assumed he'd found out about her spy mission, despite turning off her location before she'd left.

Her skin was still damp when she slipped into her terrycloth robe, pulling her hair out of its grasp as she entered the common area of the suite. Unlike Emery's, this house was new, and quiet; she had to clear her throat to get her father's attention, who was sitting on the living area's loveseat.

"I'm done," she murmured.

He stood, only able to meet her eyes for brief glances.

"Few things," he started, licking his lips anxiously. "I don't know what happened at dinner, but your mom came home pretty upset, and had no interest talking to me. I just wanna make sure you're ok. If there's anything I need to hear..."

"You mean you wanna make sure she didn't cause a scene?" Lennon's burning eyes challenged him. "That she didn't hit me?"

"Did she?"

Her jaw flitted as she stuffed down her misdirected anger. "You know most people don't have to have these conversations, Dad."

She caught his eyes soften before he dropped his head. Lennon didn't know why she was being cruel; he was not her enemy. "No. She didn't," she conceded.

"Good." He stepped back, relaxing a little. "Good."

"So...cool if I go to bed?"

"Not yet." He walked past her into the room, stopping next to her bed.

"I got an email from your guidance counselor today." His voice hardened with disappointment.

Shit.

"She's been trying to get a hold of you for two months."

"C'mon, Dad. It's late," she pleaded.

"You still haven't picked a major?"

"I've been a little preoccupied," Lennon spat.

"*Don't* do that." He pointed at her sternly. "She sent that email before you even got home, I checked. You've been struggling all year, so don't you dare you use your sister as an excuse."

She stood frozen, unable to argue.

"You're on scholarship, Lennon," He continued. "You were valedictorian, one of the top of your class last year. What's going on?"

"I don't know what I want to do." Vulnerability shrunk her voice.

"So you're giving up?" he asked incredulously. "That's not you. Your counselor wants to help, *I* want to help! Why aren't you asking?"

"I don't *know*." she groaned, pressing her fingers against her temples. "And she doesn't know how to help me, not in the ways I need. I'm an email on her mailing list."

"What about us?"

"You guys have enough on your plate."

"You *are* my plate," he said firmly. "So talk to me. Why are you hesitating?"

"I—don't—know." Her wall was stone cold, turning his arrows into dust.

"Not good enough. Try again."

She scowled. How could she explain that choosing a degree felt like finally signing the contract to life, something she'd been running from since she was four? There was pain and evil in living, and she was already tired. Once Lennon chose her path, she would be subjecting herself to terms and conditions she didn't trust.

"What do you want from me?" she asked coldly.

"Not this, Lennon." He shook his head. "You can't give up. Which you're trying to do...why, because it's hard? That's not our way, we don't quit."

"Why not?" she challenged. "Sometimes it's good to quit things, Dad. You and Mom could benefit from knowing your limits."

"Don't be cruel," he said sharply. "And don't talk to *me* about quitting."

Her jaw worked under her skin. She didn't want to anger him—she needed him on her side. She stood statuesque, refusing to indulge.

"Look, if you can't give me an answer, I'll have to resort to my own theories."

She crossed her arms, raising her eyebrows. "You're really gonna make me ask?"

He stared at her for a moment, shadowed with disappointment. "You're on drugs again."

The tension snapped like a rubber band. She thought they were speaking as adults, but now, in one sentence, he'd shrank her into a kid again. She tried to recover. "Weed's legal—"

"I know that." He pointed at her bed, and her body turned ice-cold, blood draining from her face. "I think you've got pills in here."

Her tongue was itching to lie. She'd manipulated men with ease since she was a teenager—teachers, law enforcement, even friends. She understood the way men thought, she knew how to act around them, how to speak. But this man knew her more than anyone else; he'd carried her on his shoulders, made her smile in the midst of tears. He knew what a mermaid promise was. She wouldn't compromise their relationship to get out of trouble. Lennon wouldn't break trust, even if he had first.

"Did you go through my room?" The question squeezed through clenched teeth.

"I saw an orange bottle under your bed. I guess you were too high to remember to put them away."

"I didn't..." She stopped herself, preparing for the pain that would soon come. "Someone gave them to me."

Stacy's face fell at the confirmation. "I thought this was over."

Her voice broke. "I know."

"You *promised* me. No. More. Pills."

"I know I did." The memory used to give her motivation, but now it weighed her down with guilt.

"How long?"

Lennon looked at him, begging. "Dad—"

"*How. Long?*"

Her tongue was too heavy with shame to form the words.

"Did you ever stop?"

She wished she could wipe the pain off his face, hug the disappointment out of him. It hurt to know that she was causing this, and even more that in that very moment, she was craving the things that hurt him this much.

"For three months," she admitted.

Missing Page

"You promised to *stop*." His voice lowered, head shaking. "She wouldn't want this for you, Lennon."

Ice blue daggers impaled him, frozen with hurt. "*Now* who's being cruel?"

She reached for the nightstand, pulling it open and grabbing the bottle between her index and thumb, shaking the pills inside. "Look, most of them are still in here. It's not like last time, I didn't even buy these! Michaela left them here, it was a shitty gift—"

"A *gift*? What do you even need these for, Lennon?" He snatched them from her hand.

Answering was impossible—she couldn't tell him this was much deeper than a rebellious phase or even a drug addiction. How would he react to her revealing that this was a seventeen-year-old wound, the same that had caused her to scream in the night with her eyes wide open? She could stand disappointing him if it meant keeping his veil of reality intact. Lennon had been holding on to this for years; she'd learned how to live around it. But it would hit her father like a truck. His world would crack, breaking whatever idea of himself he'd built. To know that things had been happening under his nose for longer than he could've imagined...

He *was* a good dad. She wouldn't be the one to make him think otherwise.

"Are you even listening to me?" His voice raised a decibel.

She nodded. "Yes, I heard you. And, for what it's worth, I'm really, really sorry."

"You...we agreed. You said..." he stammered, as if afraid to hold her to her word.

"That I'd go to rehab," she finished. "I remember."

Before Page died, Lennon couldn't say she understood the pain he was feeling. That ache when you know you've done everything you could, and it still wasn't enough—even if she was put in the best facility, it was an admission of failure, of dysfunction. But now she recognized the look in his eyes, and she would be strong so that he didn't have to be.

"Then I'll go. I'm not going to fight you about it." Her words sounded detached, but she meant them. She was sure to regret it later, but had bigger things to worry about.

"You're not?"

She nodded hesitantly. "But can I ask one final favor?"

He waited, and she uncrossed her arms. "You can toss the pills. Toss the weed, too, I don't care. But I just need two more days."

That was the first lie she'd told. She *did* care; the idea of throwing out the only fix she'd known for nearly a decade terrified her. It made her want to scream, cry, kick her feet like a toddler getting their bottle taken away. But she could do it—she *would* do it, if it bought her time.

"I won't run away," she assured, reading his mind. "You have my location, remember?"

She'd make sure to leave it on from now on, to stay true to her word. His eyes darted around, thinking.

"Just two days," she repeated. Her lips subconsciously rubbed together as she willed the words out of his mouth.

His eyebrows furrowed, confused, but Lennon had a habit of only letting people know what she wanted them to know, when she wanted them to know it. It was a take-it-or-leave-it offer.

"Mermaid promise." she said, laying out her final card. It was the one she'd hidden under the table the last time they had this conversation.

The beat before he answered was misery. But finally, he sighed. "On two conditions." He tucked the bottle into his pocket. "One, you email your counselor first thing tomorrow morning. Make a plan you can work on once you're...out."

Ugh. She'd thought he'd forgotten about that. How was she supposed to pick a career—a life—when she was still figuring out if she wanted one? Though it wasn't ideal, she could have that drafted in the next hour and still have time before having to commit to a major.

"Okay," she relented. "What's the second one?"

"You gotta get rid of these friends," he said gravely. "I mean, these could've killed you Len, what the hell were they—?"

"One step ahead of you," she interrupted. "Kinda came to that conclusion on my own after last week."

"All right." He nodded, believing the conviction he heard in her tone. "Then I'll giving you three days."

"But I only need—"

"I know. Your, uh...Hart called me yesterday."

"He did?" Her heart leapt at the sound of his name, but was quickly consumed with confusion. Since when did he and her father talk? She'd made an intentional effort to keep Hart as far away from her family as possible. Lennon wasn't even sure when—or how—they'd exchanged numbers.

"You've been pushing him away, but he's been a real friend to you, Len."

"Dad, I love you, but it's really none of your—"

"Your wellbeing *is* my business," he insisted firmly. "I think he's good for you. That kid cares about you, Lennon, I could hear it in his voice. I think you'll be much happier if he's around."

She paled. "What are you saying?"

Stacy scratched his whiskers. "We uh...*I* got him a ticket...here."

Her dad was dropping an atomic bomb on her chest like it was a water balloon.

"*Why* would you do that?" she exploded, lifting her hands to her head. "You're gonna bring him *here*? We're not—I...."

"For you, John." Stacy said with utter confusion.

"He's not supposed to see all of this!" She gestured around her, blood rushing to her cheeks.

"Well, baby doll, this is your home, your family. This is you."

He wasn't wrong, which was exactly why she'd worked so hard to conceal Hart from it—this ugly truth. All she could think about were the twinkling eyes and boisterous laughter in the Rogers' home; one night in the Mayfield House of Horrors would send him running. It would have been a death sentence for their relationship, if Lennon hadn't already killed it.

"Does Mom know?"

"She's excited to meet him. But she won't be here long, she has her conference in Sacramento this weekend. She's leaving Thursday afternoon."

It was Tuesday. Off her look, he crossed his arms. "How much damage can she do in forty-eight hours?"

Lennon side-eyed him. "Are you *seriously* asking me that?"

Touché, his expression said. "I'll make sure things go smoothly. Can you trust me on that?"

She sucked her cheeks in, still stuck in her honesty-only policy. "I want to."

He took her into a tight hug, resting his chin on her wet hair. "Ok. We can work with that."

24

Lennon kept her fingers interlocked over her bouncing knee as she waited in the private airport lounge. She was trying not to rip the skin around her healing nails in anticipation of his arrival, which would be happening any minute.

"Do you know when the next flight's getting in?" she finally asked the employee hunching over a monitor next to her. His wrinkled face looked one second away from falling asleep, but he blinked himself awake at her question.

"Looks about...five, ten minutes, give or take."

"Thank you." She nodded. Seeing old people working made her sad. It was ten; there was no reason a man in his seventies to be on the clock. "You, uh...you almost outta here?"

He smiled tiredly. "Not quite."

A woman passed her, hovering in front of the coffee machine. It screamed while hot brown liquid dispensed into the cup, though she pressed a finger to her ear in annoyance as if someone else had caused it. After the high-pitched squeals relented, she moved the cup aside, reaching for a few creamers. She flicked a few of the straws around in search of something, eventually swiveling her head to find help.

The man next to Lennon lifted his head at precisely the wrong time, making eye contact. She abandoned her coffee, striding over to him. "Hello," she said quickly. "I'm having a little trouble finding paper straws."

He looked behind her, squinting. "I think we're out."

She looked dumbfounded. "You don't have any paper straws? Even in the back?"

"I'm sure we *have* them, but if you didn't see any—"

"Do you mind checking? I know I'm being a pain, I'm sorry."

He nodded stiffly, shuffling from behind the kiosk and hobbling toward an Employee's Only marked door. Lennon stared at the ground, feeling the woman's eyes move to her. There were no headphones to protect her from smalltalk this time.

"I hate being that girl...they're just *so* bad for the environment."

Lennon scoffed under her breath, a corner of her lip twisting. The woman continued, pouncing on the opportunity to educate the naive girl. "They're killing sea creatures by the hundreds, you know? It's the least we could do."

"No, I believe you, it's just..." Lennon trailed off, shaking her head.

"What?" she pressed.

Lennon sighed, but it was too late. "You know the fuel for these things come from offshore sites, right? Big drills that are leaking a bunch of oil into the ocean you say you're worried about?"

The woman's mouth snapped shut, furrowing into a scowl. "Well, *I* can't help that."

Lennon nodded pensively, resisting a grin. "Right, right."

The metal *Arrivals* door swung open then, and the first few bustled in with their luggage in tow. Lennon scoured their faces with a pounding heart, waiting for a familiar one. Nerves prickled her skin with each passing stranger; a part of her was jumping at the idea of seeing him, and another was bewildered that he was coming at all. A smaller, less rational part worried he'd come just to tell her how shitty

Missing Page

she was, and yet that seemed the most palpable. She would probably let him—it was the least she deserved.

He was the seventh in. She found him the second he crossed the threshold, towering nearly a foot above the woman who came in before him. She remembered how easy it was to find him in a crowd and how safe that made her feel, though now it only sparked a stomach full of nerves. He found her a few seconds after, their eyes meeting in a time-stopping moment.

Hart's irises were a swirls of of rich chocolate and warm caramel, better than any coffee; they clashed with the cold, reflective metallic color of Lennon's. Even looking into them felt like she'd been smacked with caffeine; her heart fluttered into a new, fast rhythm, and she blinked in quick flutters. Hart's inviting warmth could swallow the world whole, while hers spit everything out.

She waited for him to make the first move, to show her what this trip was supposed to mean. He side-stepped out of the slow traffic, dropped his bags, and rushed her, enveloping her small frame in a bear hug. It was long, warm, and slightly crushing, but somehow not tight enough. Despite her aversion to touch, she would rather die than be the first to pull away. The scent of cologne filled her nose, and her muscles instinctively relaxed.

"Oh my God," he murmured, voice muffled as she squeezed him back. "My girl."

She wondered if she was dreaming. He wasn't yelling, he wasn't spouting off every single horrible thing she'd done to him. His arms were still filled with the same love when they said goodbye at the airport over a month ago—it was like their last conversation had never happened.

She burrowed her head between the zipper of his Carhartt jacket, resting her ear just over his heart. *Du-dum, du-dum, du-dum.* Though a little fast, it was strong and steady. She'd been thrashing and trying to hold everything above water for so long she hadn't realized it had already pulled her to the bottom. His arms felt like a life vest bringing her back up to the surface, a gasp of air. She took it as deep into her lungs as she could, filling herself with him.

"I can't believe you're here." That's all she could utter.

It hurt more than she'd imagined when he'd pulled away. But it only lasted a second—his eyes found hers again, and his large hands cupped her cheeks, brushing his thumb over the soft skin. "Where else would I be?"

Her nods were disconnected, unable to process the depth of his words.

"Wanna go home?" he whispered.

The honest answer was no. The thought made her lip tremble, but she tucked her head into his chest again before he could see. He bent to grab the strap of his duffel and slung it over his shoulder, hooking an arm around her as they walked out to the cover of the Mercedes.

"Where's the Jeep?" he asked.

She shrugged. "Dad took the top off. Gets too cold at night."

Her fingers were timid weaving in with his once they were inside. She'd done it without thinking, and waited for his rejection, but it never came. Normally she didn't mind the silence—preferred it, actually—but they'd only made it three blocks before it became too much.

"I'm happy you're here," she said softly, keeping her eyes to the flitting yellow dashes.

He squeezed her hand, shoulders relaxing a bit. "I thought you'd be mad."

"Seeing you wold never make me mad," she frowned. "You're my best friend."

He smiled softly. "I come all the way here, and you friend-zone me?"

She rolled her eyes, but secretly appreciated the normalcy. The unsaid was still hanging over their heads, mixing in with the stale scent of alcohol—the car smelled like Cash. Eventually that conversation would come, but she'd hold onto this moment as long as he allowed.

"You put up a pretty good fight keeping me away."

"I didn't want to. It was to protect you."

"I don't need protecting, Len. I can take care of myself."

She flipped the blinker on, pressing her foot against the pedal to pass the car in front of them. "To protect us, then. Or your image of me."

"I already know about your parents. And I know that you're not them—"

"But they're a part of me." Her voice shook as it came out. "I've kept my life with you separate from the one I live with them for so long, and it was working..."

"**Until it wasn't**."

Her worried fingers twisted around the leather wheel. "I've always been scared that when you see my mom, you'll see me in her. You'll see something that I can't take out of me."

"Someday you'll understand that I want you, and everything that comes with it. I *want* to be a part of—"

"You want to be a part of this? *This* is what my family is, Hart." She tugged at the collar of her shirt, revealing a fading bruise. "I had to clean beer cans out of my mom's car before getting you. Even my dad's given up on her. My sister..." Lennon grit her teeth, forcing herself to stop and recollect. "I don't think you understand that bringing you into this is *exactly* what I'm afraid of."

Pain hardened his voice. "Because you think I can't handle it?"

Because you don't deserve it, she wanted to scream. "Can we not do this right now?"

Hart's nose twitched in frustration. "We've been 'not doing this' for ten months, Lennon. I'm trying to figure out exactly what the hell we *are* doing. I've done things your way, I've always been open with you. But you can't have one foot in and one foot out forever. At some point, you're gonna have to decide whether or not you trust me. Because I'm not leaving until you tell me to, and I...I l—" He sighed, looking to the window to escape her unreadable gaze. "Something's gotta change."

Lennon knew this would come someday—The Ultimatum. Though she thought she'd have more time to prepare. She'd been pushing her life back for too long, and it was all coming down now with deadly force, crashing over her. That four letter word felt like a tug-of-war between them, but her muscles had exhausted, growing tired of of the game. An unexpected dread settled into her stomach; soon he too would slip through her fingers, and it would be no one's fault but her own for not tightening her hands.

"Okay," she said, a part of her feeling strangely defeated. "I hear you. You're right."

"Do you care about me?"

His expression was as raw and honest as the question. It wasn't a plea for sympathy, it was a demand for the truth. When she looked at him, she saw a soul swimming in a rare vulnerability she'd been too selfish—or perhaps too scared—to reciprocate. But not anymore. She could see now that it had been inevitable from the start; her heart had jumped in long ago, and she was drowning herself trying to pretend otherwise.

"More than anything." She breathed. "And you do deserve that. I *want* to give that to you."

"You'll talk to me?"

"Not tonight." She felt his disappointment as his fingers released their hold, and squeezed in response. "But I will. You've done more than enough, been more than patient. Just give me—give us tonight."

He chewed his lip in thought, doubt hanging over his brows.

"I promise." she said, glancing away from the road for extra conviction. She knew she was asking something of him that she herself couldn't give in that moment, how incredibly selfish she was being.

Ever so slightly, he began to swipe his thumb back and forth over her knuckle. A sign of resignation, of trust that she didn't deserve.

"Tomorrow." he said, with a tone of finality.

"Tomorrow." she promised.

She wasn't sure how much she could give him; there were things she'd held onto herself for the better part of two decades. But if she wanted a future with him, she had to be willing to give him her past. If she couldn't do this for him, for the man she loved so deeply, she wouldn't be able to do it for anyone.

Lennon had started comparing their arrivals before she even killed the engine. Not a single light in her house was on—no silhouettes waited for them from the entryway, but the quiet came as relief to her.

Kaiser sniffed his palm cautiously as he stepped inside. "He's okay, Kai." Lennon whispered, seeming unfazed by the dog's guardedness.

Kaiser licked his hand once before losing interest, rubbing his head against Lennon's leg instead. Hart followed her lead, slipping off his shoes and glancing around the dark room for life. The glint of moonlight bounced off the waves in the distance.

"They're bigger than I thought," he mumbled under his breath.

"We're upstairs. C'mon," she whispered.

She flipped the light once they climbed the single flight, gliding into the bedroom. All of this was so surreal—she wanted to roll a joint more than ever, pass it back and forth until giggles or sexual tension took over. But she didn't want to risk her final three days of freedom in case her dad and him had made some kind of alliance. She didn't yet know whose side Hart was truly on.

Her bottom lip was crushed under her nervous teeth as he peered around the room.

"Pretty cool space you've got here," he noted.

She nodded, crossing her arms over her chest. "Yeah. It's...away."

"*Away*," he repeated quietly.

She reached on her tiptoes, helping him pull the duffel over his head. His hoodie followed, and he shook his hair once it was free. "Are you hungry?" she asked.

"Nah. Ate before I boarded."

"That was, what, two hours ago?"

"I'm fine, b—Len."

She was more preoccupied with his slip up. Her finger trailed up his shirt, resting over his chest. "You almost called me baby."

A subtle red flushed through his cheeks. "Habit. Sorry."

"Don't be." She peered up at him, feeling his heartbeat quicken under her hand. "I missed it."

He swallowed, looking down at her soft features. His hand lifted to the high bone in her cheek, swallowing at the warmth spreading from her skin to his. "Me, too."

Her eyes closed, breathing him in. "I missed you."

In a slow, aching movement, her hand carefully covered his. When her eyes opened, he'd lowered his face within inches of hers. She could already feel her lips parting, aching to be touched by his.

She expected *some* kind of attempt... After all, they'd been apart for over a month. She was sure he'd missed her breathless pants in his ear, the way her necked tasted under his wet tongue. But Hart's initiation never came. "Are *you* hungry?"

She breathed, feeling her heart puttering beneath her ribs. He was going to make her pay, after all.

"Not at all." Her words were barely a whisper, weak and shaky.

"Then we should get some rest." he murmured, and in the next second had returned to his place next to her.

Though she didn't try again, she missed the way he felt so much that it burned. It'd be a lie to say she hadn't thought about the way his skin had felt over the past few weeks, the way they fit perfectly into each other. Plus, Lennon *did* love the feeling of his chest rising and falling against her back; she had learned to pinpoint the exact moment he slipped into unconsciousness. It gave her something to mimic, a thing to focus on besides her dread of sleep.

Once they were snuggled together, he pressed his lips to the back of her neck and inhaled deeply. A faint smile touched her mouth when a hum rumbled from his chest, satisfied knowing his desire matched hers. He'd always been the one with better self discipline.

Missing Page

Hart sang her to sleep as if they'd never been apart. Elvis, no less—she wondered if his choice of *Now Or Never* was intentional or not.

"G'night, honey." he sighed before losing consciousness. She tightened her fingers in his, feeling something inside of her chest open.

Hart was right. If anybody deserved the truth after all these years, it was him—he *could* handle it. Better than her parents, or Conrad, or anyone else. And though she was scared of the nightmares that were to come, there was now a small comfort knowing he'd be waiting when she woke.

"G'night, Hart."

WHOOSH

25

The sun had only been awake for a few hours when she finally escaped from the claws of her nightmares. Lennon gasped, ripping away from the body next to her for a split second until she remembered who it belonged to.

He's safe. I'm safe.

Still deep in his sleep, Hart stirred from her movement, a raspy groan rumbling from his chest. "Y'okay, baby?"

"Mhm," she said quietly, blinking the sleep out of her eyes. He hummed, tightening his arms around her.

She watched him and his peaceful expression with a soft curiosity, unable to remember the last time she'd wanted to return to a dream. Carefully slipping from his hold, she stretched in the sunlight, tattoos contorting with her skin. Toiletries in hand, she padded excitedly downstairs to the master bathroom—it was the best in the house, and letting Hart sleep a little longer was a perfectly viable excuse.

Her focus was interrupted with mouth-watering smells of breakfast foods. Thinking she'd been the first one awake, she let her

Missing Page

curiosity pulled her head around the corner. Stacy was scrambling a large pile of eggs in a skillet, supervised by a red cotton robe leaned against the counter. Cashmere was still waking up, huddled next to their coffee machine. The caffeine hadn't yet erased the grumpy lines on her face, nor the puffiness, but.

"Morning," Lennon uttered, surprised. Her parents both looked to her, and then straightened, expecting Hart to follow.

"He's still asleep," she murmured, suppressing a grin when both of their shoulders fell with relief. "I just came down to shower."

"God, you scared me." Cashmere pressed her hand to her heart. She noticed the towel in her daughter's hand and started down the hall. "I better get ready, then. You can use the guest shower."

Lennon scowled, fleeting away to the tiny bathroom just off the entrance. It was her least favorite in the house–it was too small, and the water never got hot enough–and her previous excitement made her extra disappointed.

Though she'd been quick, there were two deep voices conversing outside the bathroom by the time she emerged. She hurried to wring the water out of her hair, scrunching while she eavesdropped.

"...oh, gotcha. Yeah, Cali's cool." Hart's muffled voice came through the door. Lennon winced right as her father's voice came through.

"California, son, not Cali. Don't let the locals hear you say that."

She smiled. *It was about time someone told him.* Lennon made it back to the kitchen before Cashmere had returned. It was just the two men talking, and they seemed...relaxed. Amicable, even.

"There you are," Hart said, smiling sleepily at the sight of her. "Why didn't you wake me up?"

"You needed the sleep," she answered simply, glancing at her father. "I see you two finally met."

"Officially," Hart corrected awkwardly.

"Right." Lennon narrowed her eyes. "How did that happen, again?"

Stacy moved the skillet off the stove, dumping yellow fluff into a serving bowl and moving on to the bacon. "Let's make things clear—he found me. The kid *Facebook'd* me."

Hart reached to scratch the back of his neck. "You told me his name a while back...it's easy to remember—"

"Why's that?" Stacy interjected sharply. Lennon looked at him knowingly, stifling a grin.

Hart stuttered. "Oh—er, it's just...y'know Stacy isn't–"

"A man's name?"

Hart paled, stammering again. "No, I was gonna say common! It's not a common–"

"Stop it, Dad." Lennon laughed, putting her hand on Hart's tense shoulders. "He's messing with you, Hart."

He didn't believe her until Stacy smiled, identical to the mischievous one that sometimes sprouted on Lennons' face. "Oh."

She leaned down to his ear, whispering as a pair of heels clicked down the hallway. "Trust me, he's not the one you need to worry about."

"We don't tell secrets in this house," Cashmere warned, fidgeting with her satin blouse. She flashed her best realtor-headshot smile as she reached out to hug Hart. "Is this the young man I've been hearing all about?"

"I hope so." He chuckled, straightening his posture. He could feel the immediate change in the air with her presence, the way everybody's backs and faces straightened out. "Nice to meet you, ma'am."

Cash winced. "I spend too much on Botox to be a ma'am. Just call me Cashmere, or Mrs. Mayfield. Nice to *finally* meet you, Hart." She shot a look at her daughter on the last sentence, batting her fake eyelashes and reaching for her mug. "You're here for three days, right?"

"Yes," he confirmed. Stacy handed them empty plates, and they each scooped servings from the bar, Hart eating a little more feverishly than the others.

"You *were* hungry," Lennon hissed under her breath.

"Not anymore," he said after gulping down his last bite.

"Lennon," Cashmere scolded as Stacy pushed the bowls of food toward him. "You're not starving the boy, are you?"

"No, Mom."

"You have a guest, now, so make sure you're—"

"Cash," Stacy interrupted softly. "Honey. He just got here."

She faltered. Lennon could feel her mother simmering under his chiding, but she let her words cool behind pouty lips.

"Don't worry, she's been great." Hart assured, nodding to Lennon.

Her mother's shoulders rolled, taking a moment before trying again. "What're your plans while you're here?"

"I didn't have much time to make an itinerary," Lennon mumbled, attempting a joke.

"Take him everywhere. You could show him your school, the gelato shop...oh, the country club! God knows we're wasting that membership..."

Lennon hadn't been there in years. She and Page used to bike there during the summers—two and a half miles, just to use their pool and sit out by the fishing pond. She'd send Page to get virgin mudslides while she took a 'bathroom break,' which really meant running to the dock to smoke before Page got back. Then they'd sit, talk, and laugh for hours. That felt like a lifetime ago.

"That could be fun," Hart agreed, taking his plate to the sink. "I'm really just here for Lennon, and to help you guys out. I don't care much what we do in the meantime.

"But if you're up to it..." He looked to Lennon, winking, and she felt something light stir in her stomach. "I'd love to get the Lennon tour."

She caught her dad's small smile of approval in her peripheral. Lennon almost snorted—he *liked* him. Despite his tough exterior, Stacy was a teddy bear.

"Sure. Let's do it."

"All right." Hart clapped his hands against the counter. "Give me ten minutes." He kissed her head and jogged up the stairs, the pipes of her shower squeaking to a start shortly after.

Lennon descended instead, pushing open the royal blue door. The air hit her, staler than ever; Page was fading. Her five tries came and went within a few minutes, and she scribbled them onto the wrinkling paper, setting it back on her nightstand in frustrated defeat.

Hart's hesitant knock startled her, and he smiled sheepishly from the hallway. "Ready?"

Lennon stood, feeling caught. "Yeah, I was just..." She trailed off, noticing his curious gaze at the room.

His voice was much quieter than before. "This is her room?"

Lennon swallowed. She forgot it was his first time here. This showed a new facet of grief, realizing he would never learn things about her first-hand. If he was ever curious about her, he could only ask Lennon.

She was unable to answer, but nodded tightly.

His eyes returned to hers with a gentle caution. "Can I come in?"

Her brain had already loaded a polite *no* into her mouth, but something in her heart made her pause.

"Yes." she said curtly, remaining still.

He crossed the threshold carefully, taking a seat next to her on the bed. "I recognize this room."

Her brows furrowed in confusion. "You do?"

He nodded to the canvas above her headboard. "The picture's different, but the bed's the same. I FaceTimed you while you were in here...it was the first time you ever let me talk to her."

Her breath hitched, overcome with the forgotten memory.

"It was a huge deal to me. I knew it was important, since you'd hidden her for so long. I was scared she'd notice the phone shaking from my hands and call me out, but of course now I know she was way too nice to do something like that. I expected a mini-you, and I guess physically, she was, but once she got to talking I realized you

Missing Page

two are *completely* different people. You don't talk about anything, she wanted to talk about everything. She even asked about Christmas...I thought she hated me for taking you away."

"Page doesn't hate anybody," Lennon had said with a sad smile.

"I believe it. Even though a phone screen, I've never seen someone with such genuine happiness. It radiated from her, it was contagious.

"But the coolest thing I noticed—" his tone changed into something even more gentle than before, placing his hand over hers— "was how much *you* changed. I felt like I was getting to see you for the first time. She brought out a side of you I'd never seen before.

"She was your world. You revolved around her like she was your sun," Hart said in admiration. "And you were her moon, her stars. Opposites, but perfectly complimentary." His words stretched over her like a hug. But as the memory faded, so did his smile. "What were you doing in here?"

Half-truths came easier than a full lie. "Had to get some work done...internet's the best in here. And it feels like her." She stood, changing the subject with a smile. "You wanna go?"

He nodded, thoughts working behind warm, analytical eyes. In that moment, Lennon felt as though he could see right through her. Maybe he had all along. Was it possible that Hart had seen every molecule of pain, love, and fear that hid behind her eyes and plastered smile, that he heard everything she was trying conceal in her steady voice? Surely he couldn't know *why* he was hiding it, though if he thought about it enough, he could probably connect it to her recurring, unexplained nightmares. Maybe there were alike in more ways than she thought, though he seemed to be the only one capable of good timing.

He threw his arm over her shoulder, kissing her hair. "Let's go."

They passed her old elementary school on the way, but she couldn't be bothered to stop. Lennon didn't want to misuse what little time she had left, and she couldn't think of a bigger waste than reminiscing on a childhood she didn't miss. She parked into her family's platinum member parking spot, and slipped her fingers through Hart's as they entered the large building.

After stopping at the bar, Lennon took him to her favorite sitting spot by the window, which harbored a perfect view of the club's crystal-clear lake. The happier Hart was, the chattier he became; with a Jack Honey and Coke in one hand and Lennon's fingers interlaced in the other, basking in Laguna's sun, he'd gushed for ten minutes straight.

"Utah's pretty, the lakes are great...but *this*?" Unwilling to let go of her hand, he used his glass to gesture toward the rolling emerald hills, the high sun sparkling against the pond. "This is paradise. You live in paradise."

She laughed humorlessly. "This place is gonna eat you right up. It's a Venus Fly Trap."

His smile morphed into something smug. "'Devil in Disguise', huh?"

Lennon grinned, but the smile didn't reach her eyes. There was too much truth to find humor in his words.

"Sorry," she uttered, watching him take another sip. "I'm not trying to be a downer."

"You have every right to be."

"Ugh." She shuddered his coat of pity off her shoulders. "Can't we just get fucked up, and worry about everything another day?"

Her humor didn't transfer well. He watched her, worry creasing his eyes.

"I was kidding, holy shit." She rushed to recover. "Bad joke."

"You *do* do that, though. We did that."

"Over homework, or finals. Nothing serious..."

"I'm not sure that's true." He was looking out the window, his mind somewhere else.

Her brows furrowed. "What do you mean?"

He fidgeted uncomfortably, lowering his voice. "It didn't always *feel* like it was just about school." He'd loved her too much

Missing Page

to risk rocking the boat before, scared he'd lose her. Now, he loved her too much not to. "You remember the first time I spent the night, and had to wake you up from your nightmare? After I left, you didn't talk to me for three days. You did the same thing after we had—"

"I remember." She cut him off, feeling the blood rush to her cheeks. She hadn't realized he'd been taking notes.

"I felt stupid that whole weekend because you didn't text me back. I figured I'd misread, that you only wanted to hook up... But then you were back to normal on Monday. Like nothing had happened." His eyes fell. "I thought it was me. Until that morning when I closed the blinds, and you—"

"*Okay*, Hart." She tugged her ball-cap over her eyes. He'd been paying much closer attention than she thought, too close for comfort.

"That's when I knew it wasn't about me. They were...triggers, almost, that made you go radio silent."

There wasn't enough THC in her system for this, and the easiest thing she could resort to was dismissal. "I have shit from my past to deal with, that's not new information. I was high out of my mind during all those scenarios, Hart, who knows what I was thinking?"

"Look, I'm not playing dumb anymore. It wasn't just a 'bad trip,' Lennon, you know that. *I* know that." He leaned forward. "You've said all these things before. But you never say what the shit you're dealing with *is*."

Their faces were inches apart. She couldn't get away from the truth if she tried; he was smarter than she'd ever given him credit for. If only she could—

"Oh—My—God. Lennon, is that you?" a shrill voice called from behind them. With a wince, she turned, desperate to jump ship. Macy tugged on her inebriated twin's elbow, pointing. "Mic, look who it is!"

Their matching faces of surprise were almost comical. Michaela gasped. "Ohem*gee!*"

The girls exchanged empty glasses for two pink cocktails and hurried over, clumsily wrapping their arms around her. "We thought you died!"

"Michaela, *seriously*," Macy hissed. "Be fucking considerate."

Horror washed over her face as she realized. "I'm an idiot. Oh, Lennon..."

Lennon waved away her apology. She could smell the tequila on their breaths when they hugged her, and it's not like they had much awareness to begin with.

Michaela's attention traveled to Hart, her eyes trailing up his arms and along the sharp curve of his jaw. It was quick, but it made Lennon squirm—they were practically eye-fucking him right in front of her.

"Don't tell me this is who I think it is!" Macy gasped, unaware she'd wetted her lips.

"Wait...*you're* Hart?" Michaela asked in slight disbelief.

"So you *have* talked about me." Hart nudged Lennon with a smirk. She could tell by the look in his eye they were in no way finished with their conversation, but he'd let it go for now.

"Only when we drag it out of her," Macy giggled, twisting a strand of hair absentmindedly. "Lennon's *very* private...she likes to keep things for herself."

"Well, I can't have anything to myself with you two around." Lennon's smile was perfectly polite as it filtered her words, transforming her bullets into flowers.

The girls took seats on either side of them, jumping into an interrogation of Hart's past, interrupting ever so often with giggles and *aww's*—Hart carried charisma effortlessly, and even more handsomely. Lennon imagined he could have a conversation with a rock if he wanted, and even then, that rock would be left feeling better than it did before.

Despite the girls' flirty smiles, Lennon was content to watch. She'd heard most of these stories from him before, but she appreciated when other people asked questions for her so she could stay in her own personal bubble. She liked listening to him—every

Missing Page

story he told was a happy one. And in every answer, he'd squeeze her hand, or lift it to kiss her knuckles. It was clear where his attention lived.

"You two are *so* opposite. How interesting." Michaela pursed her lips around her pink straw, squeezing her elbows to her sides to boost her tits.

"So she's always been this quiet, then?" Hart asked, resting his arm on the back of Lennon's chair. "Glad it's not just me."

Michaela giggled. "I think so. We met in middle school. Were you different before—?"

"No," Lennon answered. She kept her eyes on her hand, currently being caressed by Hart's thumb.

"But you're not shy." Macy raised her eyebrows suggestively, finally looking away from Hart. "We've seen *that* first hand."

"Silent, but deadly," Michaela added.

Lennon wrinkled her nose. "Like a fart?"

"Like a gun," Hart corrected, understanding exactly what they meant.

Presently, Lennon looked nothing like the party animal they were describing. She had shrunk in her chair, sweeping her fingers absentmindedly over knuckles freshly healed from the last time she went out.

"Hey, you wanna head over to the lake soon?" Hart squeezed Lennon's thigh, sensing the energy shift.

"Yeah," She blinked. "We should get going."

He took her hand, lifting her to her feet and nodding to the girls. "It was nice to meet y'all."

"You, too..." They both watched him stand, in awe as all six foot four of him towered over their seats. Lennon gave a small wave goodbye, feeling Michaela's mischievous eyes lingering.

"Before you go...did you ever get my little gift? I didn't hear anything from you. I mean, not that I was *really* expecting you to share." She laughed then, as if it were an inside joke. Lennon felt the hairs on her arm prickle at Michaela's question.

"How're they treating you?" Michaela's mouth circled around the vowel, holding it between her lips. Lennon stared at her, recognizing her game. Michaela always got what she wanted—of course she wouldn't let Hart leave when Lennon was still the apple of his eye.

Hart looked back and forth, picking up the vagueness. "How is what treating you?"

Lennon remained silent, deferring to Michaela. It wasn't anger she felt, but disgust, and even pity. These girls didn't care about her because they *couldn't*. They were robots, programmed only with small talk, social-climbing ambitions, and dopamine addictions. If she wanted to make Lennon look like some kind of junkie, fine—but Lennon wouldn't do Mic's dirty work for her. Macy stirred her empty drink, ice clinking against the glass.

Michaela laughed awkwardly. "It was something take the edge off, with everything—"

"A few happy pills," Macy added, nodding innocently.

Hart blinked, his smile fading. "Sorry, did you say pills?"

"Nothing crazy." Michaela's voice raised an octave as she tried to recover with a pageant-level smile.

"Just a bottle full," Lennon said dryly.

He looked to Macy in confusion, and then let out a strangled laugh. "I can't tell if you're joking."

Michaela's face blanked as realization settled in the creases between Hart's brows. Her plan had backfired. "Oh my God, you're serious."

"What's the big deal? You're acting like we gave her heroin," Macy finally said, taking a defensive stance next to her twin.

He turned to Lennon. "Did you take any?"

A pang of guilt threatened to cement her teeth together, but she forced the words through them. "A few."

The vein in his throat pulsed, and a dark expression took over his face as he turned back to Michaela. "She's been sober for almost four months. Her sister just *died*...if she was having a bad night, those

Missing Page

could have killed her. I mean, are you fucking crazy? What's wrong with you?"

"*Excuse* me!" Macy sneered, while Michaela stood wide-eyed.

"Hart," Lennon said softly, taking his elbow. "Let's go."

Michaela's eyes narrowed into slits as they walked away, fury contorting her lips into an uneven scowl. Lennon heard her voice again just before they reached the door.

"So what, that's it? You're done? You can't just walk out on ten years of friendship, Lennon!"

Lennon turned, piercing her with a knowing gaze. Michaela's bravery instantly evaporated, and she stepped back. There was nothing she could guilt her with; of course they never really friends. The twins used Lennon for excitement, and Lennon used them to survive. It was purely transactional, and she wouldn't let her pretend otherwise.

"Have a good one, Mic," Lennon said. The door swung shut, severing the last string holding them together. *It was done.*

She held her hand out to Hart for the keys once they reached the parking lot, and noticed worry still creased into his otherwise handsome face.

"Hey," she said softly, hoping her calmness would ease his anxiety.

"Hey," he murmured, tugging gently on her hand.

Her gut twisted at the pain he was feeling at her expense. She needed him to forget, to feel as okay as she did—relieved, even.

"If I ask you something, do you promise to be honest with me?"

"Of course," he said instantly, brows furrowing.

She paused for effect. "Do you think Michaela's tits look like mine?"

He blinked. "What?"

"Apparently I was her inspo photo."

He shook his head, but something happy touched the corners of his lips. They shared a laugh, and she felt the air lighten.

"I'm sorry," he added. "For going off back there..."

To his surprise, she smiled. *Of course he thought her anger was directed at him.*

"Don't be," she said with conviction. "Seriously. Long overdue."

At his hesitancy, Lennon reached to place a kiss on his chin. "It was kind've hot, honestly. But don't tell Hart I said that."

The look he gave her might as well've been a kiss, but instead he squeezed her fingers, shaking out their hands. He hadn't forgotten, after all.

We're not out of the woods yet, the silence said. These moments, however nice, were only precursors to what she'd promised him—the truth. Hart couldn't go forward without it.

He'd hoped the prolonged tension would wiggle its way under Lennon's tongue during the drive. His doubt grew with each turn of the wheel, in every gear shift. Then again, he should've known better than to think he could ever win a quiet game against her.

As she pulled into the lot overlooking the coast, his willpower crumbled to the ground. But just before he could get the question out, she looked to him.

"I don't have those pills anymore. Just so you know."

His voice was quiet, but relieved she'd followed through. It was a step in the right direction. "When did you relapse?"

"The day after Page..." She couldn't say the word, but he understood. His nods were slow, his eyes far away. "She kept offering, so I kept going back."

His fingers inched over hers, cradling them like water.

Lennon looked out the windshield, taking in the picturesque view of the beach. She wanted to remember this moment, the *before*. Before the toxins that had poisoned the wells of her heart and mind for years spilled out and leaked into whatever—or whoever—was near. That dark, festering truth pushed uncomfortably at the seams, using all its might to escape.

She wondered for so long who, if any, would be the one to extract this from her. They were always cold listeners—psychologists, her mother, God. For some reason, in all of those scenarios, she'd never

Missing Page

imagined it'd be someone whose hand she could hold, and feel safe when it squeezed back.

Her pounding heart clung on to the confession, begging it to stay inside. She'd carried this secret like an infant, long past due, because she didn't trust the world enough to take care of or understand it.

"Do you know where we are?" she finally asked.

His head swiveled, eyes hidden beneath his cap. They trailed up the coastline, settling on a small cove tucked into the curve of rocks; a gaping mouth invited entry, but there was an eeriness around it.

He swallowed. "Is that...?"

"Yes." Her tone was monotone, giving no tell of the catastrophe happening inside her. Hart reached across the console, taking her hand in his.

"This place used to be a really happy memory for me and my family. I've thought that's maybe why she ended up there that night." Lennon shifted, wrapping her arms around her legs. "My dad used to take me to get comfortable with the water again. The day she was born, I started asking when we could bring her along." A distant smile touched her lips. "She called them mermaid lunches once she could talk. They got so much fun after she started coming. It really did feel magical."

"What do you mean, get comfortable again?"

The palms of her hands grew damp, and her eyes unfocused. "My friend fell off his family's boat on a lake trip when I was four... his name was Wyatt. He had been my best friend. My only friend, actually."

There was a beat while she worked out the words in her head.

"I was little, but I knew my clothes didn't look like the other kids'. Neither did my toys, or our house. It'd never bothered me, but I'd heard my parents fight about money, so I knew the differences were a bad thing. And then my mom got pregnant, the same year we were supposed to move. My dad was taking every gig he could get, and my mom was busy trying to get her real estate license. There just wasn't time for me...but I hated that daycare, every moment of it. The only good thing about it was Wyatt. And he's the one who—" She broke off, waiting for the lump in her throat to pass.

"We'd just dropped my mom off at the dock when it happened. She'd gotten seasick, but Mrs. Bates wanted to practice driving. So we went out, for one last lap." She blinked, struggling to form the words. "We heard the yelling first...then the propeller—"

Hart's eyes widened.

"There was blood *everywhere*." Lennon whispered. "On the boat, on Mr. Bates, in the water... My dad covered my eyes the second he realized, and kept them there until we got back. I never saw the body. I just had to listen, and it was all *loud*, all of it. Everyone was crying, shouting, there were flare guns, sirens... I'd never heard cries like that." Her eyes shut, voice shaking. She wouldn't hear them again, either, until they came out of her own mouth at her own loss.

"Oh, honey." Hart uttered dolefully.

"They wrapped him in tarp. It was all they had." Her voice shrunk, barely above a whisper. "And I've always thought...it would've—if he hadn't... It's my fault that he died, because it should've been me." The secret finally crawled out, weak and malnourished from years of imprisonment. It hung on to her words like a parasite, grasping for its last moments of life.

"He'd switched places with me. Mr. Bates was watching me while the boys and my dad went to the front to look for dolphins. I was making such a fuss about wanting to go with them, but my dad only had two hands, and Mr.—Devin, that's his name, was talking Mrs. Bates through the driving—"

Her heart was tearing, but she couldn't stop the tumbling of words. "I cried so much that Wyatt offered to switch me. It wasn't even five minutes after..."

Hart leaned over the console, his expression agonized over the tears building in her eyes. He wanted to wipe them away, but she was gripping his hand so tight that her nails had begun to leave half-moons in his skin.

Her teeth held tight to her wavering lip. It was finally out, in the

Missing Page

open for Hart to see in all its wretchedness. She was scared that if she moved too much, it would make everything real.

His face fell. "Who let you think that was your fault?"

She remained frozen, the air trapped in her lungs starting to burn. His response had surprised her again, and her brain was still processing.

He reached forward, cupping her face. "I've always been honest with you, haven't I? Lennon, you did *not* kill that boy."

"I think I did," she whispered, gasping. The air had gotten so sparse all of a sudden; it felt like no matter how much she invited oxygen in, it still waited at the door of her mouth, as if scared to enter. She clamored for the handle, nearly falling to the dirt before she found her footing. She edged towards the horizon, taking a seat just before the edge of the cliff. Lifting her hand to her heart and her eyes to the ocean, she saw a dying sun greeting her, its orange rays bleeding into the water.

From the Jeep, Hart's feet followed small dirt imprints, until he found a seat next to her.

"Since Page, it's all I think about now." She swallowed, eyes hurting from holding back tears. The truth stung her throat like acid. "It feels like I poison whoever I touch. There has to be something that I can't see, right? But then I look in the mirror, and it's just me." Tears stained her cheek. "I just see *me*."

The ocean crashed against the shore like thunder. A setting sun cast a glowing finale over Hart's face, warming his irises to a shimmering bronze. His lips pressed into her hair, and she settled her head in the crook of his neck.

"I've always been sad. I think I was born that way. Wyatt and Page were some of the happiest people I've ever met, and *you*..." She wiped her eyes, willing her control back. "I've never met someone like you. I didn't know people like you existed. But I haven't been able to admit it because I'm terrified that when I do, I'll lose you too."

Once his arms wrapped around her, she completely unraveled. She'd done enough today; it was time to set the scalpel down.

"Can we go home?" she pleaded softly. Hart walked back with her to the car, taking the driver's seat. Lennon's forehead rested against the window, letting it cool her sweaty skin. Sobriety made sure that every ounce of pain could be felt—getting that out took more strength than she thought she had. She made it through, though. That counted for something.

26

Stacy was grilling tilapia and salmon when they returned. He was sunburned from an afternoon shoot, but otherwise seemed in good spirits. A faint, familiar odor wrinkled Lennon's nose and entranced Hart's, drawing both of them to the cooler and tackle box by the door.

"Going fishing, Dad?" she asked, meeting him on the deck. Hart's hand pressed against his growling stomach, and Stacy handed them serving plates.

"Yeah, before the weather gets bad. Freezer's getting low." He wiped his brow with the inside of his arm, hot from the grill. "You two wanna come?"

Hart couldn't help his excited grin. "You know a spot?"

"I know a few," Stacy said proudly. "You fish?"

"You know, Stacy, I think this is the beginning of a beautiful, beautiful friendship," Hart said genially, eliciting a loud laugh from the large man. Though obviously eager, Hart deferred to Lennon, their conversation still fresh on his mind. "You wanna go, baby?"

She glanced between the two of them, wanting to laugh at their matching hopefulness.

"Sure. Sounds nice." She stabbed a small piece of meat, the metal clanging against the ceramic plate. For the first time in weeks, she actually felt the calls of hunger poking from the inside. "So what am *I* gonna do?"

They were quiet as they ate, all hungry from the long day. Lennon was full after the one plate and started on the dishes while Hart and her father scarfed down seconds.

Stacy saluted the two goodnight. Soon Hart was next to her with a drying towel, and the two shared looks and smiles under the window light.

"Think I'm gonna hop in the shower," she whispered, carefully placing the last plate in the cabinet. It felt strange to go without him, but she didn't want to overstep. He nodded, watching her with a pained longing as she faded away.

Soon the knobs of her shower twisted, freeing a stream of hot water from overhead. Her clothes fell from her bony figure to the floor in a heap, and she flinched away from the mirror at her reflection, tearing a robe from its hook to wrap around herself. She kept her eyes down as she took a brush to her knotted layers.

The knocks on her door came just before Hart's head peeked in. "Mind if I come in?"

She nodded, reaching to tighten the straps around her waist. He watched her through the mirror she was avoiding, stopping behind her. Every snag of the brush sent a vicarious wince through him, before eventually becoming too much to bear. Even when it was self-inflicted, he could not tolerate her pain.

Gently, he moved his hand over hers, wrapping his fingers around the handle of the brush. "Could I try?"

She looked at him through the foggy mirror, taking in the way his eyes washed over hers with pronounced adoration. Her hold on the brush relaxed until it slipped out of his grasp, and dropped to her side. He pulled the bristles through her tangles with unwavering patience and ease that spread through her jaw and shoulders. It

Missing Page

wasn't long before her eyelids grew heavy, threatening to close in the warm fog.

"How's that?" he murmured, his lips brushing her ear with each syllable.

"Good." she hummed, suddenly feeling a pulse between her legs. "It's good."

Her fingers lifted unthinkingly to the fluffy straps around her waist. The terrycloth fell free, dropping to the ground, and she turned to him, tracing her nails up his chest.

"Come with me," she said, pulling him toward the shower.

Against her expectations, he faltered, as if expecting a different trio of words.

"Len..." he said, holding her wrists before they could travel lower.

"What?"

His eyes were burning when they found hers. "What are we doing?"

Remorse shadowed her thin, beautiful face. "Hart..." She lifted his hands to her lips. "I'm sorry. I know this must all be confusing, and has been for a long time. And maybe I'm saying this too late, but I have to. Because if we never speak again, and you go on never knowing the way I feel about you..." Her lips pressed together, but she forced the vulnerability out before she could swallow it. "It's something I've never felt before, with anyone, and won't ever feel again. I...I care about you, *so much*, and I—"

She didn't know how to properly explain the love she felt for him, which was so strong and selfless that she was willing to stay away to keep him safe. Four letters seemed meager in comparison to what burned in her heart for him.

"I'm yours," she professed. "Whether that's your friend, your girlfriend, I'll take whatever you'll have me as. But I can't keep pretending to not feel the way I feel about you, and I won't try. I have ran away my whole life, but you are the only person I've ever wanted to run *to*."

She felt like she'd flipped her heart inside out, bared for all to see. After a painstakingly long moment, he lifted her hand to his lips.

"Say something," she begged, after his continued silence.

"I liked the way girlfriend sounded," he mused, his lips traveling over her knuckles. "Should we start with that?"

Before she could think about it, she rushed forward, clashing her lips against his. The soft, warm flesh drew a hum of pleasure from her the moment she made contact, It was water after a drought, sun after a storm. He reached forward, cupping her face as his lips worked tenderly against hers.

She purred once they were both under the water. His skin suctioned against hers, and his large, gentle hands slid over her waist and up her shoulders, grazing her nipples with his thumbs. She gasped when his lips touched the tender skin beneath her ear, feeling a tingling sensation shooting all the way down to her toes, and arched against the tile.

Hart moaned when he tasted her, stepping forward and pressing her against the icy wall. Her arms wrapped around him like vines, growing feverish as she felt him harden against her abdomen.

"I missed you," he said into her neck, his fingers teasing the flesh between her thighs. She gasped softly, her head thudding against the wall.

"*Please.* I want you," she breathed. Another sigh escaped as his fingers slipped inside her. He flicked upwards, and she dug her nails into his bicep, feeling a wave of euphoria roll through her. His teeth pulled at her earlobe, baring in a smile when she trembled with pleasure. His hand lifted to her mouth just before she came, muffling her cries in his palm.

"Fuck, Lennon," he growled.

She needed their bodies to be together, to feel him as closely as humanly possible. Her leg hooked around his waist while he settled between her, but the momentum stopped there. After a painfully long beat, he finally mustered the words.

"Are you *sure?*"

Missing Page

"Yes," she said, her eyes locked onto his. "Nobody's ever been more sure than I am right now."

He wrapped her other leg around him with ease, kissing her deeply as he sank into her. The groan that followed rumbled from his lips into hers, and at once, their bodies were intertwined in a beautiful mess of skin, sweat and soap.

"Jesus *Christ*," he whispered, pressing his forehead to hers.

Lennon would say the thing if she could speak—she was currently overwhelmed with the raw, stretching feeling spreading through her entire body.

He stopped at her silence, finding her eyes. "Are you okay?"

"Please," she panted, parting her wet, swollen lips. "Don't stop."

Hart pressed a kiss to her nose and lifted her arms over her head. The wall thudded rhythmically as he rocked into her, clenching his jaw to distract from the immense pleasure filling every muscle. Lennon knotted her hands in his hair, eyes rolling as the pressure built. She peered up at him from under her dripping lashes, watching him hold off his own to keep going.

"I want you to," she breathed. "With me."

Though he was the stronger of the two, even he had his limits. Within minutes, the two had been reduced to a symphony of breathless pants and tangled limbs. And for the first time in a month, Lennon felt a moment of true, genuine happiness.

She only noticed his red, angry skin after he turned, and quickly stepped to block the scalding water from doing more damage.

"Go ahead," she murmured, once they'd caught their breath. "I'll be out in a minute."

She faced herself in the mirror once alone, taking in the color that had returned to her sallow, hollowed cheeks. Even that moment of pure, complete bliss couldn't erase the last month from her face. In a matter of moments, all the happiness she'd felt had disintegrated, leaving dust and emptiness in its wake. It was a comedown worse than drugs, being alone after feeling so close. Lennon crossed her arms over her chest, feeling the void more than she had in weeks.

Suddenly there were tears welling in her eyes, and she was unable to stop the dam that had broken. Her grief was everywhere, even the good parts. All she could do was hug herself, trying to calm her convulsing body and hold it together at the same time.

Hart would come knocking if she didn't come out soon. She wasn't ready when her feet stepped out, but most of her emotions and tears had made it down the drain. She scrunched her hair into a towel before entering the bedroom, finding her near-unconscious boyfriend burrowed beneath the comforter. "Asleep already?"

He turned to face her, raising the blanket like a wing for her to lie under. "Not yet."

Lennon slipped into one of his t-shirts and crawled into the space, nestling against him.

"I'm glad you're here," she whispered. Although whatever had attacked her in the shower still lingered in her mind, she already felt much better wrapped in the arms of someone who cared for her the way Hart did. His love was light, and that looming void Lennon felt could only grow in darkness.

"I'm glad you're glad." He kissed her wet hair, inhaling. Lennon's cheek settled against his chest, listening to his heart beat in her ear.

"Hart?"

He hummed tiredly. "Yes, darling."

"I love you."

The air stilled. "Sorry, what did you say?"

"I said what you think I said."

He bent his chin to look down at her, unable to hide the boyish smile spreading on his face. "Really?"

She nodded slowly, feeling almost as surprised as he looked. "Yeah."

"Can you say it again?"

Lennon turned her head to fully meet his eyes. "I love you."

His pupils swelled with adoration. "One more time," he pleaded, slightly more playful.

"You haven't even said it back!"

Missing Page

He cupped her cheeks in his hand, leaning forward to plant a kiss on her nose. "I've loved you since the day I met you, Lennon Mayfield. I've just been waiting for you to catch up."

Damn him and his contagious smile. "*Blegh*. We're a couple of cheeseballs."

"Who cares?" He sighed contently. "My best friend is my girlfriend, and my girlfriend loves me. Nobody can tell me anything."

It didn't take long for Lennon to drift once they said goodnight, falling into a black nothingness. That darkness was something that not even love could protect her from.

Deep asleep, Hart stirred, moving his heavy arm around her. Once craving it, she now felt like a trapped animal, fighting to breathe against her captor.

"Shh...s'okay, honey." he mumbled. "Go back to sleep."

27

WHOOSH

"Our sand's actually chocolate-milk flavored, you know."

Lennon looked doubtfully at the half-full purple cup she was holding. If she and Wyatt's older brother had been making castles and drawing tic-tac-toe in the sand for the past thirty minutes, why was he only *now* divulging this information?

"No it's not." She wrinkled her nose.

"I swear!" Conrad promised, eyes wide. Freckles splashed over his nose like constellations under a pair of mischievous hazel eyes.

Still unconvinced, she turned, looking for Wyatt—he always told the truth. But he and a few other kids had gone with Mrs. Bates to walk through the gardens. This was only Lennon's fourth day at daycare, but she couldn't imagine choosing a boring garden over a place like this. Only Conrad and two other children seemed to think the same.

Wyatt's home was like a castle, filled with trinkets and toys she never knew existed; they even had stars in their ceiling in the movie room. Lennon's home looked small and cramped in comparison, and she woke eager to leave every morning, wondering what adventure

Missing Page

she'd get into. So, while her flags were raised, it didn't seem *impossible* that a house of this grandeur had something magical like chocolate flavored sand.

"C'mon, just try it," Conrad insisted, nodding for emphasis. Lennon glanced down once more. It *was* kind of tempting, and the color matched his promise...

She bent over almost immediately, hacking and spluttering for air the sand had stolen. Conrad clutched his stomach, doubled over with laughter. "You did it! You actually did it!"

Lennon glared through watery eyes, wiping the clump of sand off her tongue. "You're a jerk!" She cried, feeling warm liquid trickle down her cheeks.

"It was just a prank, jeez," Conrad breathed, still recovering. "Not my fault you're so gullible."

Lennon ran for the house, red with humiliation. How could she have fallen for that? If she were five, she'd know better...

"Lennon? You okay, sweetheart?"

Her head swiveled to the living room, to where Wyatt's father stood. She shook her head, her tongue still hanging from her mouth.

"What's wrong, pretty girl?"

"Water," She would have laughed at how funny she sounded it if it weren't for the circumstances. Mr. Bates walked with her to the kitchen, setting her on the counter and filling a sippy cup. She swished the first gulp in her mouth and spat into the sink, watching the small particles trickle into the drain.

"Get some sand in your mouth?" he asked, smiling. She shook her head, but her tongue was too dry to say anything else. Everyone had called Hadley a tattletale when she told on Conrad; nobody talked to her for a whole day. Lennon wouldn't risk that, not when she was so new.

"Hmmm..." Mr. Bates flipped his wrist, checking his watch. He looked out to the yard, counting the children with his eyes. His tongue *tsk'ed* a few times.

Mr. Bates pulled her from the counter and led her down the hall, into the bathroom. She jumped when the water started, spooked by how loud it was. He bent and grabbed something from beneath the sink that crinkled like plastic, silver and transparent. Before he stood, she watched him flick the doorknob, clicking the lock into place. Something strange bubbled in her stomach.

"C'mon, let's get you undressed."

She swallowed, trying not to show her discomfort as her Blues Clues T-shirt slid over her head. "Why do I need a bath?"

Mr. Bates grabbed a hair tie, twisting her waist-length hair up before setting the crinkly thing over her head. Why wasn't he answering?

"Don't want to get your pretty hair wet..." he said gruffly, setting her in the water.

Her body clenched at the temperature, immediately shivering.

"It's cold!" she gasped, crossing her arms.

"I know, I know, we gotta be quick," Mr. Bates said, concentrating.

In those seven minutes, Lennon had never felt more exposed. For some reason, this felt like a secret. Her dad never gave baths like this, with so much haste and fear.

As long as the bath had felt, she wasn't ready when he pulled her from it, shocking her skin with the brisk air. Mr. Bates wrapped her in a towel and carried her down another hall; this one led to his and Mrs. Bates' bedroom, which she'd never been inside before. There'd been no reason to.

"I'm c-c-cold," she said through chattering teeth after he laid her down on the bed.

Mr. Bates approached her with a bottle in hand, squirting a thick white cream from it into the other. "We just gotta put some lotion on. You can't have dry skin, you'll get itchy."

She was starting to feel sick. But he was a dad, and she was only four. Dads knew way more than she did.

She could hear the laughter from the other kids in the backyard. Lennon craned her neck to look toward the window, try to pinpoint

Missing Page

who was having such a good time. The hair cap crinkled as she moved, and Mr. Bates' eyes darted, quickly walking around the bed. His hands reached for the curtains, and with a quick jerk of his wrist, the dark material swung shut, erasing any light from the room.

WHOOSH

∼

"Get away from me, get away from me!" she screamed.

Lennon released her hold on Hadley, the adrenaline from her chase fading fast at the sight of the girl's arm. Dirt had clumped over her scratches, but dots of blood were already starting to poke through.

"I'm sorry, I'm sorry!" Lennon said fearfully, trying to calm the tattletale down as her whimpers grew in volume. It was too late—the damage was done. Hadley wailed, and Mr. and Mrs. Bates came running.

"What on Earth!" Mrs. Bates gasped, holding Hadley's arm. She turned to Lennon, who wilted. "Did you do this?"

"We were playing Jungle... I was the tiger," Lennon mumbled guiltily.

"Oh, no." Mrs. Bates clicked her tongue, lifting Hadley into her arms. "C'mon honey, we'll get this cleaned up."

Mr. Bates looked at Lennon, shadowed with disappointment. But she recognized the glint in his eye that always came when she did something bad. One that almost resembled success.

"We've told you before, no more roughhousing." he warned. "You'll have to stay home from the park today."

"I said I was sorry," she pleaded.

Lennon's heart plummeted. She didn't want to stay with him. "No, no! I'm sorry, I'll be good—"

"This kind of behavior has consequences, sweetheart. We can't hurt our friends." Mrs. Bates placed a hand on her small head.

She hung her head once he walked away, turning to the last person there. "I didn't *mean* to hurt her. She's such a baby."

"You can make her a cawd," Wyatt suggested. "I have constuction paper."

"Construction," Lennon corrected.

Wyatt smiled, and his cheek bloomed with red. "Constwuction, sowwy."

"They won't care," Lennon muttered. She let him walk with her back to the yard, feeling her mood sour with every step.

"I'll stay with you."

"Really?" She looked at him, hope widening her eyes.

"Yeah." He shrugged. "No pwobwem."

She hugged him tightly, filled with gratitude. Wyatt always knew how to cheer her up. He made the best silly faces, helped her in the prank war against his brother, and now was sacrificing his park trip so she wouldn't be alone.

As much warmth as it brought her, it all froze over once Lennon watched the kids file into the suburban one-by-one, and Mr. Bates' hand on her shoulder.

"Nap time," Mr. Bates sang.

She was the last one awake in Wyatt's room, hearing Wyatt's soft snores on the bed above hers. She couldn't fall asleep with the TV playing in the other room, knowing Mr. Bates was so close.

She froze when the door creaked open, hearing soft footsteps cross the wooden floor. Her body lifted, and hot breath hit her face. It was too scary to open her eyes. But she was sure she wasn't messy, she always made sure. What was he taking her for?

He walked for too long for the destination to be the bathroom. Maybe he was moving her to a different room, but she couldn't come up with a logical reason. Mr. Bates lied her down on something soft, sinking with the weight of her. In the next moment, the footsteps faded away.

Lennon was able to muster courage in her solitude. She cracked her eyes open, but just barely. Even with skewed sight, she recognized the ceiling, as well as the dark brown dresser, the lotion bottle...

Missing Page

She was in Mr. Bates' room again. Just like before, her stomach twisted into hard, painful knots, full of shame and fear.

She felt him sink into the bed next to her, but she remained frozen.

Summoning all of her courage, she squirmed, yawning as if she was waking up.

"Shhh," he whispered. "Go back to sleep."

She wanted to whimper, but her voice had left her. He reached forward, grasping the long string of the blinds.

WHOOSH

~

"Hey, Ang?" Cashmere touched Mrs. Bates' arm as Lennon walked into the home. "I wanted to talk to you for a moment, about Lennon..."

Mr. Bates hand felt like a flame on Lennon's shoulder as he guided her in. Wyatt looked up from his roadmap rug, glasses lopsided, and waved excitedly once he saw her. It gave her an excuse to duck out of Mr. Bates' grip, grabbing a toy car as she joined him on the floor. She didn't really like playing cars—she preferred Barbies, or tag—but she hated Mr. Bates' touch more.

It took a few minutes for Mr. Bates to notice his wife's absence. He turned, pausing at the sight of the Mayfield's concerned expressions. His heart picked up a few paces seeing Cashmere's mouth move so fervently, and rushed back after his wife glanced at him.

"...no, she's been sleeping fine," Angie assured, and then chuckled. "I've watched that girl drool more times than I can count."

Cashmere joined, but couldn't hide the worry tucked into the creases of her eyes. Mr. Bates placed his hands on his wife's shoulders, smiling at the couple. Stacy was large, thick with muscle, but too kind for his own good. Cashmere, on the other hand...

"Something wrong with Lennon?" Mr. Bates asked, frowning.

Stacy shrugged, a little embarrassed to have another witness to their parenting troubles. "It's probably growing pains. She's crying a lot, not wanting to go to bed... We thought she might just be fighting nap time. She's had night terrors for a while, but they're getting worse."

"She cries for hours." Cashmere looked helplessly at her husband, and then to Devin. "*Screams.* I can't tell you how many miles I walk a day with her in the stroller until she falls asleep. I mean, I'm in the best shape of my life, but at this point I'm getting concerned for her vocal cords."

"Hmm. She's been much better behaved since Hadley... We'll keep a closer eye on her, of course." Mrs. Bates said, looking into the house.

"Okay," Cashmere breathed, relieved. "Thank you."

Lennon yawned again and again as she played monster trucks with Wyatt, ever so often glancing at the group of adults gathered outside the door. She could see their mouths moving, but couldn't understand what they were saying. Wyatt had noticed her distraction and followed her gaze.

Lennon turned, confused when his worried expression matched hers. Did he understand more than she did? What exactly did he know?

"Do you have to go his room when you get in trouble, too?" she asked, keeping her voice low.

Wyatt paled with terror, and quickly shook his head.

She stuttered, the humiliation quickly turning into anger. "What?" she asked defensively.

Wyatt spoke just above a whisper, his voice shaking. "It's a secwet. We'll get in big, *big* twouble."

She'd never seen Wyatt so serious. Lennon stared at him, frightened by his sudden change, and full of questions. But before she could open her mouth to ask another, the creak of the entry door silenced her.

"Who wants to watch Spirit?" Mr. Bates called, reaching for the remote. All the kids yelled in excitement—all except for Wyatt, who was still shaken, and Lennon. She didn't look or react much to Wyatt's dad anymore—she didn't want his attention. She didn't know why it was her and not the other kids, but it was.

After lunch, Mrs. Bates released the kids to the backyard, tasking her husband with watching them while she cleaned up the kitchen. Lennon was red-faced and shiny when Mr. Bates waved her over, slowing her in her running.

Me? She pointed to her chest.

He nodded. *You.*

Not expecting her sudden stop, Conrad slammed into Lennon's back, nearly knocking her to the ground with his velocity.

"You're it!" he yelled, grinning as she regained her balance.

"She's not playing right now, Con." Mr. Bates called, his tone hard enough to crack the smile on his son's lips.

She carefully walked over, looking anywhere but his eyes.

"Lennon..." he began.

"I'm being good! I'm—"

"Are you not sleeping during nap time?" His question took her off guard, froze her heart.

How did he know? He couldn't...could he?

"I am," she lied, nodding earnestly. Lennon had been on her best behavior the past few weeks, seeing the mansion more as a jail instead of a castle. Despite her obedience, Mr. Bates was an expert at finding things to keep her home over. On those days, she never slept; she was too anxious, especially once she heard the footsteps approaching.

"I don't think you're telling me the truth." His voice came as a growl. His fingers tightened around her small arms, too much for comfort.

"Lennon, if you're not napping, you'll be in big, *big* trouble. Not with me, but with your mom and dad. They already talked to me about it this morning, you're not behaving at home—"

"I am!" she insisted, heart pounding against her tiny ribs. "I am sleeping, I promise." She'd tell him anything to make him let go of her; it was *really* starting to hurt.

He watched her for a moment, searching for any sign of weakness. She thought back on what Wyatt said and promised herself right then, that for her sake and everyone else's, she'd never tell a soul.

Finally, he released her arms, leaving wrinkles in the sleeves of her shirt where his fingers had been. "You can go play now."

She started feeling sick after that. By the time nap time came, she thought she was going to vomit while she waited for Mrs. Bates to announce where they were going. But it didn't matter; she would be left home with Mr. Bates that day, to make sure she was catching up on sleep. Wyatt and Hadley had stayed too, passed out before Mrs. Bates even left.

The slow footsteps came like clockwork. *Don't throw up*, she commanded herself. *Go to sleep.* Her breath halted as the footsteps slowed next to her, and his arms swept her from the couch. She bit down on her cheek, trying to exert the nervous energy somewhere other than her shaking legs. *No, no, no!* She didn't want to go. Maybe it'd just be a bath today...

After a few agonizing moments, she felt the mattress beneath her, and crushed the flesh of her cheeks between her teeth to resist crying out. Her heart pounded while he removed her shirt, worried he'd notice at any moment. *Take me back, I promise I'll sleep!*

"Daddy?"

She didn't need to open her eyes to recognize that small, brave voice. The voice of her best friend, who had always saved her bad days.

His footsteps circled around her, stopping on the other side of the bed. "Wyatt, what the hell are you—?"

"What are you doing?" Lennon could hear the tremble in his voice. She wanted to call out to him, to thank him, to cry, *something*. But she was still paralyzed on the mattress.

Missing Page

"Lennon hasn't been sleeping, we're giving her the bed," Mr. Bates explained. "Go back to bed, *now.*"

She didn't hear anything for a moment; it seemed as though everybody, event time, had froze.

"Wyatt," he commanded, his voice a petrifying snarl. The tiny footsteps padded away, cut off by the door shutting and locking. Lennon gulped, her throat painfully dry. Wyatt hadn't been able to save her. She heard Mr. Bates circle, like a lion with his prey, until he was on the other side of the bed.

Just don't close the curtains, she begged. *Just don't—*

WHOOSH

WHOOSH

WHOO—

28

Lennon sat in the lounge chair facing the magic mirror window, a hollow shell of herself. Hart stirred, moaning quietly as consciousness took over him. He extended his arm to pull her loser, waking abruptly at the emptiness his fingers closed around.

"Len?"

She was deaf to his words and the world, too deep in her own thoughts. Bags tugged at her eyes, a light purple color. In fact, it was the only color on her pale face—she looked ill.

"Lennon," he repeated, louder. She jumped, eyes darting to him. "Are you okay?"

"Couldn't sleep," she rasped, her attention returning to the window. He followed her gaze, feeling a coldness drape over them when the cove came into view. Hart peeled the sheets from his skin, swinging his long legs off the mattress and walking cautiously. Instead of reaching for her, his hand unthinkingly went to the curtain rod to ease the sun glaring in her face.

"Don't!" Lennon begged, putting her arm as a barrier between the two. He'd forgotten that strange, unspoken rule.

Missing Page

"You're shivering," he noticed, concern sharpening his senses. She closed her eyes as he lifted his palm to her forehead, checking for a temperature.

Lennon had truly thought that getting at least some of the poison out would heal her, would remove some of this weight she'd never asked to carry. But only getting part of it out left her wound open to infection, and she was paying dearly.

He took a seat at the foot of the chair, gently squeezing her knee. "Did you sleep?"

"A little—not really. The nightmares are back."

His eyes softened. "Ah, man. Thought we got rid of those."

She nodded tightly. They'd never gone away; she'd just gotten better at hiding them.

"You should've woken me, I would have sat with you. Let me get you some melatonin...do you want tea?"

"Those don't work for me." She couldn't speak too much at a time; most of her energy was being used to work through the havoc going through her mind. "They haven't for a while. Thanks, though."

"What can I do?"

"I need to be alone." She hated the bluntness of her words, but she didn't have the emotional capacity to cushion them. "Please."

Lennon was struggling enough, on the brink of a breakdown, but the *last* thing she wanted was for Hart, or anyone, to witness it. She was hungover from toxins that had been fermenting in her for seventeen years.

"All—All right. I'll leave you be. If you need anything..." He trailed off, already knowing her answer,

"I'll be okay," she insisted, putting on a weak smile for extra assurance.

His lips pulled to the side, eyes earthy and grave. "You know you don't have to be, not all the time. Especially for me."

Her lip betrayed her, beginning to quiver. She'd reached the edge of her mental cliff. "I know."

And she did. Which was exactly why she was pushing him away, before she exploded. Flesh and bone would tear as easily as paper once she did.

Hart retreated in defeat, his hand lingering on the knob before he shut it. "I love you."

She didn't move until his footsteps had completely silenced. It took everything in her to remain still, even holding her breath. But as soon she heard the second door close, she exhaled loudly, lifting her hands to her temples. Each inhale was shakier than the last.

Shh...go back to—

"No, NO!" Lennon pounded her fists against her temples, trying to silence the voices in her ear. "Shut up!"

You can't tell anyone. Bad things will happen....

She shook Wyatt's voice from her mind. She shouldn't have let her dad take her stash, or at least not all of it. If she could just have one, measly joint to silence that low, terrifying voice—

Go back to sleep...

She stood up as if the chair itself had whispered to her. Her breath was labored, unable to find a steady rhythm. There was no help this time, no aid to cushion her nightmares. Feeling helpless, she fumbled with the shower handle, her hands damp before the water started. There wasn't time to wait for the water to get hot, eliciting a gasp from her at the ice-cold water. She lathered body wash against her shoulders while the water slowly warmed, soap slapping loudly against the tile. Every noise was magnified, and overpowered the voices in her head, but this relief was temporary—it'd only last as long as her shower did. Lennon made sure to go through all the steps: shampoo, conditioner, hair mask...

Downstairs, Hart and Stacy were talking about their favorite fishing trips, their best catches. Stacy glanced toward the railing and then to Hart with a tight smile.

"We might've gotten bailed on, kid."

"I don't think she slept much last night." Off his look, Hart rushed to explain. "She was having nightmares. Might be sick, too. She wasn't looking too good when I talked to her."

Stacy nodded with a new understanding. "Poor girl. She's been struggling with those since she was little. The withdrawal probably isn't helping, either."

Hart nodded absentmindedly, thinking of the day before. So, *that* was what had plagued her nights all year... It broke him even more to know it wasn't new. He was too deep in his revelation to even process her father's last sentence. "I'll go check on her."

Stacy looked down at his watch. "We gotta leave in five. It's gonna storm this evening."

Hart nodded, ascending the stairs two at a time.

"Baby?" Hart called. "Your dad's wanting to leave soon... The weather's gonna get bad later."

"Just go without me," Lennon called back. This worked better for her, anyway. Time had so far been her enemy, but in this case, she was willing to call a truce.

"What? We're not leaving without—"

"It's fine!" she insisted. "Just tell him I'm not feeling good."

"He knows." Hart scratched his neck. "I'm here for *you*, Len, not the fish. I won't be mad if you want me to stay."

"Hart, it's fine. You'd just be stuck downstairs without me, anyways. Go, have fun."

"Are you sure?"

She paused, trying to work through her frustration. *It's because he loves you*, she reminded herself. "Yes. I just need a nap, I'll be better when you get back. I love you."

"O—okay. I'll, er... I'll go tell him. Love you, too." Hart left for a final time, shaking his head once he met Stacy's eyes. A heavy air hung over them while the boys as they gathered their gear, eventually heading for the Bronco.

Lennon rinsed the suds from her hair, still shivering despite the scalding water scorching her. Even the sanctity of her shower was weak against her trauma, rolling through her like a snowball.

The phone chimed outside, opening her eyes faster than her thoughts could leave. A pair of hazel eyes stared over her shoulder in the mirror, ripping a scream from her throat. Lennon whipped around to defend herself, but the enemy had only been in her head. She lifted her hand to her chest, struggling to find her breath. *I'm going crazy,* she thought. *This will drive me insane.*

While she recovered, she realized the mistake in her imagination. Only one man in the Bates' family had a light hazel tint, and it wasn't the one that usually visited her dreams. Lennon felt incredibly guilty; every time she looked at Conrad, she only saw the other two men in his family. Why couldn't she ever see *him*?

She thought back to their recent conversations, how strange they both became when either of them came up. Was it possible? Could he know what was buried so deep within her conscience that it only came out during the night?

Lennon twisted the knobs in a race to get out, wrapping a towel around her torso. She picked up her phone, water dripping from her hair onto the screen. A text message paused her and her quick fingers.

> **CONRAD**
> Haven't heard from u in a bit. Wanted to check on u

She dried her fingers and phone on her towel, typing out a response.

> Can we talk?

Knowing she'd left him stranded the last time they spoke, she wasn't sure how he'd respond. But this was no time to nurse her ego or insecurities; she needed to know if she was alone in carrying this burden. Before she could set it down, a chime rang through the bathroom, his name lighting up her screen with a red location pin.

Missing Page

> CONRAD
> Sure. I'm home, come on over

Lennon zoomed in on the location, squinting. It was an apartment complex, less than ten minutes away.

> Be there soon.

She threw on a loose pair of jeans and another of Hart's T-shirts, plucking a jacket as an afterthought to protect her from the rain to come. Before she headed downstairs, she set her phone and watch on the nightstand. It was too much to explain if he checked her location and saw her at a random house; it was almost preferable to think she was off sneaking drugs.

The drive was quiet. She kept going over what she could say in her head—did she ask questions until he said something first, or did she just spew the truth at point blank range? There was a chance that this would all be news to him, and she didn't know if she could bear the guilt of tearing his world apart like that.

She passed the park next to Emery's house, watching the trees fly by her in quick streaks. Groups of kids were sprinkled throughout the clearing, chasing after each other or sun bathing on picnic blankets. After a few minutes, her Jeep slowed outside the address his pin led to, passing a row of cars and a bike rack. She climbed the stairs to the second level, taking a deep breath. A half-railing provided a clear view of the park and its flourishing plant life, trees bending to the wind's warning. A wall of gray clouds was approaching slowly in the distance, but she still had the sun—for now.

Knock, knock, knock.

"Coming!" Conrad called.

Her heart sounded like was pounding everywhere: in her head, her ears, her stomach. Conrad opened the door, mouth moving, but she couldn't quite hear him over her own body.

"What?" she finally asked after the ringing dulled.

"Come on in," he repeated. Lennon kept her focus strong as she entered, taking in his rugged appearance. Red and puffy eyes, skin sullen, a thin sheen of sweat building above his brow. Even his curls had lost their liveliness.

Say something, idiot.

"This is your place, huh?"

Stupid.

Lennon looked around, stuffing her hands in the pockets of her jacket. It was small, a typical bachelor pad. A black leather loveseat faced a small TV, parallel to a worn-down lounge chair was tucked in the corner, guarding the large hutch next to it. She squinted, eventually recognizing the different liquors and bartending supplies stocked in the glass cabinets.

The door shut weakly behind her, and she could feel the wind as he passed her into the kitchen. "Water?"

Lennon's head shook back and forth. "Oh, no. I'm good."

His movement slowed, already having reached for the cabinet.

She could smell the staleness of his apartment, the faint scent of alcohol seeping from every wall. Something was off. *He is a bartender,* she thought in his defense.

"You look like shit," she murmured, taking a seat at his table. "You feeling okay?"

He laughed at her nonexistent filter, though there was no humor in it. He was so weak that the expel of breath dropped his head, eyes peeking at her beneath his hair. "I was gonna ask you the same thing. Didn't sleep much last night."

"Me neither."

Conrad left the kitchen for the hutch, reaching for a bottle of bourbon and a rocks glass. "What was your reason?"

"Nightmares," she answered vaguely. She was still building courage to bring up her reason for coming. "What about you?"

His expression shifted, and he folded his hands on the table. "You didn't hear?"

Lennon held the question between her brows. "Hear what?"

Missing Page

Conrad sighed, sucking in his cheek, but Lennon waited patiently, having grown comfortable in her seat. He finally met her gaze, eyes a little glassier than before. "He, uh...my..."

His voice broke off, and he shook his head, looking down at his hands. "Dad had a heart attack last night. He's dead."

29

Lennon had to lock her jaw to keep it from falling. Every nerve was tingling, like lightning was about to strike. "He's dead?"

Conrad held his head in his hands, unable to look at her. "He was coaching his church's little league game. He just turned fifty-five—" A weak breath shook through him. "In March. Fifty-five. That's not even...."

March 18th. She remembered—she'd had to go to daycare that day.

Lennon knew she was supposed to comfort him. Right now was the time to offer a hug or kind words. She swallowed, scrambling for something honest to say. "I can't believe he's gone."

Mr. Bates was dead. It was difficult to cover her processing as mourning. She couldn't possibly tell him now, when she was still coming to terms with what this meant—Lennon had been condemned to suffer his sins alone.

"What the fuck is happening?" He looked to her hopelessly. "Wyatt, then Page, now my dad? God, this—it feels like—"

Missing Page

Devon's name didn't belong with theirs, but she let it go. "Like what?"

Eyes once full of warm bronze were now dulled, rusted over. "I used to think it was the town that was cursed. Maybe it's me."

Lennon swallowed the lump building inside her throat. Conrad's eyes traveled down to her exposed arm, a thick line of ink tattooed down her major vein. That arm was the one she reached forward, wanting to comfort him. "Conrad..."

He lifted his glass towards his lips just before their skin met. Lennon pulled away, rejection flushing her cheeks only for a moment. Before anything else, she was an information gatherer, crafted from a talent for detachment—feelings took second place to that.

"I'm gonna use the restroom real quick." Conrad swished the last of the bourbon between his teeth before excusing himself.

Lennon watched him slip into the bedroom, closing the door behind him. So *private*, she observed, thinking back to the way he corralled her to the dining area, steering her away from the two rooms or the kitchen like a ranger. Now, the curious sheep was left to roam free.

She walked around the living room, taking her time with the picture frames hanging on the wall. A graduation photo, a picture of him and what must be his college friends locking arms with their faces painted in school colors. And, at the end, a collage of film photos collected into one frame, slightly yellowed from time and its poisonous oxygen.

They all had the same date—March 18th. She'd remembered Page's journal entry, dated on the 16th, though it'd been made last year. She knew there was something about that time that had prickled her skin. Her body remembered, even when her mind didn't.

Only a few photos had all four family members in them. Most were snapshots of two young boys cheesing widely at the camera, their young, sun-kissed skin speckled with sand. Her eyes lingered on the one where Wyatt looked the most familiar, his tiny arm slung around his older brother. Lennon's breath caught as nostalgia filtered her memories, coloring her vision in shades of pink.

"Hi, Wy," Lennon whispered. She lifted her fingertips to the glass, letting them rest over a face she hadn't seen in years. Her head tilted to look at Conrad's happy expression, frozen in the youthfulness of 2004. She'd seen slivers of this nine-year-old boy during some of their talks or moments spent together; he existed, somewhere, though she saw no trace of him today.

The hutch reflecting off the frame caught Lennon's attention. She turned, closing the distance between her and the old oakwood. It was kept well, unique to his taste—it told stories. She quietly opened the cabinets, a messy collection of different cups and shot glasses. A broken glass hid behind the rest in the back, too dark to pick out any details. She'd been so curious with the cabinet's contents, she almost missed the glass countertop, showcasing the inside of a large drawer.

Rows of shot glasses lay face-up, stained glasses glinting in the fading light. They were arranged in a beautiful, diverse collection, ranging from alien heads, to detailed cowboy boots, to glass-blown flowers. She took her time appreciating each one, wondering what meaning they all held for him, what memories they carried.

She paused her venturing at a perfect, elongated space toward the bottom, tucked between a Washington State and a glittering, rectangular disco ball. It wasn't waiting to be filled—something had been removed. Her stomach seemed to notice first, flipping before she could understand what she was looking at, or *not* looking at. Did this space belong to the broken one hidden in the cabinet? Lennon side-stepped, pulling it open again in one swift motion. Her hand reached in cautiously, weaving a large shard through the extra glasses until it reached light. The piece stilled her along with the rest of the world; even the trees had grown quiet under her revelation.

An ocean-blue piece of glass painted with tiny fishes glinted up at her, it's base colored moss green. Lennons's eyes widened in horror, stepping back as though it had burned her.

It was not exactly the same, but it was close. Much too close.

Missing Page

Her brows knitted together, mouth growing dry. She hurried to put the piece back, now looking at the other glasses with a new alertness. A mushroom, five different state-themed glasses...

There. This one had no fishes painted on, but instead was speckled with golden flakes, in between the bubbles. This was the missing piece to the pair in Page's order, the same shot glass she thought Emery had placed on the table at Page's funeral, now hiding in Conrad's cabinet. Gravity swung the cabinet closed with a quiet click, and she stumbled backwards.

The door behind her creaked, and she whipped around, meeting Conrad's gaze.

"I thought you didn't drink?"

How long had he been standing there? Her eyes darted to the door, still swinging shut. His eyes held something bordering accusatory, but she forced it out of her head. *He's just drunk.*

"I don't," she said innocently. "I'm conducting a self-guided tour."

"Well," he mumbled, stepping out lazily. He'd tried to pull the door closed, but it stopped just before it could latch. "If you want some, I'm happy to share. It won't kill ya."

"Sometimes it does," Lennon said robotically. She couldn't remember how her normal voice sounded. He gave her a look, and she held his gaze, trying to keep her eyes soft. She was burning with questions, but something inside was screaming at her to stay quiet, hold her cards close. Conrad stumbled into the table, muttering under his breath.

"Are you okay?" Her eyes poured over him as if she were analyzing a stranger instead of a boy she'd met in childhood.

"No," he said gruffly, rubbing his hip. "I'm having a pretty shitty day, to be honest."

"I can imagine," she said quietly. Lennon wished she could get inside the cabinet again. Surely she'd made a mistake; it *couldn't* be the same one. Nothing made sense if it was. She tethered her eyes to his while her mind worked, willing all her manufactured innocence to seem unbothered.

"What did you want to talk about?"

"What?" She swallowed, unable to think straight.

"You said you wanted to talk...is it about the other night?"

She blinked, trying to collect her thoughts. "Oh, no. I'm sorry about that. I shouldn't have left you, I had a lot of stuff going through my head."

"Like what?"

"I—" she stammered. "I misunderstood our relationship."

It didn't come out the way she'd meant it, but he seemed to understand.

"I thought we weren't friends," he said dryly.

In that brief, fleeting moment, she saw a grieving, hurting boy from her childhood. "Of course we're friends."

Conrad tilted his head, taking another step toward her. "Since when?"

"Since always, Conrad."

He was quiet for a moment, pouring over her expression. "Why're you looking at me like that?"

"Like what?" Adrenaline sent another spike through her, worried her face wasn't blank enough.

He was close enough that Lennon could smell the ninety proof on his breath. Her chest rose and fell like a cresting wave, brushing against his at its peak. She feared he could hear her thumping pulse beneath Hart's t-shirt. The only thing concealing it was the growing winds outside, whistling in an eerie chorus. Conrad's eyes grew fuzzy, mistaking her nerves for tenderness, and lifted his hands toward her cheeks.

"Conrad..." She breathed nervously. He didn't stop. "Conrad, no."

She ducked under his arm, tripping on something as she put distance between them. It chimed as it rolled, under the cover of the table. When she finally looked at him again, her flight response eased. A look of horror had spread over him, realizing what he'd done.

"Oh, my God. Lennon, I'm so sorry—"

Missing Page

"No, don't be, it's fine." She shook her head, crossing her arms over her chest.

"I'm not in my right mind right now." He pressed a palm to his forehead. "Shit. I misread that, I'm sorry."

"It's okay. I think you've just had a little too much to drink." She threw forgiveness to him like a life ring. "I'm fine."

The bedroom door cracked open, and she pivoted, expecting another human. But only a ball of fluff strolled in, flicking its orange tail as it rubbed against her leg.

"That's, uh...that's Carrot." Conrad sniffed, taking his glass to the kitchen. The faucet ran until clear liquid touched the brim of the cup. He began humming a distantly familiar tune as he did this, but it was too off-pitch to recognize.

"You have a cat?" she asked, trying to see what had rolled under the table.

"Oh yeah, this girl's been with me through it all." Conrad gulped down the water, droplets trickling down his chin. He stuck his hand out, motioning; she watched the cat glide over to him, rubbing her head against his sweatpants. Conrad poured more water over the melting cubes, too preoccupied to notice Lennon scooting her chair to get a better look beneath the table.

All she could think about was that shot glass and how much it looked like the one sitting in her sister's room. Her stomach was in a full-blown panic, threatening to expel its contents at any moment.

No, no... Her head spun, the room melting around her. *It's Conrad, he wouldn't...*

She finally saw the silver that hid behind the dining chair. It was a metal bottle opener, engraved with two small letters at the top. She squinted, leaning closer.

C.B.

Conrad Bates. Etched onto the bottle opener she thought had belonged to her mother, which Lennon vividly remembering stashing in her glovebox the day she came home.

"You feel okay?" Conrad's voice startled her. "You're pale."

Her body turned automatically, on autopilot while her brain worked inside. "This news, it's just...it's a lot to process."

"You're telling me."

Lennon needed to see her glove box. Once she saw it still inside, her fears would be relieved, and she could tell the self-preserving voices to stop screaming for her to run. But before anything else, she needed back in that hutch. But *how?*

She winced at the idea that popped into her head, but couldn't think of a better one in the short period of silence.

"Could I try some, actually? Whatever you were drinking?"

Conrad's ears perked up, his walls lowering again. "Yeah?"

She nodded, knowing this would buy her a few extra minutes. She stole a glance at the cabinet while he busied himself with the glassware in the kitchen, trying to squint through the shadows.

His approaching figure didn't register through her concentration, causing her to jump when their fingertips met. Conrad dropped a few ice cubes in her glass, humming that same off-kilter tune.

"Thank you," she uttered, lifting the cup to her lips.

He chuckled. "Well, you gotta put liquor in there. That's just Coke."

"Oh. Right."

Thing had changed so quickly; she'd thought her skin was prickling from the incoming storm, but maybe it was trying to warn her of what dangers lay inside instead rather than out. Lennon had come to share her wounds, half-expecting that he'd lift his sleeves to reveal the same. But she'd never considered that she was putting herself in the den of the lion. Every fiber of her was trying to give him the benefit of the doubt, but her faith was declining with each passing second.

The display waited behind her, begging her to look, but she couldn't risk it yet. If she was right, it would mean Conrad was capable of more evil than she'd ever imagined. Instead she reached for the bottle of bourbon, starting to pour.

Missing Page

"Whoa, that's good." He nodded once the amber liquid passed the three-quarter mark.

"Sorry," Lennon whispered. Her fingers shook as she sipped, and she winced once the alcohol slid over her tongue.

"How is it?"

"Kinda sweet...mostly bitter. Still don't understand the whole appeal."

"Probably doesn't come til you're drunk," he teased. "You checked out this collection, yet?"

Conrad gazed down at the display with a sense of pride, dragging her eyes from the cabinet.

"Yeah, it's pretty cool," Lennon murmured. *What circumstances would place Page in this apartment? How had she broken a shot glass if he hadn't put one in her hands?*

He chuckled, scratching his neck. "My dad's actually the one who started it."

Conrad pointed to one toward the top, in the shape of a fish. "He got me that on my birthday. This one's from Germany..."

She listened idly as he told her the backstories of his favorites. His fingers went back and forth, conveniently skipping over the only one she was interested in, the space without. Hoping it'd come off as innocent, she lifted her hand to the cabinet, opening it to reveal the stragglers. "What about these?"

Conrad took control of her curiosity, fishing one of non-interest and holding it in the palm of his hand. "These are where the boring ones go to die."

His eyes followed her as she reached for the broken one. She brought it into the light, her heart jumping again, trying to morph her voice into something innocent. "What happened to this guy?"

He took it into his free hand. A practiced, confused expression shadowed his reminiscing before he chuckled nervously. "Oh—must've forgotten to throw this away. Don't ask me to explain drunk decisions."

She watched him carry it to the kitchen, whistling the tune

instead of humming. Rather than throwing it in the trash, he set it on the counter just next to it. *He's keeping it,* she realized. *It's sentimental, somehow.*

As she came back into her body, his whistled tune finally pierced her ears, now much more recognizable. It vibrated through her in a painful epiphany—*Beautiful, beautiful, beautiful...*

"You like John Lennon?" Her voice sounded strangled.

"Oh. Yeah." He shrugged, stopping. "I didn't even realize he sang that. Pretty catchy, huh?"

The way he glanced at her made her wonder if she'd said too much. Her skin was on fire, screaming for her to run. She didn't know if she fully comprehended how much danger she was in. They stood for a moment, taking turns sipping, waiting for the other to speak. Lennon's stomach grew warm, her surroundings beginning to relax at the hands of fermented rye, though her adrenaline kept her alert.

"What are you thinking about?"

"Just, uh..." Lennon's head didn't move, but her eyes looked to the ceiling for guidance, and then the window, watching the trees bend to the winds' command. "I was thinking how unlucky my life has been. How both of our lives have been, our families..." Her eyes settled on the picture frame, looking at the smiling faces. Her eyes lingered on Devin.

When Conrad looked, his attention found Wyatt. "It hasn't played out at all how I imagined. That's for sure."

She nodded. After a moment, she set her glass on the table. "I, er—I should probably go—"

"You're not gonna waste that, are you? That's top-shelf stuff, right there."

She stared at the glass, tilting it in the light. His eyes scoured over her, searching for any hint of deceit. Lennon felt four years old again; she could practically feel his fingers digging into her arm like his father's had. Hesitantly, she lifted the glass to her mouth and took another swig, looking at him as if he was forcing her arm.

"I hope I didn't scare you earlier, or make you uncomfortable."

Missing Page

He sucked in his cheeks. "I'm sorry, I...I have a lot going through my head."

"Don't worry about it," She assured him, spine prickling. "Me, too. I just have errands to run today, get back before the boys. Buzzed driving's drunk driving, right?" Lennon smiled for extra conviction. She made sure her eyes never left his, burning through with an uncomfortable intensity.

It was strong enough for his gaze to fall, taking a step back. "Well, I just meant...I'm not trying to keep you hostage. If you need to go..."

She forced a smile, letting out the breath she'd been holding. She set the glass on the table, pushing it to him. "Thanks for understanding."

She was barely able to utter a goodbye before she closed the door, trembling as she peered out towards the park. Emery's house sat on the other side, hidden behind the thick brush. She pictured Page's bicycle cruising down the path, stopping at the bottom of these stairs.

Lennon found Page's bicycle tucked beneath her creaky deck, the one Emery swore to know nothing about. She'd said it must have been left there from the day before. As Lennon descended the stairs, her attention found the complex's bike rack with fresh eyes. And in the space closest to the stairs, a blue ribbon knotted around the rusted metal waved to her as she passed, as if recognizing old friend.

Rain began to fall as she sprinted to her Jeep, fumbling for the glove box. It fell open with a thud; her registration, insurance, and papers were all accounted for. She sifted through, feeling for metal, but there was none. It was gone.

Shoving her gearshift into first, the Jeep engine snarled as she tore away from the curb, not touching the brakes until she turned into her driveway. Lennon took the steps two at a time down to Page's room and burst through the door, worried the room had been raided just as her Jeep had been.

The gift pile remained exactly as they were left—untouched, except for a thin layer of dust starting to gather on the surface. Lennon pushed the bags aside, searching until the glass came into view and holding it tight in her hand. She pulled the note from her nightstand next, smoothing it over over her duvet.

Sorry about my clumsiness—I was kinda nervous ;) I got them online, but I hope its cl

An image of the broken shard flitted behind her eyes, and she clutched her chest, struggling to find her breath. *Page had been at his house. She'd broken the glass and got these as a replacement.* But there was no reason Page would be at his house...unless they...unless he—

Though her stomach was challenging her, she forced it into submission so she could grab the laptop, opening Page's secured documents.

Every password had something to do with what Page was hiding in that entry. There was only one word that came to Lennon's mind now—the only possible answer.

c...o...

Lennon typed in the letters one by one, her teeth sinking deeper into her lip with each consonant. The second entry, Page talked about him celebrating his dad's birthday. It had been dated March 16th.

n...r...

If this was the answer—if this name opened the document, it meant Lennon had failed more than she could've ever imagined. She'd failed her sister, her parents, Conrad, and also failed the four-year-old that lived inside her. The little girl who had been reaching, stretching out her fingers for a hand to hold for so many years. Lennon tipped her chin up every time, acting like she didn't exist. She'd chosen to focus on the girl who used to sleep in this blue bedroom, but maybe if she'd given herself even a sliver of the same protection...

a...d

Would things be different?

Lennon hovered her ring finger over the enter key, holding her

Missing Page

breath as tears streamed down her face. She'd been so sure it was Emery. Now she realized why that had to be the only option. If this opened, it would be a brutal reopening of old scar tissue, it'd rip her apart like a cosmic blow. She couldn't handle the emotions wracking through her, and she hadn't even pressed enter.

Do it, she hissed at herself. *Press the button.*

She was petrified, more than ever before. Lennon was sure this truth was capable of killing her. But somewhere, deep in her weak, frightened state, she was also sure her sister deserved justice more than she deserved peace of mind. Lennon's finger weighed down on the key, wincing as the loading circle rotated.

The date loaded first. May 25th, a few days before Lennon returned from college. Her eyes poured over Page's words, anxiously picking at her nails.

5/25

This is gonna be short one, sorry. I'll make sure to give details tomorrow! Just don't have a lot of time.

I don't really know how this all happened. I think things changed after I snuck to his house during that big fight between Mom and Dad. I couldn't listen to Mom scream another word and needed to get out, so I walked through that park near Summit Place, next to Emery's. I almost went there, but then I remembered Conrad—formerly known as Twofor2, I'll explain tomorrow—talking about his new place. He told me a while back I could always call him if I needed anything. So I went over, he made a pizza, and I ended up staying way longer than I'd meant to. I didn't want to leave, honestly, but it was past midnight. He hugged me for a long time and said I could come back anytime. No one's ever been that nice to me.

I know it's kinda weird, technically he's my tutor, but I didn't see it like that. It's not like he's a stranger, he's been a family friend since before I was even born. And he really does feel like a friend, he's nicer and cooler than any of the kids at my school. I went back again a few weeks later, and then the third time, when he wasn't home, I went to Seadog's. I could see him through this big porthole window in the front, so I watched from the trees. it was so interesting to see him that way. He was so different, so serious.

I caught him before he left, he said we could talk but it had to be back at the apartment. I guess he could get in trouble for me even being the parking lot. This time he showed me his shaker tin tricks and his shot glass collection. It was so cool. You know what's coming—right after he asked if I wanted a drink—but ugh, I still cringe thinking about it. The most important glass, the first one he ever got, is the one I dropped. Why, God?? He was so nice about it, he still made me a lemon drop (which was delicious by the way) but I wanted to die, I felt so terrible. He hasn't been talking to me as much after though, so that's why tonight's happening. I got the glasses and card ready, now I just gotta execute. If I can get past Lennon and Emery doesn't catch me, I think I might get my friend back :)

So, Emery hadn't been the last one to see Page after all. Lennon's chest tightened, agonizing over this final hope-filled entry. Page had no idea that these plans she'd written about, with a smile on her face and hope fluttering in her stomach, would be her last.

And yet, Conrad had not been the first to take advantage of a Mayfield's innocence.

30

The printer whirred to life in Page's room, pushing out a sheet of paper in a rhythmic chorus of ink and machinery. Lennon stared lifelessly at the pages as they fluttered into the tray—her sister's final journal entry, copies of the receipt and Etsy purchase, the letter Page had started to write, and the online name Conrad used to conceal his identity.

She still couldn't understand why this had to end in her death, unless something happened in that cove that he couldn't let her go over. Maybe Page had finally come to her senses and realized how wrong this was; she'd always had a strong sense of good and bad, and Lennon couldn't imagine she had the intuition to leave without mentioning it. There was no telling what Conrad was thinking—shame and fear could turn people into monsters.

Anguish ran hot through her veins. Lennon was disgusted with the last living Bates man, but even more so with herself. How could she have ever allowed herself to trust someone who came from Devin's flesh; how could he do this to her, to Page? What kind of inhuman monster could sit across from a grieving girl, knowing he was responsible for her pain?

As the final sheet of paper floated on top of the stack, Lennon took a moment to look them over. It seemed so clear now that they were collected into this neat little stack. She took them into her hands, hurrying upstairs. Lennon remembered that look Conrad had given her the first time they ate together, after mentioning Emery. She had mistaken his relief as innocence, probably thankful she was making things so easy for him. Was her finding the bike at Emery's a happy accident, or by design? Either way, it was what made him able to sit there so relaxed, because he knew any trace of him was wiped clean. He'd played her like a fiddle.

Her phone camera sounded off as she snapped photos, sending them with a short message. She needed to hear the truth from his mouth, but he wouldn't talk unless they were alone. *Alone* was a hard thing to be in this town; she was sure he knew that.

> Come to the cove in thirty minutes. Don't try anything stupid.

Lennon watched, waiting impatiently. Within a few minutes, the read receipt came through, stopping her breath in anticipation. Three dots played peek-a-boo on the screen, disappearing and reappearing every few moments, but nothing came. She'd have to trust that her threat and reputation was enough.

Lennon looked over everything a final time, nodding to herself. There were no lines she wouldn't cross for her sister, even after death. She knew what she had to do, though it hadn't sunk in until now. Her knees bent, lowering to plant kisses on Kaiser's head and scratch his favorite spot behind his ear. He whined, as if knowing she wasn't planning to return.

"I know," she cooed, planting a kiss on his long snout. "But I have to. You know I do."

She avoided his concerned, too-intelligent stare, and locked the door behind her, sticking her phone in her back pocket. Rain pelted from above as she walked down the driveway, trying to get her to stay. But Lennon would put one foot in front of another

Missing Page

until she couldn't anymore—her negligence deserved worse than rain.

The walk was agonizingly slow. It allowed time to reminisce about when she and her dad would drive down this road with Page squished in the middle, lunch boxes in hand. They'd sing and laugh while Lennon took in the view of the sunsets, always presuming it'd be her last. She wished she'd looked more at her family instead. Presently, her hand found the rusting railing at the end of the road leading to the beach.

There was once a time she'd been hopeful Hart would walk down these hidden stairs with them—that she'd be able to finally show him a family tradition she was proud of. But, like the shards of glass in Conrad's cabinet, her little family was too broken to be put back together. She was finally accepting that they'd never be exactly the same, nor should they want to be.

On the last step, she slipped off her shoes, setting them next to the wood fence. She remembered how smart her dad had been searching the night Page went missing; she trusted he'd find her breadcrumbs eventually. Lennon hiked through the sand, pausing for a moment at the mouth of the cove.

Water had already began washing inside, darkening the sand into a cold brown. The walls served as a stabilizer, but a few steps in, her hand slipped on a piece of wet rock, and she hissed, pulling her cut hand to her chest. Thin lines of blood began to seep from the flesh beneath her thumb, and she stared down in another blow of realization.

Conrad's hands had similar cuts that day at the gas station, just hours after they'd found Page. *Surfing*, he'd said. Lennon couldn't stop the scenarios plaguing her like nightmares. Those scratches could have been from the jagged walls, but Page's nails would've fit the lines just as perfectly. Did she die fighting to survive? Lennon's feet found dry sand at the end of the cove, alleviating the numbness spreading through her toes. Winds from outside whispered to her in warning, summoning a cover of goosebumps over her arms. She closed her eyes, wondering if she was imagining, or really feeling, a faint presence of her sister.

"I'm so sorry, Page." She pressed her palms against the damp wall. The rocks scratched her skin, but she remained—she'd take anything that felt like her sister, even if it was pain.

"Wow."

She whipped her head with wide eyes to find the tall, fair-headed man, drenched from the storm outside and looking strangely cautious in comparison to her smaller frame.

Conrad took a breath, eyes dewing. "You look just like her."

She snarled, anguish filling her lungs like water. His hands rose, fingers stretching out in submission.

"It's not how it looks," he said shakily. "I know what you're think—"

"It was you," she growled, throat closing with a mix of adrenaline and fury. "*You* were with her that night. *You* ki—"

"If you let me explain," he interrupted, shaking away the curls sticking to his forehead. "I promise, Lennon, I *promise*. I'll tell you everything. Please listen to me. I've done some bad things, but I swear—"

Nothing was absorbing. There wasn't a thing he could say that would change how she saw him now. Redemption wasn't possible with something like this.

"There's *nothing* to explain!" She glared at him through red vision, hands shaking. "I opened up to you, and you *used* that, used *me,* to clear your own name. You listened to me grieve, you saw how much pain I was in, and you *watched*... How could you just watch?"

Conrad lowered his hands, taking a step toward her. "I want to tell you everything. It's so complicated—"

"It's not!" she snapped. "Nothing about this is complicated. She's... She was *fourteen*, Conrad."

"She doesn't act like it, she's got an old soul—"

"She was *four—teen!*" Lennon shouted.

Missing Page

"I wish you'd... I had nothing but good intentions. It wasn't like how you think it was, nothing happened."

"You gave her alcohol, Conrad. You had her alone in your apartment."

His eyes widened, confirming what she already knew.

"I'm not a bad person," he insisted. "I'm not a killer. If I was, I would've left you in here that night of the funeral, but I *didn't*."

His words stopped her for a moment, leaving her processing with paralyzing confusion. "That was you?"

Of course it was. It made sense—he knew their door code. It must have been how he'd gotten into her glove box, too.

"I came here almost every night after. I lost some stuff here that night..."

Her lip curled. "You had to make sure your tracks were clean."

"I'm not a bad guy." He shook his head frantically, trying to believe it himself.

"Good people don't do things like this. You're a bad person who's done some good things. But you are not *good*."

"You know how special she was, Lennon."

She twisted her head back and forth in disbelief, unable to follow his delusion.

"That's why I wanted to be there for you," he continued. "You were the only one who was going through the same thing as I was. We felt the same pain—"

"*Nothing* about us is the same!" Lennon bellowed. "She was a *kid*, Conrad, a little girl—and you..." Her lips twisted with anger. "You took that from her. You killed Page—"

"No!" The guilt left his face, replaced with conviction. "You can think whatever you want about me, but I swear to you, Lennon, on Wyatt's grave. I *did not kill her*." He faltered then. "I was with her when she died. But I tried to... I would never..."

Lennon's blood ran cold at his confession, a chill sweeping through the cove. He'd confessed—Conrad had seen Page in her final moments. She watched him in confusion, waiting for him to continue his psychotic spiral.

"She came to my apartment that night. She biked over from that girl Emery's, she'd had this whole plan."

"But it wasn't the first time she'd come over," Lennon said.

"No," he answered, watching her warily. "She waited for me at the bar, once before. I told her if she wanted to keep hanging out we should go somewhere else—"

Lennon snarled, disgusted at the way he was retelling it, as though it were a bittersweet memory. "I *know* all of this, Conrad."

He blinked. "It wasn't planned. I just meant to give her a safe place—"

"Is *that* what you're telling yourself?" she breathed. He stood silent, and she clenched her teeth. "So then why'd you go to the least safe spot in Laguna?"

"She said that since I'd shown her something personal to me, she wanted to, too. We took a few shots, and I offered to drive us over there. I'd never been in, I didn't know the tide was gonna get so crazy..."

The missing pages of the story unfolded before her, flipping like a horrific picture book. Tears welled in Lennon's eyes. She imagined Page's small body in the passenger seat of this man's car, her hands twisting each other out of habit. She was so innocent; too naive to realize that he couldn't possibly love her. She was too good to see him for what he was.

"I don't know what happened," he continued, rambling nervously. "I wasn't thinking straight. I was drunk and got the wrong idea, like I did with you—"

"You kissed her?"

The question echoed through the cave, leaving them in a cold silence. Storm clouds darkened the sky, casting a dark glaze over Lennon's furious eyes. Page had been so desperate for friendship, she'd ignored every red flag sprouting along the way.

Conrad swallowed, continuing despite her rising anger. "She

pulled away and started to leave... That's when the current swept her. She fell, but it didn't look bad..." Tears leaked from his eyes. "I laughed at first. I *laughed...*"

Ice-cold waves splashed up against the cove's walls, sizzling with disgust. Lennon wanted to press her hands to her ears, deafen herself against the story he was telling.

"I swear on everything, Len, I—"

"Stop calling me that!" she shouted. "Stop talking like we're friends!"

"Okay," Conrad said calmly, lifting his hands. "Okay."

"Then what?" she said through clenched teeth.

"Then I saw the blood in the water." He closed his eyes. "That's when I realized it was serious. She got swept out so fast, and the current was so strong... It took me a while to get her. I think I was just a minute too late, and it—it *kills* me, Lennon. She'd already lost so much blood, I couldn't wake her up—"

"Why didn't you take her to the hospital?" Lennon demanded. "She could've survived!"

"What was I supposed to say?" Conrad begged. "How was I supposed to explain what we were doing alone, *together*, at midnight? I'd have to explain the alcohol... It could shut down Seadog's, put everybody out of a job—"

"*Stop.*" Lennon shook her head, backing away in disgust. "Stop acting like you ran for anyone other than yourself. You're a coward, Conrad. You liked that she was innocent and easy to control. You don't let the people you love die."

Conrad's vision blurred with tears. "I wasn't thinking straight."

"*I—don't—care,*" she snapped.

"I'm so sorry, Lennon, I'll be sorry for the rest of my life—"

"I don't want an apology!" she shrieked, shoving him as he stepped toward her.

"Please—" A sob broke from him.

"I want my sister back!" She shoved him again, but grief had sapped her strength. She stood seething, repulsed by the sight of him. "You're sick, Conrad. A coward. That's all you are."

Conrad's cries ceased, eyes traveling up to hers. They held such darkness that her breath caught, fear striking in her chest.

Wind carried her whisper to him. *"You look just like him."*

"I am *not* my father," he seethed.

His defensiveness confirmed everything she'd feared; he knew. And yet, he did this anyway, repeating the cycle without even trying to stop or question it.

"You're *exactly* like your father, Conrad. You like little girls who can't defend themselves, and you'll let innocent people die to make sure it's kept secret."

Conrad's fists twitched. "He didn't kill Wyatt, it was an accident."

"I guess we'll never know." Lennon refused to let him twist this into something innocent. She wouldn't let him avoid his shame. "But I *will* make sure everyone knows exactly what you are. Even if you refuse to."

Lennon started to sidestep him, but Conrad blocked her, his fingers flexing with adrenaline. "I can't let you go, Lennon. Not when you're like this. I need you to understand."

"I will *never* change my mind about this," she snarled, bringing herself to her full height.

He swallowed, a tinge of sadness twitching through his face. "Then I can't let you go."

Electricity pulsed through her, standing the hairs on her neck.

"I'm sorry," he whispered.

Lennon lunged first, scraping the skin from his cheek with her nails. She felt his fist crack against her shoulder, and they became a frenzy of kicking, punching, and scratching.

Maybe he would kill her, but she was done making things easy for him.

The two tumbled to the ground, where Conrad could use his weight to get over Lennon. Water soaked through her clothes, made her splutter for air. He pinned her to the sand, leaving only her feet to kick helplessly beneath him as his hand closed around her neck. It took only seconds for the gasping to start, her hands beating at the python tightening around her throat. She twisted her knees through the sand bank, trying to get them underneath her. The edges of her vision began to blacken, centering a view on his animalistic, red face. Bloodshot eyes and spit trailing from his mouth made him look more monstrous than human.

She stopped beating at his hands and swiped her nails across his face, drawing blood with the flesh. He cried out angrily and wrapped his other hand around her throat as punishment, shoving head back against the sand.

Without air, most of her senses were depleting. The roaring ocean settled into a dull ringing, and she was only able to make out dark, blurry shapes; the curtains would close soon. She was almost too dazed to notice when her knee finally broke free, but in her last moments of clarity, she throttled it upwards, landing directly into his scrotum. His knees snapped together with a blood-curdling scream that echoed through the cave, and he rolled off her. Finally free, Lennon struggled to her feet, choking on the same air she'd been so desperate for.

She wanted to kill him. Everything in her wanted vengeance, but her brain had switched from fight to flight. She wasn't strong enough to execute her desires, even before he choked her—now it was a fight just to push oxygen through her starved veins. Lennon coughed out saltwater that had filled her mouth, lifting her fingers to her tender neck with a wince. There was no time for revenge. She wouldn't get out if she didn't leave right then.

The tide worked against her as she waded through, stumbling once it got to her knees. Her foot sank into the sand, twisting excruciatingly. She cried out, catching herself just before her head slammed against the stone wall. She gasped in shock, adrenaline and pain tingling through every limb, but forced herself forward, limping; she couldn't stop for anything. Nearing the mouth of the cove, she opened hers to scream. Somebody had to be close by, somebody would hear—

"Lennon, wait!"

She startled, turning, just as Conrad's fist made contact with her temple. The world went black, and she sank into nothingness.

31

DEATH HAD ALWAYS SEEMED LIKE A PEACEFUL IDEA. THE WORLD Lennon lived in was cruel, unforgiving; she had to make herself colder than her surroundings to survive. That would take a toll on anyone—especially a child.

She didn't know where she was now, but it was light, without fear or sadness. There was no happiness, either; she was floating in a sea of tranquility. Without an earthly body to protect, she was finally allowed to relax in this new oblivion. Death was quite pleasant, just as she'd thought; if this was the eternity that had been promised by prophets and preachers, then she understood why generations had lived and died over it.

A small twinkling in the distance drew her attention just before the new darkness she was in rocked with an unknown force. It seemed as though the two forces were competing for attention, but the flashing lights were magnetic, impossible to ignore. From it came a muffled, excited scream, calling out across the dark space. Lennon stepped forward, pausing in surprise at the flash of blue that surrounded her feet. It struck like lightning through the limitless space, again and again with every step. The twinkling lights stretched into little specks, expanding into a vast night sky in front of her. The blue bursts around her feet spread out like veins, wrapping around the frameless oval, mirrorlike in shape, and yet was unable to enter. Lennon slowed as her eyes adjusted, now able to see what—or rather, who—waited on the other side. Recognition hit, and disbelief froze her in place.

It was the beach that lived beyond Lennon's balcony. She recognized that white sand, the water glistening black under a full moon, its waves frothing against cold sand. After a moment, a burst of glowing blue shot through a cresting wave, its light piercing the dark. *The algae bloom,* she recalled.

"It's beautiful. Like magic," a small voice breathed.

Lennon turned her head. More than the view, more than her own reflection, she recognized that voice. It belonged to the brunette standing off to the side, pointing out to the ocean.

"Isn't it?" Page twisted her body to face her older sister. Amazement lit her face with childlike wonder, sparkling in her eyes.

Lennon's lip trembled, taking another step toward the mirror. "You can see me?"

Page's eyebrows knitted, laughing in confused amusement. "Of course I see you, silly. Look, it's in the sand too! We're mermaids!"

Her younger sister danced over the shore, igniting the algae into an electric blue. Lennon couldn't stop staring, the otherworldly glow taking up the least of her attention.

This was an old memory. The girls had checked for the bloom for days, practically camped on the deck. When Page had seen the first light from her bedroom late one night, she ran to tell her sister. Soon enough the girls' feet flew down the steps, giggling as the ground below them lit with angry algae.

In the real version, Lennon had stared at the ocean for what felt like hours, worried she wouldn't remember the details. Now she couldn't look away from her sister, living and and breathing with an elated smile on her face. She looked so *real*; her cheeks were rosy like Lennon remembered, dimpled on one side. A gentle wind breezed

Missing Page

from the beach through the mirror, sweeping their hair at the same time, and everything became alive again. If Lennon took a few more steps, she could reach out and touch her.

"Page..." Lennon uttered. Her sister turned again.

Her smile faltered ever so slightly. "Why are you looking at me like that?"

"I..." Lennon was at a loss for words. Finally, she smiled, forcing down her tears. She didn't want to scare Page or taint the smile she'd been aching to see just one more time. "I've just missed you."

Page's eyes softened, giving Lennon the strangest feeling that maybe Page knew this was a memory, too.

Lennon felt another ubiquitous rocking sensation, though her current entity remained still. She turned to search for the culprit, startling when the earthquake happened a third time, coming from every direction. *It's from the other side*, she realized. Page looked, too, a new expression washing over her cherubic face.

"You're early, aren't you? I thought you looked the same."

So, this wasn't a memory. It was a reenactment. This Page wasn't the same from before—now she knew the horrors the world hid behind unassuming faces.

In Lennon's peripheral, another mirror glinted like a star in the distance, though that word had no meaning in this new realm. It seemed lightyears away, but Lennon remembered it had taken mere seconds to reach Page.

"What do you mean, I'm early?" Lennon asked.

"It's easy to lose track of time here," she sighed. "I should've known, though. You look the same." she said, her hands twisting in each other. "I've been waiting for you."

Lennon ached to ease whatever was paining Page's angelic face. "I'm here—"

"Don't!" Page cried, rushing from the chair with her arms extended. "Don't come through."

Lennon's brows furrowed, looking identical to her younger sister. "What? Why?"

"You can't, not yet. You have to go back."

"I don't want to," Lennon admitted. She wanted to cross through the mirror that was both impossibly far and an arm's length away. Page's eyes caught on something behind her, and she turned, watching her stayed limp as Conrad set it in the rocking boat, tossing a few bags of sand after. Before Lennon could realize why his foot reared, he'd kicked the lower half of the body, waiting for movement. Page winced, but Lennon was holding her breath, bracing for pain or a pull back to her body. However, there was nothing; she couldn't even remember what the word pain meant in this place. Lennon watched while he dug in the storage compartments, pulling out rope and a tarp.

Lennon turned to Page, scolding herself for wasting a second away from her. "I'm staying here, with you."

"What about Mom and Dad? Hart? He loves you, Lennon, I've seen it."

Lennon looked to her feet, watching the iridescent teal swirl around her toes in intricate designs. She felt no fear, no guilt. She lifted her arms, blank of ink, out to her sister as she stepped forward. Page mirrored her movement, but raised her hands defensively instead, keeping her from entering.

A growl of frustration ripped through Lennon. What she wanted most in the world, what stood than less than five feet away, was keeping her from itself. "Let me in, Page!"

"I...I can't."

"Why?" Lennon frowned, her thoughts immediately turning inward. "Do you not want me to?"

She would understand if she didn't. Lennon had let her down so massively—of course she'd be angry.

Page's lips twisted wistfully. "You're my sister. I could never want to be away from you. But don't you see? You're being given a choice, Lennon. I'm not letting you make the wrong one."

"There's nothing for me back there." Lennon gritted her teeth.

"If that were true, there'd be no choice. There wasn't for me—"

Missing Page

"What am I going home to, Page? Our family is ruined, it was done even before you left. Mom and Dad are one fight away from divorcing. Hart's young, he'll find love again." Lennon smiled sadly as crystal tears leaked from her eyes. "It's over, P. Honestly, it's long over—"

"Stop that!" Page said, her eyebrows creasing with frustration. "You have to start protecting yourself the way you've protected me. I know you think you've already failed, but it's not true, not in the slightest. But if you do *this*, Lennon, you *will* fail yourself. You won't want to live knowing that—*I can't* live knowing that."

"There's nothing I can do about it!" Lennon said, exasperated. "Maybe if I'd told someone things would be different, but I didn't. I *did* fail, Page, and the only thing I'll have to live with is knowing that I saved that man from himself."

Page's eyes hardened. "And if you take another step, you'll be doing it again."

Lennon paused.

"Conrad is going to leave you exactly the way he left me, and he won't think twice about it or who it hurts. He'll do it again, and again, and again—he's made his choice. You still have yours, Lennon, don't you see? You can make sure he doesn't do it to anyone else!"

Despite everything, Page was still selfless, kind; that hadn't changed. The girl took a step forward, her toe just behind the line between the wood deck and the pitch blackness. There was a calmness around her now.

"You have chosen me my entire life." Page stared at her for a moment, her face full of loving gratitude. "My biggest regret is not choosing you that night. So please..." With a small grimace, she reached her hand through the mirror. Lennon watched in horror as it morphed into a bruised, wrinkly version of itself, swollen as if it'd been sitting in water for hours.

"Page—"

"It doesn't hurt," she assured, slightly strained. "It's just difficult."

Lennon didn't think twice, taking her sister's cold hand into both of hers. She wished she could warm the death out of her fingers.

"Please," Page pleaded. "While there's still time, please choose you. Before you can't anymore."

Lennon took in a deep breath, feeling the weight of her words in her chest. She held her sister's hand tight in hers for a long moment.

"I love you. I love you more than anyone has loved anyone."

"I could think of somebody," she whispered with a small smile.

Lennon stood there, unable to let go. How could she possibly let her sister go for a second time? She hadn't been able to survive the first.

"You better not come back 'til you're old and wrinkly," Page said through tears.

Lennon's throat grew tight with guilt. "I don't want you to be alone."

"I'm not," she assured. "Wyatt's here. He stayed in Laguna. He's somewhere around here...stops by every now and then. He actually thought I was you when we first met." Her laugh rang through the air.

Lennon couldn't believe what she was hearing. Her mouth opened, but disbelief had stolen her voice.

Page nodded encouragingly. "I'll wait for you. We both will."

Lennon squeezed her sister's hand, who was careful to keep it outside the mirror. "You will?"

"I promise."

Lennon eyed her doubtfully, waiting. Page smiled, her large doe eyes turning glassy.

"Mermaid promise."

Lennon's doubt morphed into bittersweet adoration. She could see her in every part of her life: a newborn, toddler, and finally, as she died. A young—much, much too young—girl.

Using every atom of willpower she had, Lennon released her sister's hand and turned to the black oblivion. The wave's song from Page's world faded, replaced with the angry crashing in Lennon's. The blue footprints disappeared as she got approached the other

Missing Page

mirror, losing the magic of Page's world. She slowed before she flew through, taking one final moment to enjoy this temporary peace. She hoped she could remember it on the other side.

It shouldn't have felt as difficult as it did. It was harder than fighting a current, trying to put one foot in front of the other. But with the encouragement of her sister behind her, and the promise echoing in her head, her heel lifted from the ground, sailing through the mirror. Lennon tasted blood as she breathed in, immediately wincing at the throbbing pain in her throat. He'd choked her, hard. Everything in her body ached, but there was no time to lick wounds.

It was hard to make any kind of plan when it was so dark. The engine was running, waves glided underneath the boat. She knew they were moving, but not much else. *Weapon. You need a weapon.*

It was no use looking around. Underneath the tarp, she might as well've been blind. Lennon squirmed in small, unsuccessful movements; he'd tied her up. Rope constricted her shoulders and legs, but she could still move her forearms, flex her fingers.

An opening was close—there was cold wind coming in from the outside, speckling rain on her ruined cuticles. It took a few precious minutes, but she was able to use her nose to push the opening wide enough for her to see through. There wasn't much in her limited vision—the floor, the boat's white interior, and a pair of feet. Conrad had put her toward the back, near the engine.

His back's to you. This was good. He'd cut corners in an attempt to save his strength, make it easier to toss her overboard. But that was also where all their supplies were. She wiggled to broaden her vision, heart jumping when she spotted the med kit strapped to the boat's wall. There could be a flare gun inside... It was a risky bet, but it was all she had besides her bare hands. She glanced up at Conrad, his shirt whipping in the storm, and scooted herself closer, holding her breath. *A little closer...just open those two straps, and it'll fall open...*

She was scared to reach out, too constricted to defend herself. If he saw her, she'd be dead—again. A rogue wave jolted her body forward before she could move, nearly knocking Conrad over in the process.

"God dammit!" he yelled, spitting out the angry rain pelting his face. Lennon froze, her fingers having almost left the tarp. Her shoulder was aching from the impact, but as she rolled back, she realized the collision had loosened the rope around her torso. She could move her arms now, enough to move fast if she needed. It seemed as though even Mother Nature was on her side.

While Conrad was distracted with regaining control of the boat, Lennon stuck out a shaky arm, unlatching one strap before retracting it back into the safety of her tarp, blinking blood and saltwater out of her eyes. Now the kit was open enough to reveal some of its contents. Bandages, ointments, sting relief... She nearly gasped at the flash of orange. *The flare gun!*

She needed to free that last latch to grab it—and then pray it was loaded. Blood pounding in her ears, Lennon waited for another rocky wave to lurch her forward. One more chance, that was all she needed.

The boat slowed, igniting panic in her stomach. Conrad stopped the engine and her heart with it as she realized they were at the end. At *her* end. Lennon stilled as his footsteps circled around her, feeling a jerk of the rope around her legs and a heavy thud land next to her head. *Sand bags.* She was out of time.

Standing above, Conrad reared, planting a final kick into the middle of the tarp. She wanted to scream from the pain, writhe, or at least ease the ache in her head with her hands. But she could feel from his sudden silence that a sign of life was exactly what he was waiting for, and forced herself to stay motionless. After a moment, he lifted her body from the ground, grunting with the effort.

"You've always been a brat," he grunted. "For someone so pretty. And those eyes...it really is a waste."

Something fell from the opening Lennon made in the tarp, clattering against the boat's floor.

"Ah, shit," Conrad hissed, dropping her back to the ground carelessly. Her head smacked against the floor, silent.

Missing Page

Underneath, Lennon was bursting with more pain than she'd ever experienced. Fire was shooting through her stomach and head. She was almost sure her rib was cracked and positive that she was concussed. But the worst was her lip, split enough to require multiple stitches. She was flooded with the taste and scent of pennies, and could see the flesh flaying apart just beneath her nose. Lennon wasn't sure how she wasn't screaming.

"'Course you brought your fuckin' phone," he muttered. "Well, maybe yours'll end up next to hers."

Through the gap in the tarp, she could see his hand pick it up from the ground, walking toward the front to throw it overboard. This was it—this was her chance. Lennon's hand shot out from the tarp, fumbling with the metal clasps as she gasped from the excruciating pain. The straps broke away from each other, and the lid fell open, its contents tumbling out. Her fingers fit the orange handle between her hands, and she clamored out of the tarp to stand as Conrad whipped around.

"*DON'T MOVE!*" she screamed as he reached for her. She rolled her cramping neck, feeling blood pool helplessly between the new valley in her upper lip.

He paused, beginning to lift both hands above his head. He'd underestimated her; Lennon was truly something to be feared.

"Hey, hey..." he said cautiously. "C'mon, Len."

She refused to blink or look away from him. She loosened the rope from her legs and moved behind the captain's seat, jerking her head to the back of the boat.

"Tie yourself up," she spat through her split lip. "Hands and feet. We're going back."

"You're alive," he uttered, still processing. She'd torn up his face bad; his eyebrow was split to the bone, though she wasn't sure when that'd happened, or how. "I thought you were—"

"Dead? Just like Page was, huh?" She held the gun tightly in pruned, red-stained hands. She could see two Conrads, and both of them looked like they'd been struck. A bolt of lighting ripped through the night in the distance, illuminating his face. Lennon had been wrong; he looked scarier than his father ever did.

"*Go!*" she shouted.

He took slow steps, facing her as he passed. "You really gonna kill me?" he asked curiously, almost amused.

"If I have to," she said, hoping he couldn't detect her doubt. She should've done it already; it was getting harder to picture with every passing second. As much as she saw the evil of Devin Bates in the face of the man sitting before her, she also saw the innocence of Wyatt's.

A knowing smile touched his lips then, erasing his brother's resemblance. "You're more like her than you think. You act like you're so strong, like you don't care about people, but your walls are weak."

"And whose fault is that?" Lennon retorted, venomous. "I've never gotten to feel safe, never been able to trust people. Your dad stole that from me, like you did from Page!" A lump formed in her throat. "Wyatt...Wyatt wouldn't even be able to look at you."

Conrad's lip curled under the aim of Lennon's gun. Electricity streaked furiously through the air, white-hot.

"It could've ended with you." Lennon had meant to only think it, but her concussion was blurring her thoughts with her speech.

"I'm sorry, Lennon. But it *will* end with me," he shouted over the storm, still holding the rope in his hands. "My mom already lost a son."

"And mine lost a daughter!" she snapped. "Don't be stupid, Conrad. Tie yourself up, *now!*"

She glanced away long enough for her fingers to find the key, twisting until the motor started. He clicked his tongue against the roof of his mouth, shaking his head. His hands moved first, launched forward by powerful legs, reaching out for her. Lennon squeezed her fingers against the trigger, popping the gun loudly as a bright light shot out.

It went higher than she'd aimed for. The bright light hit his face, twisting his body violently. Lennon's mouth opened in horror as he lost his balance, falling backward. The gun dropped from her hands in a desperate attempt to save him, but she was a fingertip's length too late, left instead to watch in horror. He tumbled into the water, and in one swift moment, his head hit the propeller, jerked jarringly to the side from the power. Lennon gasped, frozen in shock as his body stilled.

It took a few seconds for the paralysis to wear off. Once she was able, she rushed to the keys, ripping them out to cut the engine, and scrambled to the edge the boat, extending her arm to his limp, floating body.

"Conrad!" she yelled. The storm rocked the boat and his body as her screams pierced the air. She moved to the edge, holding on to the railing with one hand and plunging the other beneath the frigid waters. The saltwater stung her wounds, but she didn't stop until her fingers closed around his arm and pulled him in, growing queasy as his head came into view.

She didn't know why she was saving him. She just was.

Lennon hooked her arms beneath his, crying out from the pain in her ribs as she lifted him back onto the boat. There was a deep gash from his forehead to the crown of his head from where the propeller had hit; tendons, blood, and fragmented bone seeped out of it. Third degree burns scorched his throat and chin, the flames exploding like red tails over his chest.

"Conrad?" She leaned him against the soaked seat. "Conrad, can you hear me?"

He coughed suddenly, blood spluttering from his mouth onto Lennon's face. She startled and slipped, her knees crashing against the floor. Even more pain vibrated through her knees, all the way into her teeth. It felt like her bones had shattered through her shins, intense enough to take her vision momentarily. But she got right back up, starting to shake him again. "Conrad, c'mon, wake up!"

They had to go home, but looking around her, she couldn't tell north from south, or land from water. She didn't even know if he was really alive, or if it was just his mind. She wasn't sure about herself, either. This could all be her body moving like a headless chicken before it puttered out. Nothing she was doing made sense to her.

"How do we go home?" she begged, panicking. He spluttered again. His gasps were hollow, rattling like death. Lennon spotted the gun on the floor and took it clumsily into her hands, loading another flare in. Arms lifting weakly above her head, she pulled the trigger, shooting high into the sky.

Conrad's dying breath counted the seconds. She needed a flare, a flashlight, a lighthouse—*anything*, as long as it gave her a way home. Lennon found a final round in the kit, trembling as she reloaded.

Please. Please don't let this be the day I die.

She covered her ear, watching Conrad's slumped body as she fired. Tears leaked from her eyes, her mind too overwhelmed to do anything else. The sky remained dark for a minute, and then two. Dread weighed over the boat—they were going to die out here.

A true cry escaped Lennon, unique from her previous tears of anger or remorse. Her cry was rare in the sense that it was not a cry for help, but as though she knew nobody would hear it, not if they were right next to her.

And then, she heard it—a high-pitched, squealing sound. Lennon turned to follow the noise, her mouth opening when a bright light shot through the sky, spreading like branches of a tree, or poison in one's veins. In the next second, it dissolved into darkness, the rain obscuring any smoke to prove its existence. *Was that real?* It seemed miles way.

As if hearing her, another flare twisted in the sky, reflecting in her eyes like yellow orbs. She shoved the key back into the ignition and pushed the throttle forward, lurching the boat through a barrage of waves. Two more lit off as she got closer, until she was finally able to see the silhouettes waving from the shore, lit from a collection of police cars and ambulances.

Her strength fell when her dad came into view, his hand jerking forward from the strength of a barking Shepherd at his feet. She

Missing Page

pushed the lever as far as she could, shaking hysterically. There was liquid pooling around her bare toes, but it was too sticky to be water.

"Dad!" Lennon screamed, ignoring the protests from her throat. "Daddy, it's me!"

"LENNON!" Stacy bellowed, waving his arms above his head. "We're here, we're over here!"

She wiped the blood from her good lip, squinting at the taller figure next to him.

"Hart," she breathed, her voice barely above a whisper.

She pulled back on the lever, letting the bow drift up onto the sand. Almost immediately, bodies and questions swarmed her. She looked down, growing nauseous at the pool of crimson filling the square, beginning to trickle toward the front. She didn't know humans had so much blood.

Lennon clamored out, letting her dad hold her in his arms as sobs shook through them. Kaiser licked away at her fingers while her dad's hand held her head, rocking her over and over.

"Thank you, God, thank you, God..." Stacy whispered, lifting his chin to the sky. "I thought you were gone, I thought you left us!"

She cried out in pain when he squeezed her, and he pulled back, realizing the severity of her injuries. "We need some help! She's hurt!"

"Dad," Lennon whimpered. She could feel Hart's fingers moving comfortingly through her hair. She ached for him, but she had to fulfill her duty, in case it was too late. "It was him. Page, that night, everything, it was all him...C–C...."

Unable to finish, she lifted her hand, pointing to the boat. All that was visible was a tuft of crimson-soaked hair, too far and too bloodied to identify. Stacy's lips hardened into a thin line. "Shh, you're okay now. You don't have to talk..."

Her eyes widened with panic. He *had* to understand; she wouldn't die holding any more of the Bates' secrets. "No, *listen to me*! Devin...he...my nightmares..."

Stacy looked again, and Hart leaned down, still caressing her head. "What are you saying, baby?"

She could feel her vision begin to tunnel and gripped her father's jacket in her hands, mustering a last breath of strength as darkness neared. "I'm sorry."

32

Across the cemetery, a small gathering of people stood around a cherry wood coffin waiting to be lowered into the ground. There was no more than twenty or so black umbrellas melting together, shielding from an unforgiving June sun.

"Are you sure you wanna do this?"

A dark head turned from the scene, her grown in mahogany roots clashing against the jet-black strands. The voice that came from it was raspy, strained from injury.

"Think so."

Lennon wasn't sure she'd ever fully recover from the damage Conrad's hands had left on her, but she'd wear them like battle scars. *I survive,* her body boasted.

"You don't owe them anything, Len." Hart's voice was gentle but guarded. It'd gotten a lower, protective tone after that horrific day on the beach.

"It's not for them." She pulled her hair loose from its ponytail, letting it fall around her face as she pushed a pair of dark shades up her nose. The passenger door swung open, allowing her feet to meet the gravel below the Jeep. She stopped under the shade of a willow, feeling Hart's looming, calming presence behind her.

Conrad's headstone marred what would be an otherwise beautiful view of the flower fields and ocean behind it. The sun was too bright to make out the words, not that Lennon cared to read them anyway. Grief had bent Ms. Bates into the shape of a broken woman; it was easy to forget that she, too, was a victim—she'd lost everything, and had no one to dispel her anger onto. Lennon was sure Ms. Bates resented her to some degree, and she couldn't blame her, for she'd done the same with Emery not too long ago.

Hart's hands cupped her shoulders, squeezing in reassurance as they watched. Lennon's fingers snaked through their spaces, squeezing as the coffin descended out of sight. Her eyes welled, but she couldn't blink—she needed to see him be put away.

Ms. Bates buried her face in her friend's shoulder, unable to contain her wails. More moved to hug her, and Lennon shifted uncomfortably, knowing she was—in some respect—responsible for that gut-wrenching sound. She'd been a fingertip's length away from saving him, from preventing more pain than necessary.

A smaller, more cynical part of her wondered if Ms. Bates was truly so innocent. Maybe she'd been purposefully naive, turning her head to her house of horrors. *Ignorance is bliss,* that was the phrase. Though Lennon wondered, and would for a long time, she would give Ms. Bates the benefit of the doubt. Because, even if she had known, Lennon supposed there wasn't a punishment much worse than this.

The funeral concluded quietly, and the small group dispensed, holding their partners close as their shoes and heels sunk into the grass.

"Ready to go?" Hart asked, rubbing her arm. She could feel the disgust radiating from him; there was not an ounce of sympathy held for the family.

"Go ahead, I'll be there in a second," Lennon said idly. She heard the reluctance in his fading footsteps, but her attention remained on Ms. Bates. Something was pulling at her feet, urging her forward.

Suddenly she was gliding, closing the distance in slow, long strides. She'd trudged through two rows of aging graves before the logical side of her brain caught up to her.

What the fuck are you thinking?

Lennon had lost a lot of her impulsiveness since the accident. She wasn't sure if it was from the concussion or the trauma, but she'd lost the desire to self-destruct. Though this might have satisfied the old masochist in her, she'd decided to try peace.

As if sensing her, Ms. Bates' head swiveled halfway through Lennon's one-eighty. It all happened so fast; the meeting of their eyes, Lennon's brain thrusting into flight. Her breath left her lungs in a quick whoosh as she walked away, cursing her impaired speed. Gravel crunched from behind, and she braced herself.

The tap on Lennon's shoulder stopped her, pivoting slowly on her heels. Ms. Bates' tired, empty eyes poured over her, and Lennon wondered what was going through her head. Was it hate she was seeing? Disappointment?

"Sweetheart, I'm..."

Lennon blinked. Mrs. Bates' mouth didn't match what Lennon had heard in her head.

"Pardon?" Lennon stuttered.

Ms. Bates reached forward, carefully taking Lennon's bandaged hand. "I am deeply, deeply sorry for any pain my family has caused you."

Lennon had no idea what to say. She was sure her silence came off as rude, but Ms. Bates didn't seem to mind. The woman nodded once, holding her wrinkling lips tight, and then backed away. Lennon watched in disbelief, unable to form a thought or plan of action until the woman ducked into a dark suburban.

"What was that?" she heard behind her. She turned again, eyes softening at his expression.

She'd already known Hart was a good man, but he flourished best when Lennon finally allowed him to take care of her. He never once left her side, never complained. Seeing her in the hospital had been gut-wrenching; the number of tubes and casts she was in overwhelmed him. Her first memory after waking was hearing him tell her how much he loved her, and wanting to kiss every part of him despite her stitched lip. She'd never felt a love like that before, so full that she could offer her own back.

He helped her walk back to the car, lifting her into the seat. "You okay?" he asked, now that they were eye-level.

She kissed his cheek, making sure to use her bottom lip more than her top. "More than okay."

∼

Eight days later, Hart held Lennon's bruised hand gingerly in his, his thumb barely applying pressure over her knuckle out of habit. July's sun was setting on the ocean's horizon, shedding its last bit of warmth over their skin. Hart was a few shades darker, since she'd been cooped up inside the hospital and her home all through June.

It was their last day together. He would fly out tomorrow morning and wouldn't be able to contact her for month. Now that she was medically cleared, Lennon fully intended on fulfilling her promise to her dad. She'd be checking in to a private rehab center after they dropped Hart off; this would be mostly good, except that it required thirty days without visitation. She understood why, although she wasn't convinced he'd be there by the time the rule lifted.

"Thanks for staying," Lennon murmured, squeezing his fingers.

"Don't thank me." His head lowered, shaking. "I wouldn't be anywhere else."

Even though it hurt, she reached to kiss his cheek. "I'm sorry I didn't tell you all this before."

"You have nothing to apologize for. I'm not angry. I love you,

Missing Page

Lennon." Hart leaned over, pressing his lips to her fingers. "I'm just happy you're alive, and here with me."

She winced as she moved to his chair, clenching through the spasm that rocked through her ribs. Once settled, she nestled her head against his chest, listening to his heartbeat to match her breaths to.

"Just so you know, if I *do* ever die..."

He chuckled at her dark humor.

"I don't ever want you to feel like you can't love again," she said. "I would want you to move on. Just make sure she's really good to you."

Hart furrowed his brows, offended at the idea. "What's the point?"

She rolled her eyes. *Ever the romantic.* "I'm just saying, in case I go before you, don't forget I gave you the okay. I won't haunt you or anything over it."

His arms tightened around her instead of laughing. "I won't, but I get what you're saying. I'd want that for you, too.

Lennon looked at him incredulously. "You think *I* would want try to find someone else? Hart, I hate people. I'm sorry to tell you this, but you were a happy, persistent accident."

He grinned. "I came bearing chips."

"*Ugh*," Lennon groaned. "You're too young for dad jokes."

Their laughter faded into the calls of the seagulls and the roaring of waves, all alive and well. It was quiet for a long time before she craned her chin up to see his eyes, knowing they'd reveal where he'd gone to. Sure enough, they were far away, staring coldly at the sunset and the cove that interrupted it.

"What're you thinking about?"

He didn't answer at first.

"Hart?" she whispered, concern rippling in tiny waves on her forehead. *Was this it? Was he getting second thoughts?*

"You deserved better. So did Wyatt." Hart tightened his arms around her protectively. "I just... I'm angry. At him, at both of them."

They held each other as the light died out, the ocean's white-maned heads crashing against the shore.

"You guys hungry?" Cashmere's voice lifted Lennon from her sinking consciousness. She leaned against the frame, holding a non-alcoholic beer close to her chest.

"Starving," the two said in unison. Lennon waited to move until after her mother left, leaning in to Hart for a deeper kiss. Her lip had significantly healed in the last few weeks—the doctor said her scar would be minimal, and his nurse and Hart promised it was a cute addition—and she was eager to use it again.

Hart had to work to hold her passion at bay, trying to set a slower, more careful pace. It was only a moment before he pulled away, leaving Lennon entirely unsatisfied. She missed the heaviness of him, when he wasn't afraid to melt into her; but, ever the gentleman, he was committed to his self-assigned nurse duty. His lack of touch was starting to remind her of her parents, who she frequently forgot were husband and wife and not roommates. She couldn't remember the last time she'd seen them hold hands, or even exchange a peck. She'd never felt less sexy, and deep down, she feared he'd lost that part of love forever.

Their entrance was awkward and clumsy, mores on Lennon's part. Once she sat, Cash took the seat next to her, reaching to brush a stray hair from her face. Stacy sat on his wife's other side, but she hardly paid him any mind. Lennon huffed, glancing at Hart warily.

"How are you feeling today, Len?" Cash asked.

"Much better. Practically back to normal," Lennon mumbled.

"Good." Cashmere nodded, distracted with the serving bowl Stacy had passed her.

At her turn, Lennon scooped a lump of mashed potatoes and creamed corn onto her plate, avoiding the hard-shell tacos out of courtesy; her jaw was still stiff from Conrad's fist. It was a strange thing, to feel somebody's effect after they were dead.

Cash frowned at her daughter. Despite her efforts, apologies still didn't feel right on her tongue. "Oh, *shit*. I wasn't thinking, Len...."

Missing Page

"No," Her daughter's hand waved dismissively. "Don't worry about it."

"I can make you something else—" She started, before Stacy's chair whined against the floor.

"Let me throw some salmon on the grill—"

"You wanna order something, babe?"

She began to laugh, but it caught in her mangled throat, morphing into a cough. The three stopped instantly, watching her like she could crumble any second. She had to hold back an eye roll at their expressions. "I'm okay, guys. *Really*."

Lennon's gaze lingered on the empty seat across from her as the others ate, and then shifted to the lounge chair outside. In some other world that was impossibly far but much too close, she could feel her sister sitting there, waiting.

As her mashed potatoes dwindled, she reached for her water, cursing when it slipped out of her twitching hand to the floor.

"Damnit—" she grumbled, reaching to grab it. Her shoulder banged against the table, shooting a rippling spasm through her that rolled her eyes back into her head. Hart got to her first, holding her head up and her seizing arm outstretched.

"Okay sweetheart, okay. Just breathe..." he soothed.

Lennon gripped his arm with the arm that wasn't writhing and squeezed her eyes shut against the pain, hissing through her teeth. "I'm *fine!*"

She let the spasm run its course, beads of sweat forming on her forehead. Blood rushed to her cheeks, seeing them all standing above her with wide eyes. She stood, picking up her spilled cup from the floor.

"Please, for the love of God," she bristled. "*Stop* treating me like glass. I can do things myself!"

Lennon ascended the stairs as fast as her legs would allow, letting the door close with a force. They couldn't end on this note; she needed him to be her boyfriend instead of her nurse, at least for this final night. She locked herself in her bathroom, letting the burning water scorch her skin until it ran cold and a plan had finally solidified.

You can do this, she said to her reflection, pointing for emphasis. Wrapped in a puffy white towel, Lennon exited, finding Hart waiting at the edge of her bed. She cupped his cheek briefly as she passed, exuding as much grace as possible in those few steps to the dresser. Her towel fell with a soft *plop,* replaced with a pair of tiny, satin shorts. She silently cursed at the cuts and bruises that were still present on her leg, but committed to embracing them. Confidence *was* a choice, after all.

She plucked a T-shirt from the drawer, making sure the material was lightweight. Her arms raised high over her head to pull it over her full chest, taking her time with each movement. Lennon spun and sauntered to him, impressed with the amount of seduction she was still capable of. The mattress sunk on either side of him with the weight of her half-healed knees, and she felt his breath rise to the surface in a shallow gasp.

"Baby, what are you...?"

Lennon's finger trailed over his lips and the curve of his jaw, drawing goosebumps as they traveled down his neck. Her nail stopped at the hollow spot between his collarbones, where she leaned forward to suction her lips to the soft skin. Her tongue flicked against the bone, feeling him tense beneath her; but not in the way she wanted. Off his expression, her insecurity doubled. Suddenly feeling exposed, she pulled away, crossing her arms over her chest.

"Do you not want me?" she asked, her voice smaller than she'd intended.

He laughed in surprise. "*What?*"

"You barely kiss me. You won't even let me—"

"You had stitches, Len," he said, taking her hands. "Of course I'm into you, but you're healing. This can wait."

Her bottom lip jutted out slightly. She'd be lying if she said she hadn't wondered how he kept himself busy during the night; was he looking or thinking about other girls, wishing he hadn't gotten sucked into all of this?

His hands settled on her hips, digging lovingly into the non-bruised skin. "You're still the sexiest, smartest, *bravest*, most beautiful woman I've ever known. But that son of a bitch hurt you, Lennon, he hurt you bad. Sex has been the last thing on my mind, and I'm sorry if that hurt you. But my number one priority is making sure you're—"

"Taken care of, I know." Lennon mumbled, bored. "But..."

She leaned forward, placing a kiss beneath his ear. "If you're gonna take care of me, take *care* of me."

He looked doubtful. "Baby—"

"You do want me, right?" she asked, lifting her t-shirt over her head.

"Always."

"Well, I know my body better than anyone, and *I* say I'm okay."

He shook his head, keeping his amusement contained in his eyes. She felt a shift beneath where she was sitting. He held his weight as he rolled over her, lowering her ever gently into the mattress. His lips worked carefully but feverishly against hers; it took only minutes for them to fall back into their natural rhythm, albeit a slower one. It allowed her to take in every detail, every emotion. She could feel her soul entangling with his, fitting even better than puzzle pieces, with no lines cutting out one shape from the other.

Though the moment ended all too soon after it began, it had been perfect, more than she'd hoped. Perfect could be found in any amount of time—if it was special enough.

"Hart," she hummed, already falling into unconsciousness.

"Yes?"

"I think you might be my soulmate."

Across the room, a breeze filtered through her bare window, soft moonlight shining through. Without the fear of seeing Devin again, there were no longer any curtains to be scared of, or sleep to avoid. Her contentedness nearly matched what she felt in that strange, timeless void, where darkness became something not to fear, but to look forward to.

And then came a dream.

Her eyes started off closed. She kept them that way out of habit, using her other senses to figure out her environment. Water rippled quietly near her feet, languid and polite. The breeze felt cool on her sweat-free skin. There was no heaviness of another's presence—she was alone. When she did open her eyes, she was met with a silver morning sky, mirroring against the water in gunmetal blue hues without a sun to warm them.

The lake was perfectly still, glasslike and pristine, except for in the middle. It wrinkled in perfect rhythm, pooling over onto Lennon's toes. Her gaze traveled upwards, toward the horizon, in search of the interruption.

A tail was sticking up out of the water, flowing back back and forth like a slow fan. Its color was a striking blue, dulling the water around it into an unimpressive gray by comparison. She thought it would dive beneath the surface once she found it, but it continued as if it had been waiting to be seen.

It almost appeared to be waving to her.

She wasn't sure why, but she lifted her hand hesitantly, waving in return. Finally, it dipped beneath the cover of the lake, sending one last ripple in her direction. Lennon watched it travel to her in a hypnotizing roll, washing over her feet with a quiet *plop*. She knew, deep in her soul, that it was goodbye.

With the lake and her soul now completely still and alone, Lennon could fully relax into herself. For the first time, she felt like she owned the body she'd fought so hard to stay in. Though it had always been hers, Lennon was now confident that she'd earned it and its trust. Nobody would take it from her again—not ever.

EPILOGUE

The sun had not yet woken the next morning when it was time for Hart to leave. Lennon offered to drive more times than she could count but, not understanding she *wanted* the distraction, he insisted that she had a big enough day as is and needed to relax. She settled for one final shower together, holding him as tightly as her arms could manage.

His thumbs swept beneath her eyes, void of their usual purple tint. She looked rested, as if she'd slept twelve hours instead of four.

Lennon could feel the difference too. She wasn't sure how to describe the relief in having a dreamless sleep without the aid of drugs for the first time in seventeen years. But she had at least thirty-one days to figure it out. There was just over thirty minutes, however, before he left.

"How'd you sleep?"

"Good." She smiled softly. That much was true.

"You feel ready for today?"

Lennon shrugged, pressing her lips to his chest. She didn't want to think about the future, but instead enjoy the present, which was now feeling very much like a gift. The two were silent as they treaded downstairs hand in hand. Hart's Uber was a Tesla like Lennon's had been, its battery humming quietly as it ascended the steep driveway. Lennon held his jacket tight in her clenched fists and pressed one final kiss to his warm, tender lips, worrying she wouldn't be able to let go.

"I'll see you soon," he said, nodding. It wasn't a goodbye, but a promise. "I love you."

"I love you," she whispered, willing her fingers to relax. Lennon felt every sense of the word as she peered up at him from under her lashes, swelling with adoration. With great effort, she finally released her hold and let him duck into the car.

It was difficult, but she'd let go of things she loved before. And so far, they'd all come back—or promised to.

She reentered her home to start breakfast, wanting to give her parents something nice to wake up to. However, there was a figure on the deck she hadn't noticed before that startled her, immediately wilting her blooming idea. It was eerily still as it faced out toward the ocean, oblivious to the goodbye that had just occurred on the porch.

Of course her father would be restless, though he was clearly exhausted with his lack of alertness. She walked forward on her tiptoes, trying to gauge his mood before he noticed her. A cool breeze rustled through his graying hair, over his closed lids. His expression couldn't be described as peaceful, but the lines between his brows weren't as deep as they'd once been.

She already missed him, and she hadn't even left yet.

Lennon paused at the piano near the sliding door, reaching a finger to the ivory chords. Stacy turned his head at the notes that played from inside, finding his daughter's soft smile peeking over the lid.

"Couldn't sleep either?" she asked. He shook his head, patting the seat next to him.

Once she was at his side, he finally answered. "No, not today," he murmured.

Lennon chewed on her cheek, feeling the old pangs of guilt

Missing Page

knocking at her heart's door. There was no way to pay her father back for everything he'd done for her, but she couldn't help trying to think of something anyway. A conversation they'd had in late May came to her then, a debt she still owed...

"I think I still owe you a fishing trip."

He looked to her, lips twisting in amused confusion. "Yeah?"

"You covered for me and Page, remember?"

He chuckled. "I forgot, actually. 'Preciate the honesty."

Lennon pursed her lips with a furrowed brow. "Well? You wanna go?"

He frowned. "Really? You hate—"

"We haven't been on an adventure in forever. C'mon," She pulled him up from his seat, both grunting with the effort. "Plus, it'll give me something nice to remember when I'm in the loony bin. And *you* can remember *me* whenever you eat the fish."

Stacy smiled at her dramatics. The center was more a resort than rehab; she'd probably like it more than being at home.

"You don't wanna drive the Bronco around? Grab some gelato for breakfast?"

"You can't break a mermaid promise," she reminded him.

"I think we can make an exception—"

"Ugh. *Dad*," she groaned, her cynicism snapping back like a rubber band. "Don't make me beg to go fishing."

"Okay, okay. I'll start the car." He wouldn't push her. This was a moment he'd been dreaming about for over half a year.

Although she was more confident than ever that this retreat would be a good thing, there was always that nagging doubt, telling her it wouldn't work. Maybe, like her voice, her mind had been permanently damaged, broken and wrongly healed one too many times. She needed this hour of normalcy more than he did, something to get out of her head before she spent a month dissecting it.

They opted to fish off the pier instead of their boat. It was too soon for Lennon—just the sight sent a shiver through her, adrenaline spiking like she was back in that storm with her murderer. *Someday*, she promised herself. Baby steps. Lennon twisted the bait on her hook with a grimace. She'd forgotten how much everything *smelled* when fishing, and how much loss of life was involved.

"You narrowing down any majors?" Stacy asked.

"A few."

"I've been thinking about it. A lot, actually...I think you'd make a real good detective, Len."

She shot him a dark look, trying to find the joke behind his words.

"I got lucky, Dad, and I barely got out alive. I'd be terrible..." She frowned, thinking of the unhelpful police. "And I don't want to work in government."

"You could go private. But you *did* figure it out, Len. Without practice, without any kind of training, you got the truth. You risked your life for it." He shook his head. "That brain of yours is pretty incredible, kid. You should use it for something important."

Another whiff of fish hit her, wrinkling her nose.

"At least think about it," he insisted, misunderstanding.

"I will. Promise." She nodded. Her career, while more important than it used to be, was still low on her priority list. There was confirmation she needed before she left in case everything was different when she returned.

She waited for their lines to settle in the water before she spoke.

"Dad?"

Stacy met her eyes a little too quickly, as if he'd been waiting.

"I just..." Lennon cleared her throat of the emotion blocking it. "I'm just worried you see me differently, now that you know."

His look was very serious, stark against his normally pleasant features. "Lennon, I want you to hear me clearly when I say this, alright?"

She dipped her chin tightly, fighting off a bout of nerves.

"The only thing that has changed, is that I have never, *ever* been prouder of you." He grabbed her hand tightly in his. "I never understood the way you worked. But you're a survivor, a fighter...and

Missing Page

despite everything, you love. Hard. I see you more than I ever have... my only wish is that I did so sooner."

She'd never pictured herself that way. Her survival looked much uglier in her mind, less deserving of praise. It's not like she'd handled things well, proven by the little trip she was about to take. But his compassion eased that part her mind, gave her more room to breathe.

There was still the *other* thing; the papers she'd found while looking for her insurance card in her mom's office. She'd been working up the courage to mention it for weeks, and though the timing was ill, there wasn't any left.

"Are you really leaving Mom?" She said it in one breath.

"*What?*" he asked, craning his head at her.

"I found the papers," she said stoically. "You filed for divorce."

He stared at her, unblinking. She tucked a fallen strand of hair behind her ear. "I'm not mad if you are. I just wanted to know if you'll still be here when I get out."

If she were being honest, it was something she'd expected long ago. Even though they were doing better lately, her father reminded her of the water in the same way her mother reminded her of metal; it only made sense that after so much time, after so much erosion, they would rust.

She fidgeted at his silence, wishing she could see what was swirling behind his dark eyes; he was probably thinking about how observant—sometimes maddeningly so—she was.

"When did you find those?" he asked curiously.

"Few weeks ago."

He *tsk'ed* with a soft, sad smile.

"So?" she asked. "You're divorcing?"

Stacy's smile smoothed out into something solemn. "We've been separated for a while, now, Lennon."

Her chest filled with a mix of emotions. Shock, relief, confusion. It explained their distance, their cold cordialness with each other. She couldn't believe she hadn't spotted it sooner.

"Since when?"

"A little after Christmas."

She blinked. "And you're still...you haven't...?"

"A lot's happened," he said, looking away. "And the house is mine. I just haven't had the heart to make her leave, I guess. Sometimes it seemed like she'd...like she was getting better."

Lennon nodded in small movements. Cash had taken large steps since her accident, but it couldn't erase years of damage. There were some wounds that could not be stitched, and instead left to half-heal in gnarled scars, festering infection deep below.

"When did you fall out of love with her?" she asked quietly.

He opened his mouth, but nothing came out for a moment. She waited patiently, sure there was complexity behind his hesitation. She had her own conflicting feelings about her mother.

"I don't think I ever did."

Lennon dipped her chin in silent understanding. Love came in all shapes in sizes, could be given from near or far. She understood all too well what was lying beneath her father's words.

"Will she be gone by the time I get back?"

He sighed, rubbing his palms against his each other. "I think so."

She squinted in thought against the rising sun, wishing she'd brought a hat as she wiped her forehead with her T-shirt. It was the same one she'd slept in—and belonged to Hart—but she did put in the effort to exchange her sweats for a pair of loose jeans. In her peripheral, Stacy leaned forward, holding something in his hand. She turned, smiling at the offering, and pulled it just above her brow with a quick *thanks* before looking again towards the twinkling ripples.

"I always wondered," she blurted, feeling more courageous under his Dodger's ball cap.

He pushed his sunglasses up his sloped nose. "Wondered what?"

She hesitated. "Why you stayed. It never made sense to me, you not leaving sooner."

"Really? After everything, *that's* what you can't figure out?"

She scowled, her lip jutting out beneath the hat's cover.

"Lennon, the only reason I would ever leave is the same reason

Missing Page

I've always stayed." His lip twitched with the thought. "When I thought you weren't coming back..."

Lennon winced, feeling his pain as hers.

"I've only ever wanted to keep you and your sister safe. Your mom, too, believe it or not. And I've been wrong, in unforgivable ways... But I always tried. I always tried to protect you as best as I knew how."

His expression morphed into a deep, paternal fury. She'd seen it only once on his face before; a few days after Conrad died, when she became cohesive enough to tell him everything. Lennon finally understood the thoughts behind his glassy, murderous eyes.

"It makes me sick, Lennon. You weren't even..."

Her lips pulled to the side, and she reached out to rub his arm. "I know."

His breath became staggered then, and he put his hand over hers. "I'm so sorry."

"I know. I am too."

Stacy sniffed, rubbing his hand over his whiskers to smooth his tortured expression. Lennon hoped that, unlike herself, he'd be able to forgive himself sooner rather than later. Eventually, he too would realize that he did not have to carry the weight of other's sins.

"By the way, I've got something for you. To take with you." He reached into his back pocket to grab his wallet, taking out a small picture folded into four parts.

A strange anticipation swelled in her chest as she closed her fingers around it. She unfolded the photo gingerly and felt the balloon burst beneath her rib cage once it came into view.

"This was the day I got back," She looked up to her dad. He nodded, and her throat tightened.

She stared down at it, taking in every detail, filling with a bittersweet sense of nostalgia. Page's lanky arms slung around Lennon's waist, Lennon's nose scrunched with an open, genuine grin. It was slightly blurry, a result of their dad's sneak attack. She remembered telling herself it'd never see the light of day, that it'd be too awkward, too insignificant to want to remember.

"I'm glad you took this." she sniffed, taking another moment before looking up at him. "I've always thought you were a good dad. We both did."

Something in the distance splashed. Lennon's eyes were the fastest, but she only caught the edge of a tail before it disappeared, leaving a large ripple in its wake. They both waited with bated breath, watching the water roll until it sunk into the sand, just in front of Lennon's bare feet.

"Seal, maybe..." Stacy muttered, still scouring.

Lennon tugged on the brim of her hat, a small smile touching the corners of her lips. "Maybe."

ACKNOWLEDGMENTS

The biggest thanks and the tightest hug to those who have brought this book to life.

Thank you to my family for being my biggest and most enthusiastic supporters. I love you, I love you, I love you.

An extra gigantic, eternal thank you to Tarryn Fisher who has supported me in countless ways, some of them being under-the-radar, and all of them with love and selflessness. You have given me a love and wisdom that I can never repay (but I hope an endless supply of Sui Pao is a good start).

Thank you to my editor Traci Finlay for the kind words, unending patience, and belief as well as commitment to making this project better. This book would be nothing without you!

To those who took time to read Missing Page before she was fully *her,* and helped me put together this puzzle piece of a book, *thank you.* This was a big book, and you women have even bigger hearts.

Thank you to Adso Piñerùa for this beautiful cover art, and to Murphy Rae for making it *Missing Page.* It was so important to me to get this right, and you went above and beyond!

Thank you to Grayson Hubbard for always getting the vision and translating my ideas so perfectly onto film. I feel so lucky to have a friend who is as passionate about creating art as I am. You are truly next-level as an artist, and I think the world of you.

Thank you to my friends near and far who make life colorful and fun. Anthony Stiriti, Bailee Read, Katia Medrano, Mary Antonovich,

Scarlett Cowan, Sydney Agudong, and Nautica Baker, I love you guys.

Thank you to Priscilla's Gourmet Tea and Coffee for providing the most inspiring and cozy public office to write in as well as the best coffee. A special thank you to my favorite baristas Bronwyn, Mary, and Devan who have always cheered me on, and to Jordan who so kindly shared his table with me.

I must say thank you to my cat Bleu, who has sat in my lap many hours while I stare at a screen and sometimes cry or yell at it. He has been my emotional life jacket through every step, and even though the whole concept is probably super weird to him, he's never held it against me.

I am eternally grateful to my muses who have molded me into the artist I am today. Lana Del Rey, Phoebe Bridgers, Sleeping At Last, Thom Yorke, Oscar Wilde, and Lorde are the rare kinds of artists that can paint a picture as beautifully as they imagine them. Thank you for serving as the soundtrack to not only my books but my life.

Author's Note

The most difficult book I've ever had to write has also been the most fulfilling, and that has never been lost on me. I know that Lennon is the voice of millions who have gone through similar tragedies or hardships and never received proper justice nor closure, myself included. I was lucky enough to have a family who supported and believed me when I came forward, but that is not the case for everyone, or even most. Many continue to carry that pain with them to this day, and many carry it alone. To those who do, please know—my heart is with you. I see you, I hear you, I believe you. You are stronger than you know.

Resources for Homeless, Male, Female and Children Survivors of Sexual Assault:
 Rainn.org
 Rain National Sexual Assault Hotline
 1-800-656-4673

SAKI (Sexual Assault Kit Initiative)
 saakitta.org

Enough Abuse Organization, a resource for Survivors of Child Sexual Abuse enoughabuse.org

ABOUT THE AUTHOR

Eden McGuire was born August 25th, 1999, and was raised throughout Oklahoma as well as Steamboat Springs, Colorado. Eden started writing as early as nine years old, and published her first novel at fourteen. Missing Page is her third title. She currently resides in Los Angeles, California.

facebook.com/edennmcguire
x.com/edennmcguire
instagram.com/edenmcguire

Printed in Great Britain
by Amazon